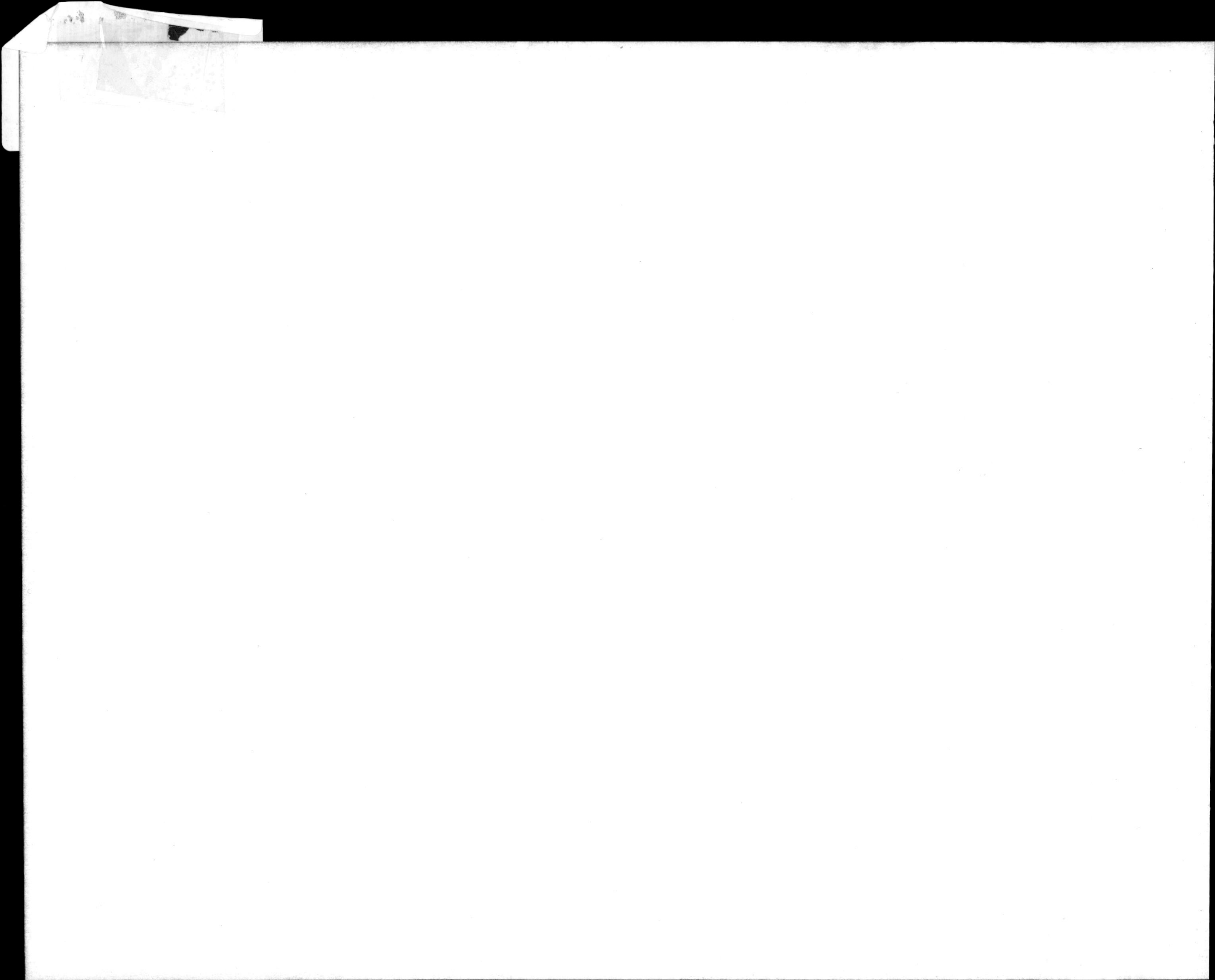

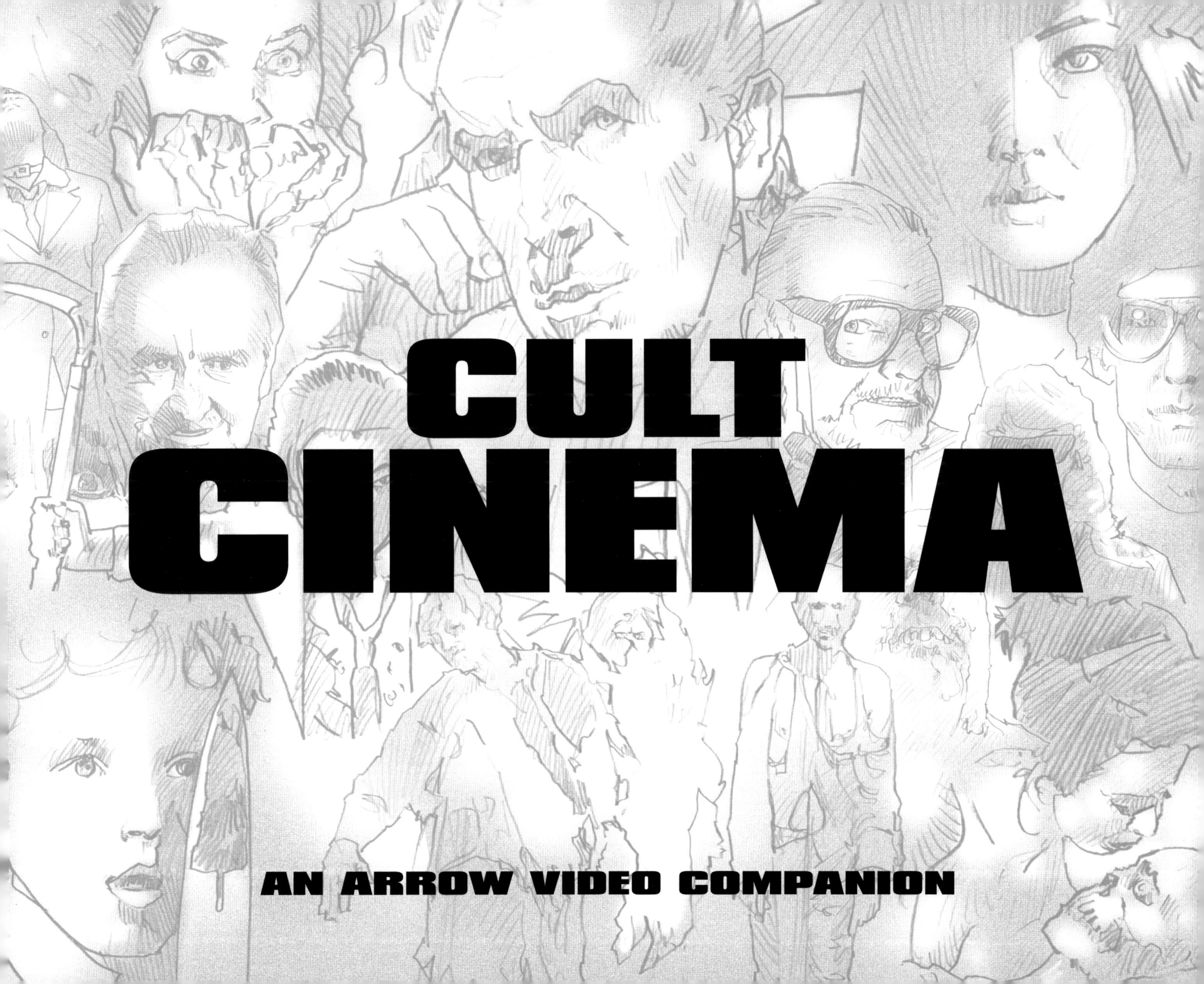
CULT
CINEMA
AN ARROW VIDEO COMPANION

CULT CINEMA: AN ARROW VIDEO COMPANION

ISBN 978-0-9933060-1-3
1st Edition, 1st Pressing
Printed in EU 2016

Published by

Arrow Films
The Engine House
Shenley Park
Radlett Lane
Shenley
WD7 9JP
www.arrowfilms.co.uk

Cover: Graham Humphreys
Design: Obviously Creative

DEDICATED TO

MIKE SUTTON

1971 - 2015

EDITED BY

ANTHONY NIELD

INTRODUCTION

Since its inception in 2009, UK-based Arrow Video has established itself as *the* go-to source for cult cinema on DVD and Blu-ray. Filmmakers as diverse as Richard Ayoade and Guillermo del Toro proclaim themselves fans, and success has allowed the label to branch out into North America. Key to this success has been the care and attention given to the films selected for release: optimal presentations, substantial bonus features and brand new writing from some of the leading voices on cult and genre filmmaking.

The book you hold in your hands is both a showcase and an expansion on the thousands upon thousands of words which have been written for Arrow Video over the years. Collected within are contributions from such names as Tim Lucas, Maitland McDonagh and Stephen Thrower, all of them writing passionately and knowledgably on their chosen subjects. This volume brings together 20 of the finest essays to have appeared in an Arrow Video release, and supplements them with 10 new commissions written especially, and exclusively, for the book.

Cult Cinema approaches its subject from five angles. Each section is devoted to a different facet of cult filmmaking – the opening chapter features seven essays devoted to key cult movies, and is followed by those on directors, actors, genres (and sub-genres), and finally distribution, which examines how different methods of seeing a film, from travelling shows to DVDs, has allowed cult movies and their audiences to flourish.

The aim is not to provide a definitive guide to cult cinema but rather, as the subtitle proclaims, a companion. Cult movies mean many things to many people – Ben Wheatley's introduction touches on the manner in which he discovered the underbelly of cinema, but it won't be shared by everyone, of course – and everyone will have their own favourites. Consider this book as a look at cult cinema through the lens of Arrow Video, which is a pretty broad church anyway: Tinto Brass, Joe Dante, science fiction, super 8, Suzuki Seijun, Boris Karloff, Battle Royale, horror all-nighters, video nasties and much more besides. Something familiar, something fresh, something that might just introduce you to a whole new world of filmmaking and its enthusiastic fandom.

CONTENTS

CULT MOVIES

CULT DIRECTORS

CULT ACTORS

CULT GENRES (AND SUB-GENRES)

CULT DISTRIBUTION

BEN WHEATLEY ON HIS INTRODUCTION TO CULT CINEMA

I was born in 1972. I can count the movies I saw at the cinema in the late seventies on one hand: Walt Disney's *The Jungle Book*, *Star Wars*, *Superman*, *The Love Bug* and *Capricorn One*. We were living in Essex just a bit too far from the local cinema so if you missed a film that was it.

1982 was a good year for me. We had a clunky second-hand Betamax player, six tapes and *Star Wars* and *Alien* were shown on TV. Ten years old. I managed to set the recorder wrong and only had *Alien* up to where John Hurt suffers from some chronic indigestion. It made for a pretty depressing short film. It was another six years before I saw the rest of it.

Star Wars I watched a lot, along with *The Ladykillers* and *Dirty Harry*. The great treat around this time was the trip to the pre-Video Nasty rental shop. Next to the chip shop in Grange near Billericay. Our first rental was *Death Race 2000* and *Watership Down*. It pretty much encapsulates my tastes. Incredibly, *Watership Down* is the real video nasty and is still one of the most complained about films to the BBFC.

Soon my mates and I were curating our own all-dayers. I remember seeing *Videodrome*, *Silver Bullet*, *Scanners* and *Magnum Force* all in one sitting. This was the big explosion of film culture for me. We would rent by the covers and the titles; we had no idea what we were getting into. No clue about genre or directors. It was a pure time before anybody noticed what we were up to.

My proper film education started with a rental of Martin Scorsese's *Taxi Driver*. (Around 1987?) I was living in London by that point and I'd seen posters of Travis Bickle in Camden Market. Me and my mate Dom rented it, not that excited. ("I mean... *Taxi Driver*? Like *Taxi* with Danny De Vito?") By the end of the film I felt like I'd had my head scraped out and reset.

1988. *Moviedrome* was on BBC2, hosted by Alex Cox, and I started to get a grasp of the context of the films I was watching. I started to go to the Scala cinema in King's Cross. All-nighters. Watching *Blue Velvet* whenever it played in London. Watching tons of Vestron movies on a Friday night.

In 1992 I went to university in Brighton and met Rob Hill who was a proper film fan. He had a photographic memory and could recall every review in the *Time Out Film Guide*. His brother Danny knew every film that was in the *Radio* and *TV Times* that had played at Christmas for the last ten years and could recall the day and time.

By this time I had a tape collection of around 20 tapes. (So sue me... I was poor.) Rob's collection was in the hundreds. I also met Andy Starke (producer of *Kill List*, *et al*) around this period. Andy's collection was legendary. A whole room in his house full of original American tapes. Basically the core of what is now available from Arrow Video. Between Rob and Andy I had hit the esoteric mother lode.

University sped by in a blur of smoke, booze and movies. All day and late into the night. We watched everything we could get our hands on. From Andrei Tarkovsky to *Cannibal Holocaust*. Cowboy movies, 70s crime, 40s detective, anime, Sirkian melodrama, *giallo*, Wes Craven, David Cronenberg, Suzuki Seijun, Troma. It was a full-on assault.

We all loved films and we wanted to make them as well. Rob and his friends Andy and Mike Hurst went on to make a feature film in their twenties. I helped them with storyboards and editing. Years later Rob, Andy Starke and I made *Down Terrace*. Many of the scenes where shot in the front room where we watched all those films.

Now this might sound like the tale of an old man lamenting the days when it was hard to get hold of movies, trust me it's not. The more these movies can be seen and the easier the access to them then the more chance they have of eroding the edges of the status quo of modern cinema.

I'm profoundly jealous of anybody coming fresh to the back catalogue of world and genre cinema, its mind expanding and fucking great. And if you are an old lag like me, then seeing your favourite films in HD and not on a wobbly third-generation VHS has a revitalising effect. Though *Cannibal Holocaust* will always be a VHS film to me.

Ben Wheatley
Brighton, December 2015

CULT
MOVIES

THE HOUSE IS THE MONSTER

Tim Lucas on *The Fall of the House of Usher*

Artwork by Graham Humphreys

"Son coeur est un luth suspendu; sitot qu'on le touche il resonne."

("His heart is a hanging lute; whenever one touches it, it resounds.")

These lines of the French poet Pierre Jean de Béranger preface Edgar Allan Poe's 1839 story, *The Fall of the House of Usher*, and so has Poe's story had resounding effect on all the avenues of art to follow in its wake. Its influence can be heard in music from Claude Debussy to Philip Glass, seen in graphic art from Aubrey Beardsley to Gahan Wilson, and read in works ranging from Charles Baudelaire to Lemony Snicket. Even Herman Melville's Captain Ahab and Charles Dickens's Miss Havisham have a streak of the Usher madness about them, and would Jonathan Harker have ventured to Castle Dracula had Poe's nameless narrator not made the dreadful trek to the House of Usher first?

Nowhere is the story's resounding effect as strongly felt as in the art of cinema, where all the arts sing as one. Since its first adaptation in 1928, Poe's story has been retold in short and long form, in live action and animation, in silence and 5.1 surround sound, its eternally crumbling pillars salting the filmographies of such diverse disciples as Jean Epstein, Curtis Harrington, Jesús Franco and Ken Russell. When Epstein made the barely-feature-length *La Chute de la maison Usher* (1928), he used the story as reason to work within the stylistic realm of Expressionism, which was dying out as sound was forcing cinema in the direction of realism. Franco's *El hundimiento de la casa Usher* (1982) unreels like a confession of the story's influence on his entire mythos, its French version going so far as to incorporate flashbacks from his first horror film, *The Awful Dr. Orlof* (*Gritos en la noche*, 1962), about a mad doctor's attempts to restore the beauty of his sister, Melissa; plainly a Roderick-Madeline relationship. Russell's satirical *The Fall of the Louse of Usher* (2002) was literally shot on a camcorder in his home garage at a time when he was considered unemployable by major studios. In a most impressive example of the career through-line, Harrington used the story to literally bookend a 60-year career in films, beginning with an 8mm short (1942), made when he was only 16, and concluding with a 16mm short (2002), made a few years before his death, in which the reticent director ventured his only public statement about his sexuality by essaying the role of Madeline himself.

Yet none of these filmmakers is so well associated with Poe in general or *The House of Usher* in particular as Roger Corman. In 1960, poised to direct his 25th film, the 33-year-old Corman proposed to James H. Nicholson and Samuel Z. Arkoff of American International Pictures that they take the money they had been spending to produce black-and-white double bills and step up to the major leagues with a single, prestigious, colour picture. When he proposed *Usher*, his producers balked, insisting that a horror picture needed a monster. "The house is the monster!" Corman famously improvised – and subsequently took the most fortuitous step of his long career, graduating to a lavish $300,000 budget and indulgent (for him) 15-day schedule.

Corman chose *Usher* because Poe had been his first literary passion as a young man – also, he knew that Arkoff & Nicholson wouldn't likely object to a property in the public domain. However, there is also something to be said about the impact of UPA's Oscar-winning animated short *The Tell-Tale Heart* (1953), narrated by James Mason, whose influence Corman has never specifically acknowledged. Yet Paul Julian, the visionary designer of that short, was subsequently hired by Corman to design the title sequences of his *Not of This Earth* and *Attack of the Crab Monsters* in 1957, not to mention two more he produced in 1963: *The Terror* and Francis Coppola's *Dementia 13*. The look and atmosphere of *The Tell-Tale Heart*, which predates *Usher* by seven years, now feel unmistakably... Cormanesque.

Nevertheless, Poe's *Usher* – with its sense of contaminated earth, corrupted lives and imminent doom – taps into something vital and personal in Corman's own output. Westerns aside, Corman's earlier films were frequently set in the wake of some apocalypse; in stark contrast to other 1950s science fiction cinema that forewarned us about the perils of the Bomb, in Corman's films it has already fallen. (His first fantasy film, 1955's *Day the World Ended*, concludes with the apt title card "The Beginning".) What arose from this landscape of cataclysm was a new breed of Poe-seeded hyper-sensitives, rebels and mutations: Paul Birch's light-sensitive vampire in *Not of This Earth*, the scientist who invites alien peril as an alternative to the status quo in *It Conquered the World* (1956), the telepathic crabs of *Attack of the Crab Monsters*. The influence of *Usher* can even be found in Corman's crime pictures of the period, with the criminal figures of *Teenage Doll* (1957), *Machine-Gun Kelly* and *I, Mobster* (both 1958) all sporting morbid temperaments and death wishes branded into them by neurotic family associations. Such evidence suggests that *The Fall of the House of Usher* was less an inspired left turn in Corman's career than a galvanising homecoming that caused all the pieces to fall into place.

Those pieces would continue to fall into place throughout the 1960s. The official run of Corman-Poe pictures – *Pit and the Pendulum* (1961), *Premature Burial* (1961), *The Raven* (1963), *The Haunted Palace* (1964), *The Masque of the Red Death* (1964) and *The Tomb of Ligeia* (1965) – were just the cobwebs on the crypt, so to speak. The real living essence of Poe was expressed through Corman's other, most personal work: *Last Woman on Earth* (1960), another post-apocalyptic tale, in which two men vie for the privilege of mating with a woman who represents life and death; *X - The Man with the X-Ray Eyes* (1963), in which a doctor's self-experimentation raises his sensitivity of sight from humorous to epiphanic and finally unbearable ends; and perhaps most intriguingly, *The Trip* (1967), in which a Hollywood director of television commercials uses LSD in the hope of gaining personal and professional 'insight' – a film for which Corman prepared by taking LSD himself. In the context of *The Trip*, the protagonist experiences visions of himself with eyes bleeding, walking through derelict houses and along Pacific shorelines, burned to death, buried alive, and (as in *The Tomb of Ligeia*) poised at emotional equidistance between two women, one light-haired and representing life in the now, and one dark-haired and representing the past and death. Attentive to the vanguard of writing being done in the fields of horror, science fiction and fantasy, Corman hired *I Am Legend* novelist Richard Matheson (who had penned an episode of the Steve McQueen Western series *Wanted: Dead or Alive* shot by his own technical crew) to script the feature. Its ear for baroque language is one of its juiciest pleasures, especially when spoken by top-billed Vincent Price, whose experience as a radio actor seldom came into more expressive play onscreen. The St. Louis-born Price was Corman's first and only choice to play Roderick Usher, but his casting was as inevitable as Corman's selection of material. Since his defining success in 1953's 3D shocker *House of Wax*, Price had become the only criterion of quality native to 1950s horror, most recently having starred in William Castle's 1959 hits *House on Haunted Hill* and *The Tingler*. Just as important for Corman's purposes, Price was an American rarity, a 'king actor' schooled on the boards of the London stage (in 203 performances of *Victoria Regina* opposite Helen Hayes), who not only brought a cultured air to his performances, but also a hint of decadence. His portrayal of Nicholas Van Ryn in the 1946 film *Dragonwyck* now seems a foreshadowing of the brooding, death-obsessed

Artwork by the Twins of Evil

bluebloods he later played in the bulk of Corman's Poe pictures.

Essential to *Usher*'s galvanising effect on the horror genre was its distinction as the first American horror picture to be shot in colour (Eastmancolor, to be precise) and CinemaScope. It is necessary to qualify that achievement with nationality because it was preceded in this regard by one other picture: the Herman Cohen production *Horrors of the Black Museum* (1959), which Desmond Dickinson shot – it must be said – with a clashing carelessness that suggests literal colour-blindness. Corman, however, had been working since his first picture as a producer with veteran Academy Award-winning cinematographer Floyd Crosby, then in his late 50s. The two men had been developing a rapport with anamorphic storytelling since the 1955 Western *Apache Girl* (also in colour), finessing it into a genuine style by the time of *I, Mobster* in 1958. Between them, on this 15-day shoot, Corman and Crosby determined the correct way to photograph horror in colour.

Usher shows its cards immediately with its title sequence, a thrilling, deep-focused barrage of neon-bright colours playing over undulating fields of smoke, subliminally encouraging the viewer to look deeper while responding to its bizarre colour chart of limpid blues, voluptuous purples, lime greens and hellfire reds. What Corman and Crosby understood that Dickinson did not was the psychological value of colour, how to suppress and selectively release certain hues, how to exclude certain colours from the story's reality and give them free reign in its dreams. It didn't matter whether the audience consciously understood this; it was information built to bypass consciousness and go directly to work on the subconscious.

The Usher house itself, so deathly obsidian on the outside, is a surprising plethora of human colours inside, its reds and beiges suggesting a dwelling of flesh and blood, a projection of Roderick's acutely pitched nervous system, the rats he hears not creeping through its walls but so much a part of him as to infest his very veins. Wardrobe designer Marjorie Corso worked closely in tandem with the production's visual planning, contrasting the cool blues worn by Philip Winthrop (Mark Damon) upon his arrival with Roderick's (Price's) enflamed red and Madeline's (Myrna Fahey's) depleted pink. By dinner, Madeline is garbed in red, as if in quickened response to Philip's now-deeper blue – chromatic opposites attracting – while Roderick seems to already be mourning her in funereal black. Note the almost complete absence of red in the scene of Philip taking a breakfast tray to Madeline's room, which underscores their unity and intimacy in ways not found in the previous scenes. As she later escorts him to the family vaults below the house, red is expressed not in set dressing but in lighting, suffusing the sequence with a sense of impending spiritual danger. When Roderick decides it is time to take Philip into his confidence, their colours are more in accord than anywhere else in the picture: dark blue and charcoal grey. In this scene, Corman brilliantly allows the voice of Price to take full sway, speaking melodically over images that lull the viewer into receding from the images onscreen as if into a hypnotic dream state. As Roderick shows Philip the family portraits – delirious works by Beatnik-era painter Bud Schonberg – he seems to be initiating him to the colours and textures of the house's subconscious, which in turn infect Philip in the movie's *tour de force* dream sequence, the one point in the picture where Corman innovates something completely new and unmistakably his own – essentially by staging in live action what Julian had done with his downbeat Dalíesque designs in *The Tell-Tale Heart*.

Just as important to the film as its colour and width is its sense of depth, which Crosby secured through the use of a 24mm lens – famously used by Gregg Toland to produce similar uncanny visual effects in Orson Welles's *Citizen Kane* (1941). In the opening shot, for example, we see Philip riding on horseback through a singed forest of damnation (the location of an extinguished fire Corman had read about in that morning's newspaper), Crosby's tracking lens keeping him in perfect focus in the distance as the closer, bare, smoking branches seem to reach out to us three-dimensionally. These opening shots very much impressed the Italian cinematographer and director Mario Bava, who recreated their effect while introducing Mark Damon in the 'Wurdalak' segment of his AIP omnibus thriller *Black Sabbath* (*I tre volti della paura*, 1963).

The film reportedly grossed nearly $1,500,000 in its initial North American release alone, and it continued to earn for the remainder of the 1960s – on drive-in triple-bills and 'Dusk-to-Dawn' shows, in television syndication and in 16mm rentals – making it the hearthstone of American International Pictures. It did no less well throughout Europe; the international success of Hammer's *Dracula* had inspired Mario Bava's directorial debut, *Black Sunday* (*La maschera del demonio*, 1960; another big money-maker for AIP), but it was *The Fall of the House of Usher*, and its follow-up *Pit and the Pendulum*, that led to the rise of the Italian Gothics, an entire run of pictures (often starring Barbara Steele) about necrophiles and prematurely buried young women that masqueraded as US or British productions and lasted through 1966. Its influence continues to resound to this day in contemporary pictures like Hammer's *The Woman in Black* and Tim Burton's *Dark Shadows* (both 2012; say what you will about the movie itself, Johnny Depp gives a classic horror performance in the Vincent Price mode), but there is no substitute for the shock of the new that can still be felt here, as Corman and company advance the horror genre into its most brilliant decade.

***This essay originally appeared in the Arrow Video edition of* The Fall of the House of Usher.**

MURDER SET PIECES

Alan Jones on *Deep Red*

Artwork by Gilles Vranckx

Deep Red (*Profondo rosso*, 1975) is Dario Argento's undisputed *giallo* masterpiece, and requires an arsenal of superlatives to do it justice. Coming between his early 'Animal Trilogy' thrillers – *The Bird with the Crystal Plumage* (*L'uccello dalle piume di cristallo*, 1970), *The Cat o' Nine Tails* (*Il gatto a nove code*, 1971) and *Four Flies on Grey Velvet* (*4 mosche di velluto grigio*, 1971) – and his later surreal supernatural extravaganzas, *Suspiria* (1977) and *Inferno* (1980), this breathtaking mystery is a clearly transitional work. With one foot in the intricately-constructed whodunits of his past and the other in the more flamboyant, mosaic style of his Grand Guignol future, *Deep Red* takes the Argento brand of technical bravado and deranged shock tactics that made him world famous in stunning new directions – to create an artistically-rewarding and truly terrifying magnum opus, a pulse-pounding descent into a baroque vortex of madness that begins when a celebrity psychic senses the identity of a murderer at a parapsychology convention, and becomes the killer's next victim.

British musician Marcus Daly (David Hemmings) witnesses the clairvoyant's brutal death and gets hopelessly embroiled in the police investigation. Obsessed with the idea that he is forgetting some crucial detail at the scene of the crime, Marcus risks becoming either the chief suspect or another fatality. From these narrow plot threads, Argento weaves one of his most imitated films, imaginatively staged with high-powered visual dynamism and choreographed to a landmark progressive rock score.

It's the murder set pieces in his films that have gained Argento a peerless cult standing. And *Deep Red*'s catalogue of carnage has rightfully become the stuff of legend. From broken glass execution and boiling water drowning to mantelpiece teeth bashing and neck chain decapitation, the terror tableaux are spectacularly stage-managed for maximum shock and awe so that the viewer won't see the obvious. For in this über-*giallo*, Argento plays completely fair with the identity of his black-gloved assassin. The maniac's face is in clear view in the key death scene, but only a second viewing (after being privy to the solution) reveals that. Because the main point Argento makes in *Deep Red* is the elusiveness of memory: how the faulty remembrance of things past can irrationally unsettle and be deadly. Cast by Argento because of his role in Michelangelo Antonioni's Swinging Sixties milestone *Blowup* (1966), Hemmings is once more plunged into a warped variation on detective fiction conventions dealing with illusion versus reality. Except in *Deep Red*, Hemmings' character doesn't gaze at an enigmatic crime photo and find no answers. He clocks what he thinks is an abstract painting and can't see the deceptively easy explanation staring him in the face.

Deliberately theatrical – the opening conference is introduced with a parting of red curtains – Argento plays with the melodrama of telepathy and the ability to see into the future with remarkable dexterity. Triggered by the genuine insights of the ill-fated medium, seen reacting in horror moments before the axe-murderer breaks down her apartment door, the precognitive theme is brilliantly carried through the entire sleight-of-hand narrative as a device foreshadowing each death. For example, Marcus is scalded by coffee machine steam prior to the boiling water death of the *Modern Ghosts and Black Legends of Today* author. And when Marcus jokes about playing the piano because it represents the symbolic smashing of his hated father's teeth, the bloody mantelpiece disfiguration isn't too far behind. With Argento's camera cruising in close-up along the keys of a piano, between toys on a floor, following a mannequin's eerie entrance and literally focusing on the killer's lost marbles, *Deep Red* takes its provocative Freudian motifs and visually elevates them into high art. With every voyeuristic nook and cranny explored by his purposeful camera, Argento renders even the daylight locations as sinister and dangerous as the Edward Hopper-inspired night-time ones, unlocking primal fears in the spectator they didn't even know they had.

Deep Red emerged from of the ashes of Argento's only big box-office failure. After *Four Flies on Grey Velvet*, the director had called time on the *giallo* and searched for a new creative challenge. "I had brought the horror thriller back into style," Argento once told me. "After *Four Flies on Grey Velvet* I felt the need to distance myself from it. Too many other Italian directors were ripping-off the genre with pale imitations and catchpenny titles echoing mine. I felt I should move in a different direction." The result was *The Five Days of Milan* (*Le cinque giornate*, 1973), a historical comedy-drama about the Italian revolution in the mid-19th century. A flop in Italy, and never given a proper release outside his home shores, *The Five Days of Milan* proved such a nightmare to make that Argento was more than happy to return to his *giallo* comfort zone.

Almost as if he had taken stock of the *giallo* explosion around him and decided to show his impersonators how it should be done, Argento went to stay at his parents' country house to write what would quickly become one of the most beloved jewels in his crown. "I returned to the thriller with a clear-headed passionate force that focused me in all the right directions," he divulged. "There's a clockwork precision to *Deep Red* and an aura of ambiguity in every single character. Everyone is a suspect with aggressive and murderous thoughts. I wanted *Deep Red* to incorporate new emotions and sensations and merge the boundaries between the thriller and horror film." Which is, of course, why it proved to be the stepping-stone to the more Gothic settings of *Suspiria* – Argento's most famous film and one that was responsible for changing the face of global horror.

To help reinterpret his characteristic *giallo* themes – Freud's 'primal scene' theory about warped childhood experience leading to disordered adult existence; the spectator made both accomplice and victim; the fetishised murder weapons – Argento chose as his co-writer Bernardino Zapponi, the long-time collaborator of Federico Fellini. Not because Zapponi had written *Satyricon* (1969) or *Roma* (1972), but because he had scripted the director's acclaimed *Toby Dammit* segment in the Edgar Allan Poe anthology *Spirits of the Dead* (*Histoires extraordinaires*, 1968). "Bernardino filled me with optimism on a daily basis and was a joy to work with. It was he who took my initial ideas for the murders and made them more effective. Why the movie is considered so sadistic is because the injuries shown are ones the audience effortlessly relates to. A tiny percentage of the public knows the pain of being shot by a gun. But everyone knows what it's like to stub your toe on furniture or be scalded by hot water. Bernardino also thought up the central misdirection device of the mirror painting."

Although *The Bird with the Crystal Plumage* was shot entirely on location in Rome, Argento had veered away from filming in the Eternal City because of the constant tourist hassle. Turin soon became his city location of choice and *Deep Red* benefits enormously from what Argento terms its "magical atmosphere". The director elaborates: "There are more practising Satanists in Turin than in any other European city and I wanted that superstitious undercurrent unfolding in the background. Turin is actually where the Italian film industry was originally based in the silent era. During the 1930s Mussolini moved it to Rome, to be nearer out of vanity, but I have always preferred Turin."

Deep Red is of utmost importance in the Argento universe for two main reasons: lead actress Daria Nicolodi and the rock band Goblin. Former stage star

Nicolodi would be vital to Argento's artistic career changes, become his lover and the mother of their now-famous actress daughter Asia Argento. Asia was born exactly a year to the day her mother walked in front of Argento's cameras during the sixteen-week shoot beginning September 9, 1974. Nicolodi first caught Argento's eye in Elio Petri's socio-political comedy *Property is No Longer a Theft* (*La proprietà non è più un furto*, 1973). The fact that she spent the entire running time naked might explain his attention more! But he thought she'd be perfect to play the lead role of feisty journalist Gianna Brezzi in *Deep Red*. On the rebound from his romance with Marilù Tolo, star of *The Five Days of Milan*, Argento was so struck by Nicolodi at her audition that the result was a whirlwind, headline-grabbing love affair. Although the relationship would end in bitter recrimination, lies and accusations (Argento was deliberately trying to sabotage her acting career), *Deep Red* was the hearts-and-flowers honeymoon period that both parties now fondly remember.

"Daria was clearly in my destiny the moment we met," disclosed Argento. "We seemed to connect on so many levels politically and culturally. It was a stormy relationship containing many highs and lows, the best one being Asia. I wouldn't have stayed with her for so many years if I hadn't thought we were two sides to the same coin though. I've forgotten the bad times now, the ultimate testament is the fantastic work we did together." Nicolodi adds: "It's true. We were incredibly happy making *Deep Red* and I think our love story shines through the finished film. My theatre friends thought I was crazy to consider starring in an Argento film. They were very snobby and dismissive over his thrillers. But I adored the script because it would mark the first time I'd be playing such a take-charge woman rather than the fragile ones I'd become known for. Dario got the stronger personality within me out into the open and helped me explore it. My arm-wrestling scene with David Hemmings is a case in point. I win by cheating, but it also underlines the possibility that the hatchet murderer might be female."

The moment Argento chose the supergroup Goblin to augment Giorgio Gaslini's score for *Deep Red* is now considered one of the most important decisions in the history of the horror genre. The pumped-up and atmospheric progressive rock became a phenomenon and a genre watershed. "I had wanted to use the rock band Deep Purple for *Four Flies on Grey Velvet* and for *Deep Red* I contacted Pink Floyd to see if they might be interested. They weren't! So I began asking musician friends for ideas and a demo tape by Goblin found its way to me. One day after

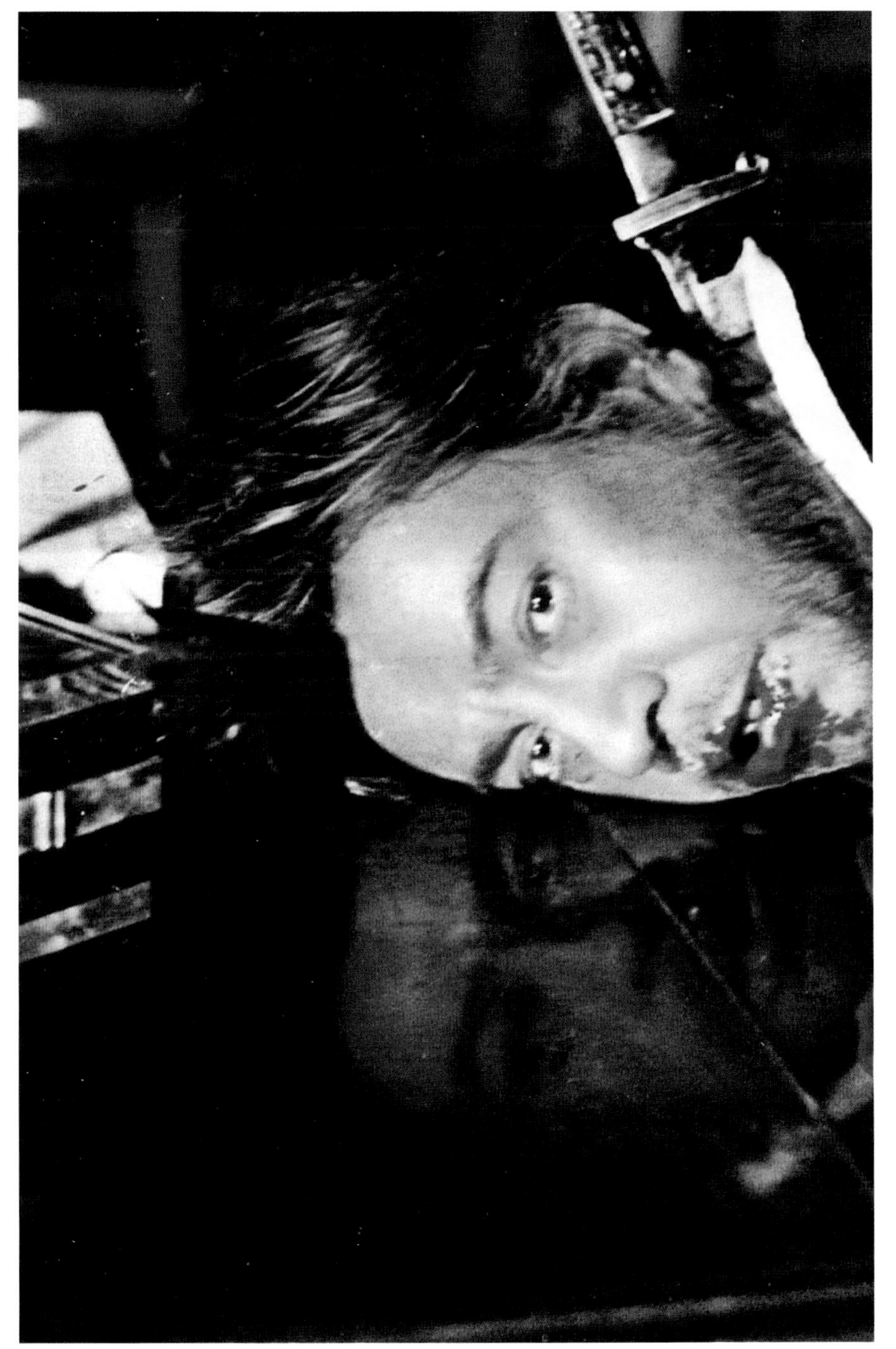

Deep Red

contacting them, two great compositions arrived in the mail. I signed them up immediately and we spent a month improvising in the studio for the final themes."

Goblin keyboardist, composer and producer Claudio Simonetti couldn't believe it when his band was given the *Deep Red* assignment. "We were nobodies and Dario was this famous director," recalls Simonetti. "For a while we just lounged around listening to Dario's favourite music by Emerson, Lake and Palmer and Genesis, and then we went away and composed the soundtrack. I think Argento and Goblin were a great marriage. Because Goblin went on to compose *Suspiria*, his production of George A. Romero's *Dawn of the Dead* (1978) and *Sleepless* (*Non ho sonno*, 2001), our success is so inextricably linked with his – like John Williams to Steven Spielberg. While I do tire of the fan boy cult built up around us sometimes, I will never be anything less than grateful to Dario. Nearly forty years after we wrote *Deep Red* we are still talking about it, audiences are still responding to it and the music is still selling. How brilliant is that?" Simonetti continued to work with Argento on *Tenebrae* (*Tenebre*, 1982), *Demons* (*Dèmoni*), *Phenomena* (both 1985), *The Card Player* (*Il cartaio*, 2004), *Mother of Tears* (*La terza madre*, 2007) and *Dracula 3D* (2012).

Another lasting legacy of *Deep Red* is that it became the name of a rare business venture Argento created with Luigi Cozzi, co-writer of *Four Flies on Grey Velvet* (and director of the 1980 alien chest-bursting epic *Contamination*). Situated at 260 Via dei Gracchi in Rome is the Profondo Rosso horror emporium, which sells Argento merchandise and other genre related products. In the basement is a wax museum featuring tableaux from Argento's best-known films. So if you're in Rome, pop along, say 'Hi' to Luigi, tell him I sent you, and he'll be happy to show you around.

***This essay originally appeared in the Arrow Video edition of* Deep Red.**

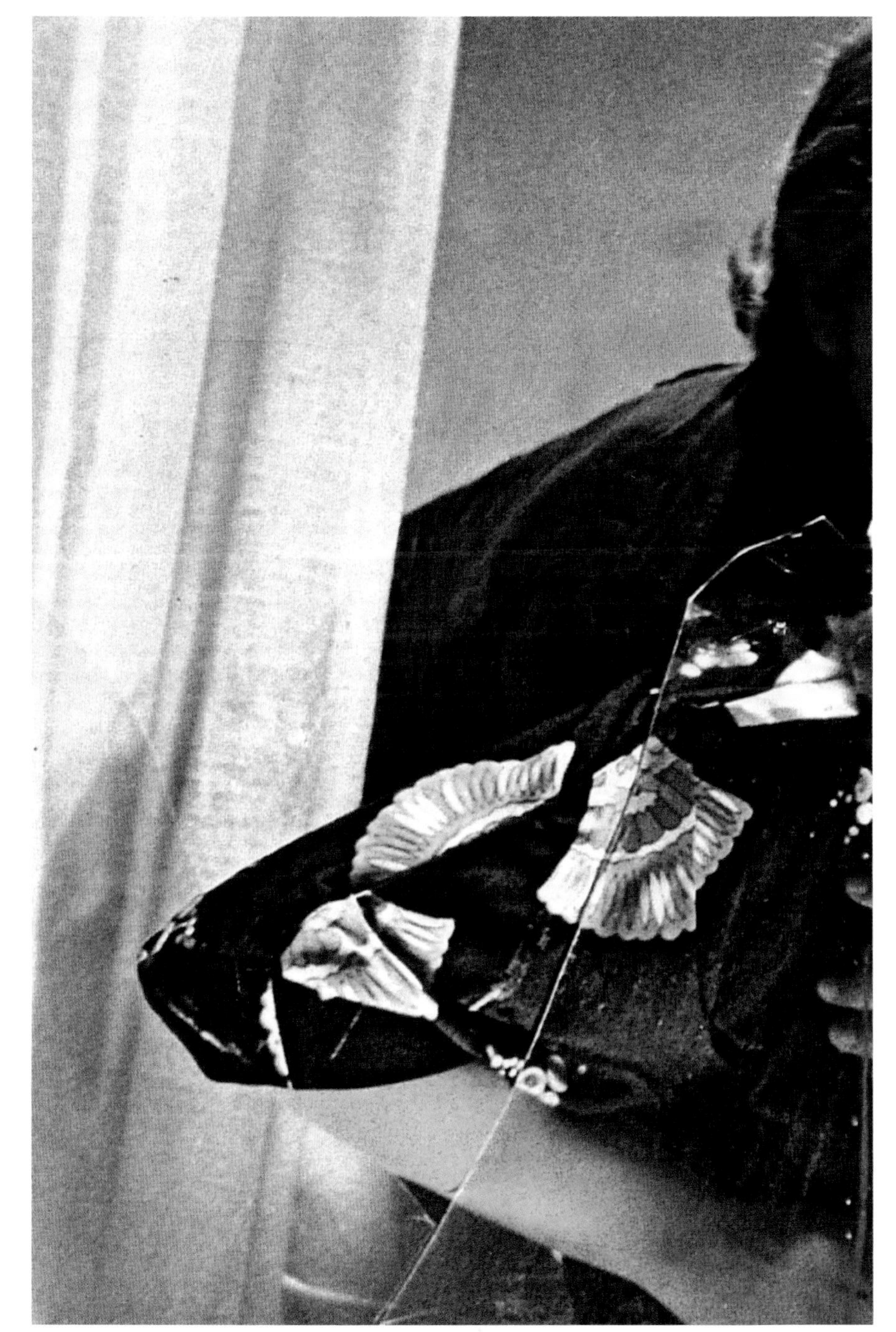

Deep Red

THE JOYS OF REPULSION, OR ANTHROPHAGY IN THE UK

Stephen Thrower on *Zombie Flesh Eaters*

Artwork by Graham Humphreys

Nineteen-seventy-nine was a revitalising year for the Italian horror film, and Lucio Fulci was without doubt the prime mover. Yet on the face of it, his *Zombi 2* – the key film in this renaissance – had all the hallmarks of a quickie rip-off, financed by producer Fabrizio De Angelis to cash in on George A. Romero's *Dawn of the Dead* (1978). To match the enormous success of the Romero film in Italy, De Angelis required a seasoned professional at the wheel. So when his original choice of director, action helmer Enzo G. Castellari, dropped out, Lucio Fulci was drafted in on the basis of two previous films – *Don't Torture a Duckling* (*Non si sevizia un paperino*, 1972) and *The Psychic* (*Sette note in nero*, 1977) – both of which featured graphic, high-impact violence. Also hired was the screenwriter of *The Psychic*, Dardano Sacchetti (although the on-screen credit went to his wife Elisa Briganti). Sacchetti himself stresses that when he wrote the script, "It was conceived as a mix of adventure and horror themes; the reference was more to *The Island of Dr. Moreau*. The film was first conceived by me with the adventurous atmosphere of mystery and thriller that gradually become horror. The idea was about someone dead, reanimated and remote-controlled by a crazy scientist through an electronic device put in the brain. I decided to return to the classic zombie tales, and we tried to use those clichés for a story which started as a mystery and became an adventure afterwards."

The script went through several further changes, but Fulci and Sacchetti embraced the opportunity to turn what could have been a simple rip-off into a nerve-wracking horror classic. The story was ingeniously set up as, if anything, a prequel to Romero's hit. *Zombi 2* would draw upon older horror-film imagery, including Hammer's 1966 gem *The Plague of the Zombies*, the Val Lewton horrors of the 1940s, and even earlier titles. Speaking in 1980, Fulci said, "I've always held great admiration for the marvellous horror classics made in America. Films such as *I Walked with a Zombie* (1941), *Voodoo Island* (1957) and *The Walking Dead* (1936) were all in the back of my mind as I made this picture."

Released in Italy in September 1978, *Dawn of the Dead* was known there as *Zombi*; thanks to the Italian legal system Fulci's movie could be released with the brazenly exploitative title of *Zombi 2*. It was shot in June and July of 1979, and then rushed into Italian cinemas in August. The film did very well in Italy and performed spectacularly worldwide. Made for substantially less than $500,000, it raked in more than three million dollars, and it was this success that provided Italian horror with a booster shot of producer confidence; the result was a gory tidal wave of trashy Italian horror epics. However, a different strategy was required to sell Fulci's film in America, where it was released simply as *Zombie*. In the UK it became *Zombie Flesh-Eaters* and in 1980 was given an X-certificate after the removal of several key scenes by the BBFC.

It would be another 18 months before British audiences could to enjoy the film in its entirety, thanks to Vipco, one of the early market leaders in home video, who took the unusual step of supplying two different cuts of the film to retailers – the BBFC 'X' print and a "Strong Uncut Version". Whilst the latter was a huge rental success (and ended up on the infamous 'video nasty' list) the cut version provided video dealers with a valuable lesson – barely a soul rented it! So much for protecting the public...

Zombie Flesh-Eaters starts strongly aboard a deserted schooner drifting into New York Harbour. Fulci immediately declares a very different identity to Romero's *Dawn of the Dead*, thanks to the bizarre zombie first encountered by two harbour patrolmen. As one of them explores the deserted schooner, we see details of squalor amid cramped quarters: rotting food on scattered paper plates; the sound of buzzing flies. On the keys of a tiny old Pianola in the corner of the cabin, lies a tangled mess of filthy black gunge and writhing worms. The information contained in the shot is negligible, yet the grossness of the image suggests that the audience beware – the film will have as much to do with gut-level repulsion as violence. When a zombie bursts out of the hold and attacks the officer, the victim tears a strip of rotten, scab-like flesh clean off and we see the intense disgust on his face. Seconds later his throat is savaged in a welter of gore. Hugely obese, with flaking skin and drooling blood, the creature then lurches onto the deck, backlit by the sun hanging low in the sky. The effect is a combination of menace, repulsiveness and out-and-out weirdness. As the zombie falls into the harbour waves, propelled by the force of the second officer's gun, Sergio Salvati's camera rises slowly from the darkened waters to dwell, ominously, upon the coastal skyline of New York, leading to expectations of an urban apocalypse. The following scene at the morgue, with the patrolman's body twitching to life, points again to the beginnings of urban destruction.

On the acting front, Fulci was well served by two British performers, Richard Johnson and Ian McCulloch. Johnson turned in a sweaty, shifty performance in a tantalising but underwritten role. He began as a stage actor at 17, before his good looks ensured him leading

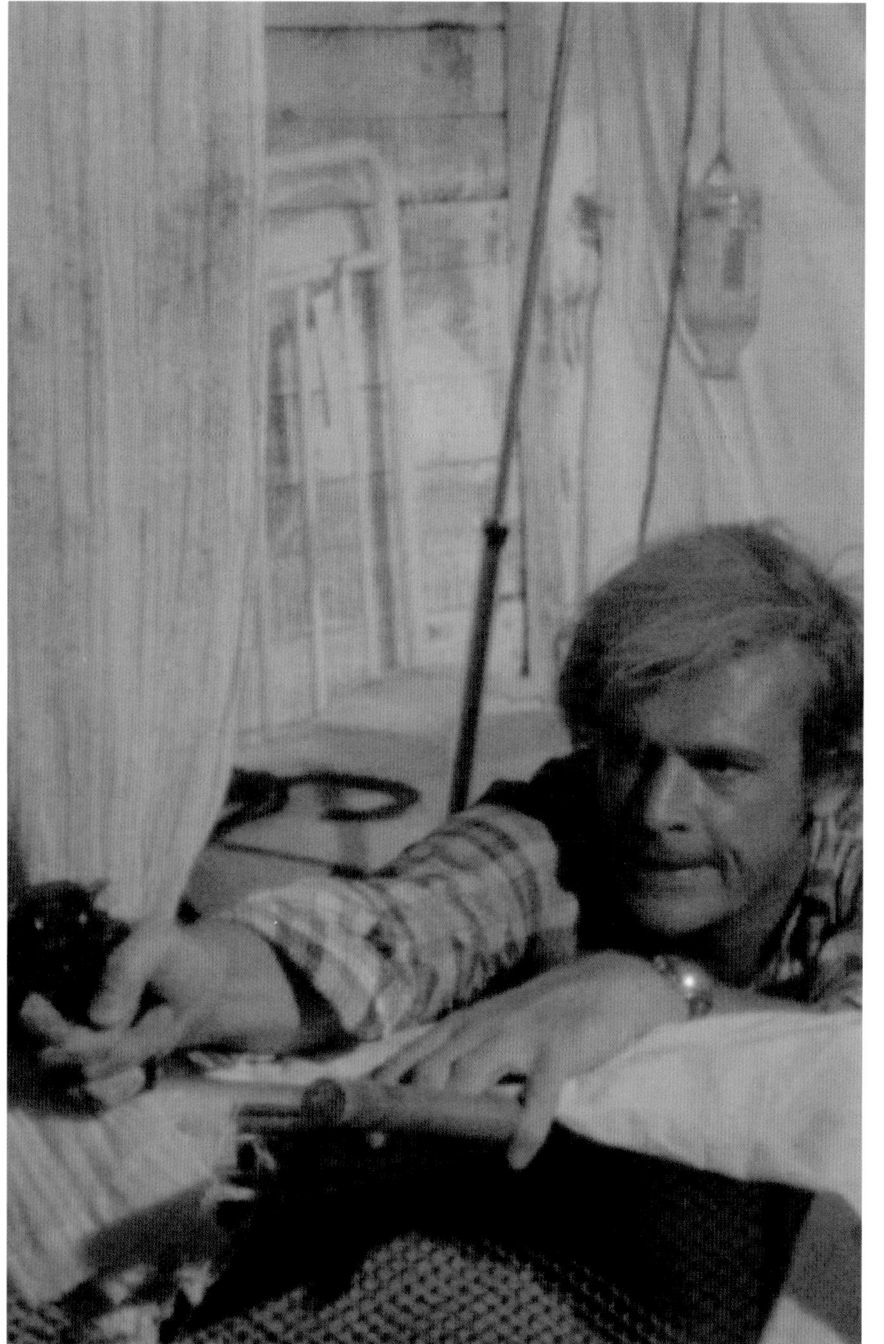

man status in a string of movies. An early showing in Robert Wise's masterful *The Haunting* (1963) lent him genre credibility, as did his frequent forays into Italian horror for directors like Damiano Damiani (*The Witch/ La Strega in amore*, 1966) and Massimo Dallamano (*The Cursed Medallion/Il medaglione insanguinato*, 1974, aka *The Night Child*). Fulci, an often tyrannical presence on set, was apparently rather in awe of the man; a rare accolade for an actor! McCulloch, a seasoned veteran of low-budget production, was given little in the way of scintillating dialogue to play with, but created a warm and likeable character. Born in 1940, he trained at RADA, worked with the Royal Shakespeare Company and made his first horror film appearance in *It!* for Herbert J. Leder in 1967. He went on to TV prominence as the star of Terry Nation's science fiction drama series, *The Survivors* (1975-77), and indeed, co-producer Ugo Tucci offered McCulloch the lead in *Zombie Flesh-Eaters* because of the series' success in Italy.

En route to the island of Matul, sexploitation thrusts its helmet above the parapet, with ogling shots of actress Auretta Gay's topless scuba diving preparations. Such tackiness is swiftly forgotten, though, as Susan is attacked by a bizarre, ragged ghoul and then menaced by a shark. What follows is a triumph of the ridiculous that seems to have stayed in the minds of all who've seen the film: a slow-motion fight between zombie and shark, with the latter tearing at rotting limbs with much gratuitous crunching on the soundtrack. The crowning touch to this balletic confrontation is the score; a gorgeously calm yet patently loopy composition by the wonderful Fabio Frizzi.

If one image were to act as the pinnacle of Fulci's contribution to cinema, it would doubtless have to be the fate of Mrs Menard, whose right eye is impaled on a splinter of wood in glorious close-up. The loving detail Fulci brings to the scene has ensured that it's firmly wedged in the memories of all aficionados of horror. Some might claim this scene indulges in a pathological hostility to women, and yet one could counter that the predominantly male audience is itself being penetrated by an image which – by macho viewing standards – they are required to keep watching. The victim may be a woman, but the audience for horror (let's face it, largely male) is forced to identify with a suffering female. Put more simply, all viewers, male and female, experience common humanity by observing penetration of the eye. Cynics will probably argue that it signals nothing more than Fulci's wish, after thirty years in the industry, to make an unforgettable impression on an audience. Well good for him – he did it!

A zombie in Italian cinema is iconoclastic, presenting something supernatural yet stubbornly corporeal: parading the flesh without the much-vaunted spirit. For Catholics, the body becomes a waste-product excreted by the passage of the soul into heaven. Fulci's zombies – far more revolting than Romero's – exude a foreboding reek of physical disgust. Nowhere is this more obvious than the scene depicting the unfortunate Mrs Menard's body being eaten by ghouls. Her flesh is unaccountably slimy and wet; closer to jelly than meat and sinew. Liquescent and undifferentiated, her organs, skin and muscle tissue are reduced to slippery pulp. The reactions of the four heroes witnessing this tableau are vital: they back off, their faces contorted not with shock or fear but revulsion. This loathing is generated by the sight of the human body as nothing but food. One is reminded of film critic Barbara Creed, who wrote: "In relation to the horror film, it is relevant to note that food loathing is frequently represented as a major source of abjection, particularly the eating of human flesh...The ultimate in abjection is the corpse. Within a religious context, the corpse is also utterly abject. It signifies one of the basic forms of pollution - the body without a soul...as a form of waste it represents the opposite of the spiritual..." She's spot on here: thus indeed do we react to Mrs Menard's body, repulsive and abject in its loss of form and integrity. For the climax of the film, the remaining humans, trapped in a wooden chapel under siege from hordes of zombies, attack these putrefied corruptions with cleansing fire, supporting Creed's notion that the popular horror film is a modern defilement rite, seeking "the purification of the abject through a descent into the foundations of the symbolic construct."

But we don't have to get that heavy. *Zombie Flesh-Eaters* is not a masterpiece, more a sort of 'pop classic' of Italian horror. Fulci crafted a memorable experience sure to excite connoisseurs of extreme imagery and the action in the second half of the film cracks along with the energy a good horror comic. Ultimately, *Zombie Flesh-Eaters* is sensational without being particularly complex, but thanks to Fulci's stylish direction, Frizzi's wonderful score and the outrageous invention of those unforgettable gore effects, it will always stay in the hearts and minds of those who love Italian exploitation cinema.

***This essay originally appeared in the Arrow Video edition of* Zombie Flesh Eaters.**

AMERICAN GIALLO

Maitland McDonagh on *Dressed to Kill*

Artwork by Nathanael Marsh

Was *Pandora's Box* (1929) the first erotic thriller? How about *Phantom Lady* (1944) or *Gun Crazy* (1950) or *Psycho* (1960)? You can play this game for hours, but the fact is that the average moviegoer didn't hear the term until the mid-1980s, well after Brian De Palma's *Dressed to Kill* (1980) had already showed them exactly what an erotic thriller was: a movie that, as Linda Ruth Williams wrote in her 2005 study *The Erotic Thriller in Contemporary Cinema*, "consistently links the violently sexual with the sexually violent." Four years later, after *Blow Out* (1981) – a high-tech homage to Michelangelo Antonioni – and the epic bloodletting of *Scarface* (1983), De Palma claimed he was making *Body Double* (1984) to show critics just how violently sexual and sexually violent a movie he could make, and succeeded in whipping up a maelstrom of crosstalk about exactly how far 'too far' was, but *Dressed to Kill* got there first. And that wasn't all it did: fewer moviegoers noticed, but it was also one of, if not the, first mainstream American thrillers to incorporate the aesthetics associated with *gialli* – baroquely stylised European shockers in which narrative takes a back seat to lavish murder numbers of near-operatic intensity.

Dressed to Kill was the very definition of a divisive hit, variously hailed as a sleek, witty entertainment by a filmmaker comfortable straddling art and commerce, dismissed as a run-of-the-mill thriller with some fancy frills and derided as a violent low in mainstream moviemaking. Some filmmakers would have blanched at seeing the fruit of their labours labelled "a master work of misogyny" by the short-lived but media-savvy organisation Women Against Violence and Pornography in Media, coupled with the warning "if this film succeeds, killing women may become the greatest turn-on of the eighties".

But De Palma was made of tougher stuff, at least in part because he was no stranger to polarising controversy. More than a decade earlier, his second feature, the Vietnam-era anti-war satire *Greetings* (1968) – which starred a very young Robert De Niro – was lauded in the alternative press as a fresh, irreverent, razor-sharp takedown of hippie-dippy anti-establishment pretentions while more traditional outlets damned with faint praise ("photographed in good colour") or slapped it down as a distasteful exercise in juvenile snark that wasn't half as clever as it thought itself. *Greetings* was also awarded an MPAA X rating (later revised to an R), a designation which, though not meant to carry the weight of a scarlet letter, was instantly associated with hardcore pornography. And that limited advertising outlets – respectable newspapers didn't run ads for X-rated movies (many still don't) – and sent legitimate cinema owners scampering for cover.

Given that *Greetings* was a $400,000 independent production at a time when indie filmmaking lacked the cachet it now enjoys, it was ideally positioned to weather a ratings hit. Few cinemas would have played it anyway and, if anything, it probably got a no-such-thing-as-bad-publicity box-office boost from the tempest in a couple of big-city teapots. Still, it's hard to imagine De Palma anticipating that 12 years later and firmly ensconced in the Hollywood mainstream, he'd again find himself in the MPAA's sights, this time defending a $6.5 million thriller featuring bona fide movie stars Angie Dickinson and Michael Caine, let alone that he'd be persuaded to make the tweaks and trims required to secure a more return-on-investment-friendly R.

But for all his fondness for provocations, De Palma was a get-the-job done guy – he averaged a feature a year for two decades and I'm willing to bet that if he'd traipsed into the jungle to shoot *Apocalypse Now* (1979), it would have been finished more or less on time and with a lot less wear on all concerned. It also wouldn't have been Francis Ford Coppola's feverish, mythopoetic *Apocalypse Now*, but the point goes is to method, not divine madness.

Dressed to Kill began in disappointment. The movie De Palma had wanted to make was *Cruising*, and he went so far as to write a what was essentially a spec script based on Gerald Walker's lurid 1970 novel about a New York City cop who goes undercover to find a serial killer trolling for victims in New York's hardcore gay underworld and loses himself in the process. Only after he was done did De Palma discover that he "couldn't get control of the rights", which eventually went to William Friedkin, unquestionably the better filmmaker for the job. It's hard to imagine De Palma, an outside-in filmmaker like his idol, Alfred Hitchcock, leathering up and prowling S&M bars to get a first-hand feel for the material.

But the book stuck with him – "mulling around in my head," he's said, along with Judith Rossner's 1975 *Looking for Mr. Goodbar*, a then-controversial novel inspired by the recent murder of 28-year-old Roseann Quinn, whose double life (special needs schoolteacher by day, sex-seeking barfly by night) led to her murder, and an idea for a scene that first came to him in college and involved "picking up a girl in an art gallery where you can see people looking at paintings, looking at each other". What brought the threads together was a 1978 episode of a popular chat show hosted by the genial but culturally engaged Phil Donohue. It addressed issues affecting transgendered individuals and featured Nancy Hunt, an articulate, witty, former-war correspondent who underwent sexual reassignment surgery in 1976 and was promoting her memoir *Mirror Image: The Odyssey of a Male to Female Transsexual*. De Palma started writing again, and eventually incorporated footage from the interview into the finished film, including Hunt's disarmingly frank declaration that both before and after surgery, she had always been "a devout heterosexual".

Stripped of its loopily entertaining digressions, *Dressed to Kill*'s plot is surprisingly straightforward. (WARNING: spoilers ahead!) Sexually frustrated Upper East Side housewife Kate Miller leaves an emotionally fraught session with her avuncular psychiatrist, Dr. Elliott, and goes to a museum to kill time before meeting her mother-in-law for lunch. She impulsively blows off the date for a tryst with a stranger. Hours later, she leaves his apartment and is slashed to death in the elevator by a tall, razor-wielding woman. Call girl Liz Blake catches a glimpse of the killer, but the police seem more inclined to consider her a suspect rather than a witness: after all, no one else saw the big blonde and hookers lie for a living. So when Liz realizes she's being stalked she begins her own investigation, and winds up working with Kate's brilliant, vulnerable teenage son, who feels responsible for his mother's death because he begged off the museum trip at the last minute. They eventually discover that Kate's psychiatrist is a deeply disturbed cross-dresser whose female persona is compelled to lash out at women who arouse his male one.

Hitchcock's influence – specifically that of *Psycho*, but also *Vertigo* (1958) and *Spellbound* (1945) – is apparent in *Dressed to Kill*'s stylish use of light and shadow, fluid camerawork, painstakingly constructed suspense sequences peppered with naughty jokes (how can you not laugh at the sight of prim, white-clad Kate at the museum, repeatedly passing an enormous painting of a woman's crotch?) and pop-Freudian underpinnings. It even has a buttoned-down doppelgänger to *Psycho*'s Dr. Richman (Simon Oakland) in Dr. Levy (David Margulies), who drops by to explain for the slow-on-the uptake all about Dr. Elliott and the killer Bobbi, a man and a woman locked in a life-or-death struggle for dominance rolled into a single, lethally damaged individual. The only thing he doesn't mention is that Caine only appears once as Bobbi; the rest of the time she's played by actress Susanna Clemm (who's credited only for her small role as a police detective).

But beneath the glib psychobabble and visual flourishes is a surprisingly sympathetic story about throwaway women: well-preserved housewife Kate (though not quite so well-preserved as she appears in her shower scene; a Penthouse Pet stood in for the "beaver shots", as DP Ralf Bode dubbed them; the doubling is dizzying) who's so demoralised by life as an accessory to her husband's upscale dreams that she'd rather be treated as a slut by a stranger; blowsy, ambitious hooker Liz, who sees selling herself as a means to a suspect end – Kate being Exhibit A in the argument that money can't buy freedom, let alone happiness; and statuesque lady-in-black Bobbi, whose very right to exist has been denied for so long that her simmering frustration turns to murderous rage.

Bobbi is, of course, a quintessential *giallo* construction, the bridge between the hand-me-down Hitchcock influences at which De Palma's detractors love to sneer and a fevered world of gender ambiguity, nightmarish ecstasies, faulty perceptions and the overall sense of a world gone mad. Hitchcock's murder scenes, however complex and stylised, elicit no joy from the flensing of flesh: the immortal death of Marion Crane is brutal but concludes on a note of overwhelming sadness, the terrible conclusion of one false move – stealing $40,000 from her wealthy, self-centred boss in the hope of escaping to a new life with her financially strapped lover.

Kate's death is sadder still – all she's done is reach out to a stranger for a few moments of connection – but it's the culmination of an escalating spectacle of humiliation. First she's spied on by a cabbie as she and her new lover start their cavorting en route to his downtown bachelor pad, then, as she's penning a polite post-coital thank you note ("I loved our afternoon..."), she discovers a health-department notice revealing that not only does he have both syphilis and gonorrhoea, but she's only one of at least a dozen women he's slept with recently. And then, after realising in the elevator that she's forgotten her engagement ring (and enduring the stink eye from a sullen little girl whose mother hisses "It's not polite to stare" to no effect), she goes back to retrieve it and comes face-to-face with the killer who carves her up, cuts her throat and leaves her body to the kindness of strangers, her bloody hand trapped limply between the elevator's door frame and the safety door gently bumping her wrist as it tries to close. Could it be any more mortifying? Well, yes actually: Kate's murder is (unsurprisingly) front-page news, which means her son learns the sordid details of her demise, information no mother would wish on her child.

That's all *giallo* territory, key images that reference *Psycho*'s shower scene – notably Kate's resigned death-slide down the elevator's mirrored wall and her hand reaching out for help – notwithstanding. Just take a look at Giuliano Carnimeo and Ernesto Gastaldi's *The Case of the Bloody Iris* (*Perché quelle strane gocce di sangue sul corpo di Jennifer?*, 1972), which opens with pretty blonde Lona (Evi Farinelli) – as carefully coiffed and made up as Kate Miller, whom she might well resemble if she lived to be 40 – entering an elevator for some manner of assignation. Lona too is carved up and left with her throat cut for a sultry model (models and prostitutes, after all, being interchangeable character types) to discover when the elevator door next opens.

Dressed to Kill is not only caught up in the same sexual maelstrom that propels classic *gialli* – woman who appear to be men, men configured as women, killers, victims and sleuths (professional and amateur) driven by impulses they can neither accept nor banish no matter how much chaos they unleash – but set to an overripe score by Pino Donaggio, in which the anti-intuitive tension between lushly orchestrated melodies and brutal visuals contribute to the overall sense of a world out of sync. For contrast, recall the shrieking violins Bernard Hermann matched to *Psycho*'s slashing shower scene – neither is inherently better, but they're deeply different.

Dressed to Kill came under fire from all directions, accused of everything from helping raise the bar on movie violence (a hard charge to make stick when it opened the same year as *Maniac*, *Caligula*, *Friday the 13th*, *Shogun Assassin*, plus a slew of Italian 'can you top this?' pictures) to pandering both to misogynists and homophobes. In regard to the former, it's only fair to point out that *Dressed to Kill*'s sympathies lie squarely with the victim. De Palma spells it out in the scene in which coarse homicide detective Marino (Dennis Franz, later of long-running TV cop shows *Hill Street Blues* [1981-87] and *NYPD Blue* [1993-2005]) asks Dr Elliott whether Kate might have been asking for it: The answer is a coldly furious no. Elliott, meanwhile, isn't gay (remember Nancy Hunt, whom Elliott is seen watching on TV?) – if he were, his self-possessed mind wouldn't be so lethally out of line with his unruly manhood.

As to the latter, whether Elliott is a thwarted transsexual or a conflicted transvestite is anyone's call, but the larger issue is that in the late '70s/early '80s the average American didn't differentiate between homosexuals, transvestites and transsexuals. They were all queers and, as such, suspect, so without imputing any malice to De Palma's part, it's fair to say *Dressed to Kill* didn't improve the image of then-unnamed LGBT community in the popular imagination.

Still, it's only fair to point out that it's less corrosive than the movie De Palma didn't make: *Cruising*, which opened five months earlier, depicted an indisputably gay world defined by self-involvement, loveless coupling and the unrelenting threat of violence. Friedkin's *Cruising* is a great movie whose tone (if not its details) comes straight from the source novel and whose troubling ambiguities are actually more potent today than they were nearly 35 years ago. Star Al Pacino argued at the time that *Cruising* was to the gay community as *The Godfather* (1972) was to Italian-Americans, a superficially reasonable argument that founders on the fact that Italians were stereotyped not just as gangsters, but also passionate lovers, devoted parents, generous friends and fun-loving neighbours. Gay men, by contrast, were typically portrayed as paedophiles, suicidal outcasts, cowards, pathetic pansies and bitchy troublemakers. When a legacy studio like Warners felt compelled to include an onscreen assurance that *Cruising* wasn't meant as an indictment of homosexuals, you know they knew they were playing with fire.

Neither film has been forgotten, but while *Cruising* is now accorded a measure of grudging and by no means unanimous respect, *Dressed to Kill* has become the belle of the (drag) ball. *Dressed to Kill* is A-list fun – sexy and suspenseful and sleek as a cunning little vixen, a virtuoso romp through a naughty New York luscious you can't help but wish it would come back... except that it never was. It's a New York of the mind, peopled by golden-hearted hookers, psycho shrinks, urban Hardy boys and tough cops in gold chains and brown-leather jackets. You can't go back again, but you can pop *Dressed to Kill* in the DVD player and pay a visit.

***This essay originally appeared in the Arrow Video edition of* Dressed to Kill.**

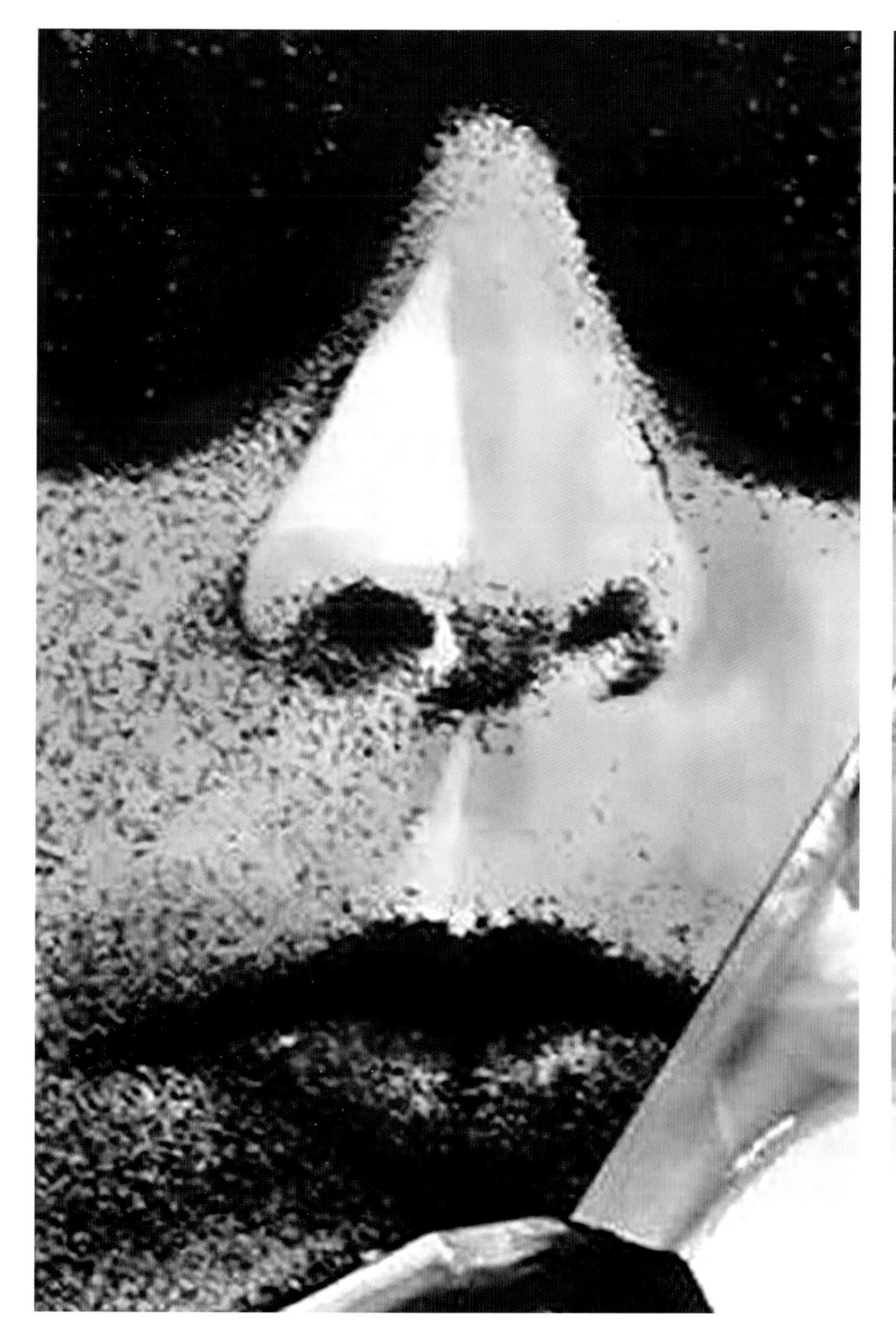

Dressed to Kill

ALMOST A COMEDY

Vic Pratt on *Withnail & I*

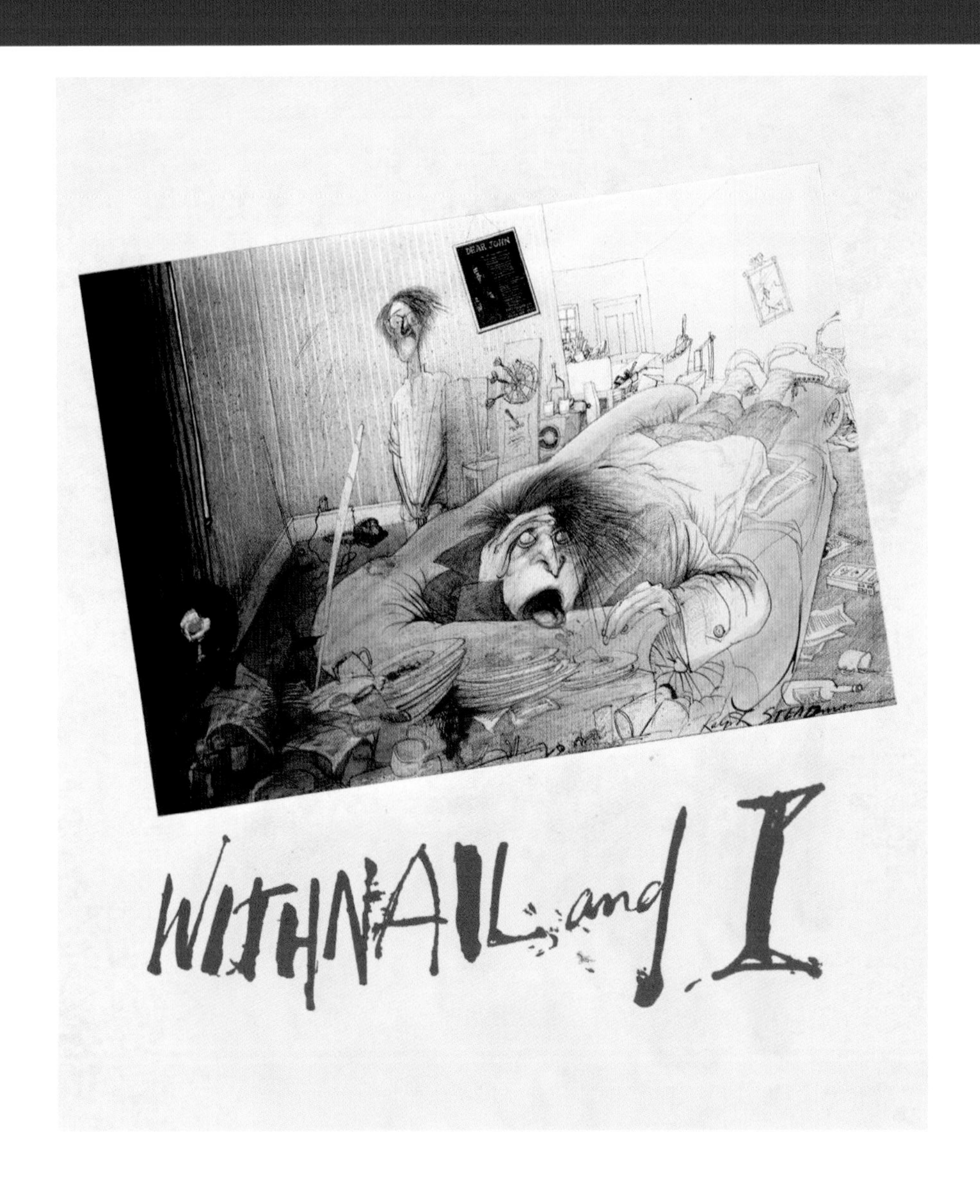

"There seem to be thousands of Withnails out there," observed writer/director Bruce Robinson, coaxed into talking about his famous creation once more for Alistair Owen's enlightening book-length interview, *Smoking in Bed* (2000). "Very weird," Bruce decided.

Weird, perhaps, but it was no exaggeration. Way back around 1990, when I was a hard-up English student, the cult had already insidiously begun to take hold, and many fans - myself included - wanted a coat like Withnail's. I couldn't find one in the local charity shop, so was forced into sartorial compromise: a moth-eaten army greatcoat. At the time, I convinced myself it was the business; on reflection, I fear it wasn't. Nonetheless, so attired, I liked to imagine I affected the same defiant air of haughty disdain for convention and the niceties of 'respectable' society that Withnail did.

I didn't, of course. I always finished my coursework on time, struggled to come up with caustic, witty one-liners, and never touched a drop of lighter fluid. Besides, who could ever be as gauntly charismatic, bloody-eyed, chisel-cheeked, unwaveringly proud, and fearlessly, funnily offensive as Withnail? Yet like so many other sensitive souls, on whom this film slowly grew, like mould in a Camden bedsit sink, I identified with him, or, at least, felt an affinity for the pain and frustration that seemed to be simmering beneath the surface. Here, at last, was a character all young, lonely, bitter aspiring artists and would-be intellectuals could relate to. Withnail - not so much played, as lived, by Richard E. Grant, and based on Bruce's "drowning upper-class" 1970s flatmate, Vivian MacKerrell - was a unique and unforgettable comic anti-hero. A tormented thespian forever waiting for that great role he deserved, watching the years drifting agonisingly by, he was stranded on the blackly humorous borders between comedy and tragedy, between success and failure. Antagonistic, acidic, pompous and relentlessly outrageous on the outside, adorned and armoured by that splendid coat I coveted, Withnail exuded flamboyant grandeur. Yet surely, I thought, deep down inside, beneath his brash finery, hid a sensitive soul, protected from the world outside only by clever wordplay, a grubby pair of baggy white y-fronts and a thick coating of Deep Heat. No wonder thousands could relate to him.

Truth be told, many would-be Withnails were probably rather more like 'I': Marwood, Withnail's more cautious and sensible chronicler, essayed with such gentle brilliance by Paul McGann. But while he sported a rather splendid pair of flip-down sunshades, and could match Withnail thread for thread in almost every aspect of the shabby-elegance fashion stakes, he just didn't have that coat.

Withnail and Marwood arrived on our screens when we needed them most. They barely registered, though, with British cinemagoers, when *Withnail & I* was quietly and belatedly released in 1988; but the 1980s were strange times. If you were there, you may hazily recall that music in the pop charts was thin and synthetic, the clothes were too, and it seemed like everything you looked at was angular, ostentatious, and in eye-scorching shades of neon Day-Glo. It was bang in the middle of the Thatcher years, to boot. Making money was the name of the game, and the aesthetics, moods, and liberal ideals of the 1960s had been laughingly consigned to the history books by the powers that be.

Then along came *Withnail & I*. Strangely out of time in the way it looked, and the way it sounded, and the way it made you feel, this was a defiantly warm, well-made, good-looking, sweet-sounding, autumnally-hued antidote to the brittle closed-circuit superficiality of the modern Britain and its shiny, quickly obsolescent artefacts; a step towards puncturing the plastic pretensions of the emptily optimistic 1980s. Here began the process of making the 1960s cool again, which would really get going around 1990 with the CD revolution – as long unheard pop back catalogues finally got properly reissued – and the release of major-studio teen-orientated '60s-themed films like Oliver Stone's *The Doors* (1991).

Don't forget, kids, there was no internet in those days, just ZX Spectrums, and there wasn't a great deal of data to go on. Pre-*Withnail & I*, many impressionable young 'uns ideas of the sixties were derived predominantly from what they saw on television and heard on the radio. Handy cultural referents included Neil from *The Young Ones*, and 'Spirit in the Sky' by novelty-hippies Doctor and the Medics. On this kind of evidence, you might be forgiven for perceiving the decade in terms of Nigel Planer's loon pants, stinky joss sticks, expressionless mini-skirted girls in black eyeliner, long hair wigs, and tie-dye t-shirts; plus Shaggy out of *Scooby-Doo*. So, thank heavens for Withnail and Marwood. These fellows were refreshingly surly, sour-faced and straight-trousered; scowling quasi-Edwardian retro-dandies, all worn-out corduroy, suits and frock coats. They looked nothing like hippy Neil; if anything, with their prescient adoption of what would now be called 'vintage' clothing, they harked back to the altogether more dapper look of the

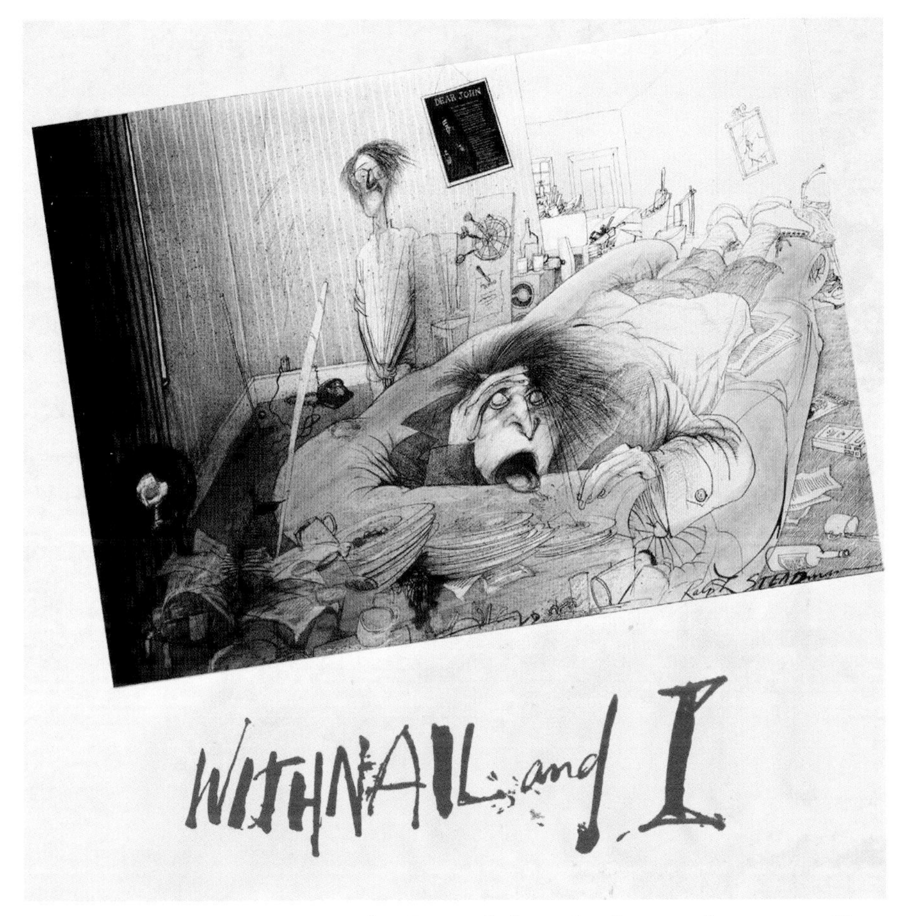

Bonzo Dog Doo-Dah Band in their early novelty-jazz days. And, defying another stereotype, but certainly appealing to us shamefully lazy, apathetic student types, they did not spout dogmatic ideas about changing the world. Rather they sought ways to enjoy and escape it. Though happy to dabble in narcotics, they primarily delighted in the age-old power of booze to this achieve this end.

Yes, these were nice boys from good homes, who wanted to avoid the nine-to-five; not social activists in the traditional sense. They were closest to what were increasingly coming to be known in the 1980s as slackers, a term returning to popular parlance describing a new generation of jaded, unemployed or under-employed apolitical youth; a lifestyle choice which would be celebrated stateside in *Slacker* (1991). Withnail and Marwood, distinctly British dandy-slackers, were perhaps more precisely what Reeves and Mortimer termed workshy fops. And at a time when Mrs Thatcher was increasingly laying down the law, and everybody was being instructed to do as they were told, work hard, smile for the cameras, and earn more, more, more, our heroes' hearty disdain for authority, refusal to pretend to feel happy, and dogged pursuance of unprofitable arts rather than 'sensible' careers, came as quite a relief; in fact, it seemed somewhat rebellious. This was a very cool film indeed, as many more viewers thankfully realised when the film began to find the audience it deserved, beginning in halls of residence around the nation, thanks to one of the more wonderful innovations of the 1980s, the VHS videotape. And so the cult grew, and grew.

But it had been touch and go for a while. *Withnail & I* caused considerable anxiety to its production company, HandMade Films. George Harrison, foremost bankroller of the project, was keen on the project from the beginning; but protector-of-the-purse Denis O'Brien had not been so sure. He was dismayed when he saw the earliest rushes, of the first scenes shot, sent back to London from a muddy location in the Lake District: shadowy sequences featuring semi-clad men prowling a remote farmhouse, and a supposedly-comic set-piece centring on an attempt to wring the neck of a chicken. From this evidence, he didn't think *Withnail & I* was going to be very funny, and only the relative smallness of the amount of money being gambled on the production prevented the plug from being unceremoniously pulled.

We all get the joke now, but it's no wonder he was worried, really. The film must have seemed specifically designed not to fit any known marketing strategy: deliberately, mischievously personal, impossible to pigeonhole, almost guaranteed not to fill the company coffers. As Richard E. Grant pointed out, looking back in a 1996 interview, the odds were against it: the finished product was a film without names, by a first-time director, with no female characters and an unfathomable title. Indeed, the first baffling poster I ever saw for it – for the video, I think – featured two scowling, mud-spattered men scowling glumly out across a gloomy, rain-drenched terrain. This was a comedy?

Almost a comedy. *Withnail & I* was black as jet, achingly funny one moment, almost unbearably sad at another. Ralph Brown, whose adenoidal tones brought Danny the Dealer so brilliantly to life, summarised its charms succinctly in Ali Catterall and Simon Wells's 2001 book on British cult cinema, *Your Face Here*: "It obviously touches a chord in people. It makes them feel sad while making them laugh." Dark and bittersweet in that unmistakeably British way, it certainly wasn't for everybody; though, funnily enough, it went down better with American audiences on its first release. Perhaps you needed to be an ocean away to truly appreciate its Englishness. Yet it wasn't in the Monty Python mould, nor was it a *Carry On*. *Withnail & I* was born of the same great humorous tradition as these now-legendary predecessors, and was similarly imbued with absurdity and slapstick, but its humour was uniquely grounded in a specifically personal, autobiographical comic realm. Its ring of truth and poignancy derived directly from the fervid pages of Bruce's diaries.

While *Withnail & I* sits in a peculiar comic class of its own, students of British comedy can, if they study hard and pay close attention, catch diverse glimpses of the glorious heritage of humour that produced it, and sense the breadth of Bruce's eclectic set of comic influences. The bawdy spectres of Chaucer and Shakespeare inevitably loom in the distance; but from more recent times came echoes of variety and music hall patter, and reflections of the great screen clowns. There's the dry, cynical darkness of the choicest Ealing comedy; and Bruce seems to have a Chaplin-esque penchant for combining laughter with tears. Would it be heresy to suggest that the end of *Withnail & I* is as tearjerking as the end of *City Lights* (1931)? I think not. Watch out for odd hints of Laurel and Hardy, too. The sight of Withnail and Marwood in bed, in an old dark house, with a rifle, no less, is the sort of thing you might almost think you'd seen in a creaky 1930s two-reeler comedy, and, as a matter of fact, you probably did: Stan and Ollie took exactly the same approach to night-time security in *Oliver the Eighth* (1934).

All this talk about chaps in bed together – strictly platonic, of course – can't help but evoke the spirits of another legendary double act: Morecambe and Wise. Marwood is essential to Withnail just the same way Ernie was to Eric. Withnail, like Morecambe, gets the lion's share of the best lines, but gentle Marwood provides the moderate marker by which we measure Withnail's excesses. Sometimes Withnail plays to the gallery like an erudite, elongated, shabby-genteel Norman Wisdom, with a debonair dash of Keith Richards thrown in. When he demands fine wines in that snooty teashop, it's a little bit reminiscent of a splendid scene in Wisdom's underrated comedy *One Good Turn* (1954). Norman's cloth-capped 'gump' character defiantly enters a first class train compartment and upsets the snooty first-class passengers by offering them swigs of lemonade from his grimy bottle, wiped off with his sleeve, before belligerently accusing them of stealing his bottlestopper. Norman is many rungs below well-bred Withnail on the class ladder, but both disrupt the polite façade of the provincial pearl-rinsed toffs to similarly exhilarating effect. And returning to Withnail, what of that wonderfully timed, wordless moment at the police station, when a screen is whipped away, to reveal our thoroughly sozzled hero spraying piss around? Wisdom never did anything so naughty, but if he had, one imagines that it might have looked like this.

Effective as the visuals are, all those who have ever wanted the finest wines available to humanity will know that it is the witty wordplay in *Withnail & I* that lingers longest in the memory. Every line in Bruce's script seems to have been carefully, delicately hand-crafted, until it is as brittle and resonantly perfect as the crystal in one of Uncle Monty's sherry decanters.

Withnail's ornate words echo the grand, well-turned phrases of Tony Hancock, as scripted by Galton and Simpson. Bruce grew up listening to *Hancock's Half Hour* on the radio, and loved how Hancock's lines were "almost jokes, but not". Withnail's speech is similarly littered with these 'almost jokes'; and Hancock and Withnail have other things in common. Both characters are tortured artistes, lazy, geniuses-in-waiting, wondering when the world will give them the acclaim they so rightly deserve; yet the viewer senses that somewhere within both there lurks an awful glimmer of self-aware doubt - suppose that, actually, they can't cut the mustard? There appears to be a fair dollop of Galton and Simpson's *Steptoe and Son* in the mix, too. Rag and bone man Harold is cut from the same cloth as Hancock and Withnail, and the faded splendour of Withnail's Camden digs isn't a million miles away from Steptoe's Yard in Oil Drum Lane. Withnail knocking back lighter fluid recalls Albert supping vodka dregs mixed with liniment; and like Marwood, he has a penchant for dinner in the bath. Aspiring actor Withnail, tormented, would-be intellectual Hancock, and frustrated aesthete Harold all ultimately find themselves trapped by a combination of mundane circumstance, malevolent fate, and their own limitations. Bleakness and misery underlines - and sometimes overpowers - the comedy: there are no happy endings for these characters. Speaking of conclusions, the ending of *Withnail & I* is as bleak as anything Galton and Simpson came up with, and as hauntingly sad.

Bruce's original script ended with Withnail offing himself with a rifle, which would have been tragic enough, but the inspired rewrite that he filmed, with Withnail left behind by Marwood, is sadder still. Even Harold Steptoe could take some comfort in the fact that his old man was just as trapped by time and circumstance as he was. But Withnail - without I - seems booked for an especially lonely, solitary journey towards oblivion. And what's more - as he melts inconclusively into the closing credits, to the accompaniment of that exactly-right theme - it looks like it's going to be an agonising, endless trip.

It's a wonderfully effective sequence. Could there be anything quite as beautiful and melancholy as the sight of Withnail in the rain? Withnail slumped over the railings, clutching bottle and battered brolly, fiercely spouting *Hamlet* to the blankly-grinning wolves; left behind, with nobody to share the struggle. The double act has disbanded and nobody cares. The world carries on, beautifully but brutally, with arbitrary disregard. Withnail may wax as lyrical as he likes; there's nobody to listen. Time whooshes past without him. We're suddenly aware of life's loneliness and absurdity.

For me it evokes a similar feeling to the equally powerful ending of Werner Herzog's *Aguirre, Wrath of God* (*Aguirre, der Zorn Gottes*, 1972) which sees Klaus Kinski's crazed conquistador alone on a river, his struggle for power thwarted by the fact that he has no-one to command. Doomed to oblivion, he's ultimately only able to bark orders at the myriad monkeys that plague his barren raft. Like Withnail with the wolves, he continues to strike grand poses in his finery; like Withnail, he has nowhere to go. It's all pretty ridiculous; and the joke's on him.

Likewise, as we watch Withnail shuffle off, shoe-sole flapping, to disappear indistinctly into an eternity of rain, we realise that for him there is no escape. Despite Hendrix's earlier suggestion that there must be some kind of a way out of here, perhaps, for rather a lot of proud, artistic souls – thousands and thousands of Withnails, in fact – the sad truth is that there isn't.

But don't be downhearted! Let's be glad that Marwood made it across the dividing line between one era and the next, even if, somewhat tragically, his hair aerials received a more severe scissoring than we might have wished. With him and his notebook lies the incentive for the rest of us to make more of an effort to enjoy the now, while we still can, for all its faults; whether we succeed or fail with our creative dreams, before the wrecking ball of passing time knocks them into the past. It's an enduring message; and wrapped up with it lies another of the many reasons why *Withnail & I* remains vibrant. For fondly evoked in this film is that never-never-land of intense experiences and seemingly unbreakable close-knit friendships, forged somewhere between youth and adulthood, an irretrievable time and place we briefly inhabit, if we're lucky, whatever generation we've been born into, before we're forced to grow up and get serious.

So here we are, nearly thirty years after release, and heading for half a century after Bruce wrote it all down. Perhaps by now there are tens of thousands of Withnails out there. Some of them might even have managed to get hold of a coat like his: in the mid-1990s, believe it or not, handmade replicas were briefly available to buy. The film has been the subject of books, documentaries, academic analysis, and Trivial Pursuit questions. There remains something rather special about it all. "By accident rather than design," Bruce has noted, "it has a timeless quality that all writers love to have built into their work."

It's timeless, sure enough, but I'm not so sure it was an accident. This is a film painstakingly built to last: as carefully constructed as a fine old piece of furniture, its charms as universal and enduring. For as long as we yearn for those irresponsible days of yore, real or imagined, and there are beginnings, and endings, people you leave behind, and great times you didn't realise were great until they suddenly slid irretrievably out of view, *Withnail & I* will, in its own peculiarly poignant way, continue to make us sad, while it makes us laugh.

***This essay originally appeared in the Arrow Video edition of* Withnail & I.**

NOT IN MY BACKYARD

Kenneth J. Souza on *The 'Burbs*

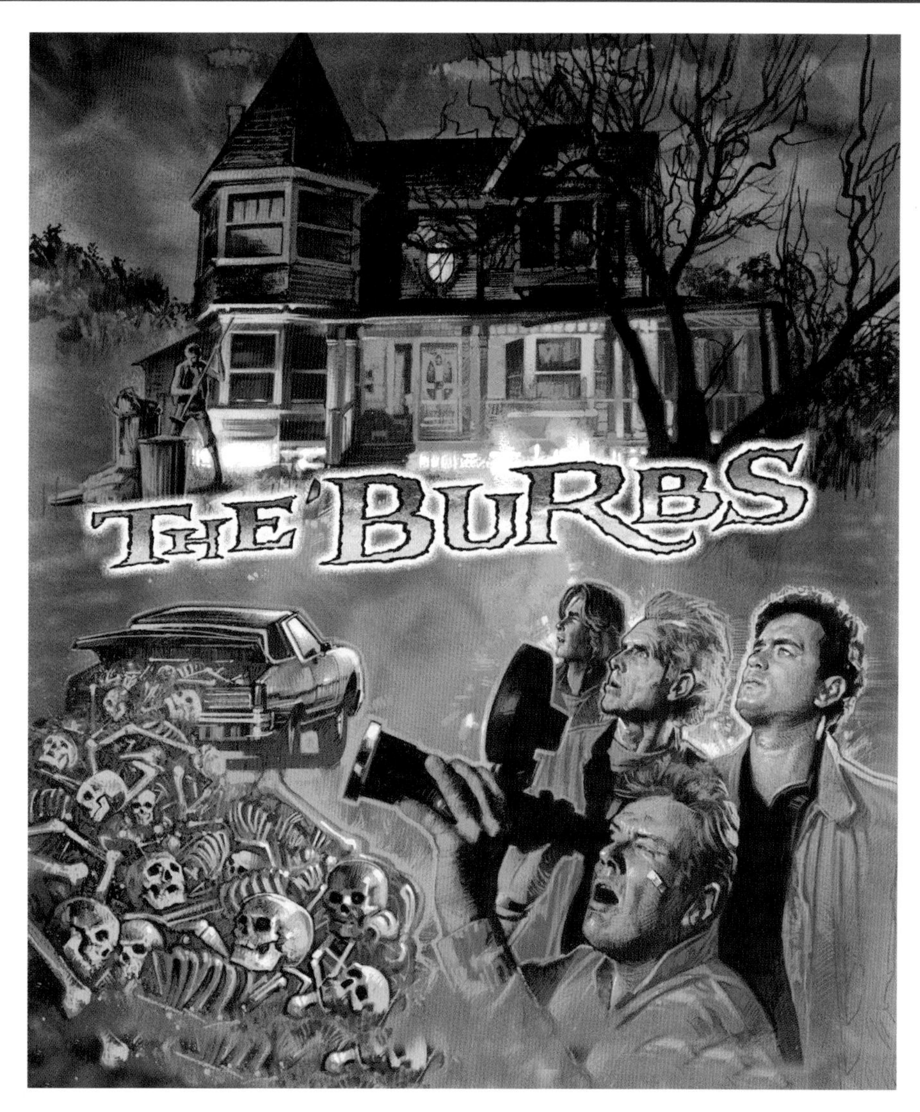

Artwork by Graham Humphreys

There's a point near the climax of *It's a Good Life*, the third segment of the 1983 feature film *Twilight Zone: The Movie*, directed by Joe Dante, where 12-year-old Anthony (Jeremy Licht) brings a manic cartoon creature to life that bears more than a passing resemblance to the classic *Looney Tunes* character, the Tasmanian Devil — although it's never called that by name. The grotesque creature comes spinning out of a fractured TV set into the living room and stops dead in its tracks, head bobbing and tongue waggling between large, fang-like teeth.

The scene is both silly and shocking at the same time, skilfully straddling the line between horror and comedy. And it's this horror-comedy hybrid that remains an indelible trademark of all of Joe Dante's films. Dante's comedies are always a bit askew, like those odd-shaped angular backgrounds of the beloved *Looney Tunes* cartoons he grew up with – and mimicked perfectly in what would arguably be the best of the four *Twilight Zone* instalments – yet they have a dark undercurrent bubbling just below the surface. Likewise, his horror films are often self-referential and satirical and are never presented without tongue planted firmly in cheek.

One of Dante's most accomplished and often-overlooked entries in a canon filled with tone-shifting black comedies and satirical horror hybrids is *The 'Burbs,* a wonderful pastiche of suburban paranoia and dark humour. Released in 1989 and starring Tom Hanks in one of his last *tour de force* comedic roles before becoming a decidedly more 'serious' actor, *The 'Burbs* may not seem to fit into Dante's oeuvre at first glance, but it bears all the fingerprints of the director's slightly off-kilter sensibilities, equally influenced by *Mad* magazine and a cadre of classic Universal monsters.

Originally entitled *Bay Window* at one point during its development, it was wrongly perceived as a parody of Alfred Hitchcock's *Rear Window* (1954) – until Dante latched onto screenwriter Dana Olsen's clever script for what it was: a comic retelling of the rumoured 'haunted house' paradigm that we all became readily familiar with growing up.

"My father was a golf pro and we kept moving and every place we ever moved, there was always this one house that everyone said '*That's* the place! Those people are weird; they never come out', and those stories were pretty ubiquitous," Dante told an audience during a screening of the film sponsored by *Rue Morgue* magazine in 2013. "When I was offered the script, I sort of sparked to it, because I thought a lot of people probably had the same experience and maybe they could relate to it."

It's not surprising, then, that Olsen based his script – which also had a working title at one point of *Life in the 'Burbs* – on real-life experiences from his own childhood. "I had an ultra-normal middle-class upbringing, but our town had its share of psychos," Olsen said. "There was a legendary hatchet murder in the 1930s, and every once in a while, you'd pick up the local paper and read something like 'Librarian kills family, self'. As a kid, it was fascinating to think that Mr. Flanagan down the street could turn out to be Jack the Ripper. And where there's fear, there's comedy. So I approached it as *Ozzie and Harriet Meet Charles Manson*."

The 'Burbs is one of those rare instances in Hollywood where the material is perfectly matched with a director who understands the interdependence of horror and comedy. As he did with *Piranha* (1978), *The Howling* (1981) and *Gremlins* (1984) before, Dante instinctively knew that humour would help ground the horror and make it all the more realistic and credible.

"I always thought all horror is comedy," Dante told author Jason Zinoman in his 2011 book *Shock Value: How a Few Eccentric Outsiders Gave Us Nightmares, Conquered Hollywood, and Invented Modern Horror*. And Zinoman correctly points out how all the classic Universal monsters were even relegated to starring alongside Abbott and Costello and the Three Stooges in tepid horror-comedy hybrids; so there's always been a fine line between horror and comedy in all of Dante's films. That line is never more blurred than in *The 'Burbs*, which, along with Dante's 1985 sci-fi film *Explorers*, has gone on to gain a level of cult status since its release.

Despite the presence of Tom Hanks for marquee value – he was fresh off the breakout success of *Big* (1988) – *The 'Burbs* failed to garner much critical acclaim upon its initial theatrical run. In fact, Dante has said the film received some of the worst reviews of his career.

But one noted critic and staunch Dante champion who appreciated the film's dark humour was Jonathan Rosenbaum. In his review, Rosenbaum noted that *The 'Burbs* "can be read as a satire about suburban conformists and snoops – xenophobic busybodies who can't tolerate the presence of any sort of eccentricity in their midst. Or the movie is a cautionary tale about the dangers of insulation and ignorance – minding one's own business and being unaware of the horrible things that are happening right next door. Or, finally, one can take the noncommittal stance assumed by the teenage characters in the movie, who are as undisturbed about the mysterious neighbors as they are amused by the xenophobic snoops trying to uncover them; the kids are simply around to enjoy the show."

It would seem that the critics who panned the film obviously didn't "enjoy the show" and were expecting more of a one-dimensional, by-the-numbers Tom Hanks comedy in the vein of *Big*. But there's much more bubbling under the surface of *The 'Burbs* — just like the mysterious goings-on in the basement of the sinister-looking Klopek house.

On paper, the plot for *The 'Burbs* doesn't really do the film justice, since it's a blended mixture of plot, performance and, ultimately, Dante's persistent point of view that make it all work. In a nutshell, everyman Ray Peterson (Hanks) suddenly becomes curious about the oddball new neighbours who have just moved into their quiet and friendly cul-de-sac on Mayfield Place in the fictional town of Hinkley Hills. His suspicions are fuelled by two nosey neighbors, Art Weingartner (Rick Ducommun) and Lieutenant Mark Rumsfield (Bruce Dern), who convince him that the new family, the Klopeks, are up to no good. As the trio — or, if you will, *three stooges* — attempt to spy, trespass and intimidate the Klopeks in escalating escapades that make them appear to be the true oddballs on the block, the film becomes a testament to the trappings of xenophobia and prejudice.

While Dante used Olsen's script as the blueprint and jumping-off point for the manic chaos that ensues, the actors and director certainly brought their own talents and contributions to the table. Some of this was by design, but much of it was borne out of necessity. Shot on the Universal backlot during a writers' strike in the summer of 1988, Dante said they essentially filmed *The 'Burbs* in sequence, which lent itself to improvisation on the set.

"I can't think of many pictures since (Hitchcock's 1944 feature) *Lifeboat* that take place in the same area," Dante said. "I thought if we could shoot the film in sequence - from the very beginning to the very end, because we were on the same location - we could do a lot of improvising and the actors would be able to come up with some different ideas about where they wanted to go. The finished version of the movie is somewhat different than the actual script, because the actors were all pretty clever and funny. It's more of a performance piece for me than a story."

On repeat viewings, however, it becomes clear that the signature touches of Dante's directorial style are what transform *The 'Burbs* from a typical situational comedy into a dark cult classic. Those tell-tale sight gags, in-jokes and "doodlings in the margins" like the cartoons of artist Sergio Aragonés that Dante so loved in the pages of *Mad* magazine are peppered throughout *The 'Burbs.* "The beauty of *Mad* magazine was that you could read it over and over and in the corner of the frame would be these little gags that you hadn't noticed when you were reading it for the continuity," Dante said.

To this end, there's the Art-shaped hole in the roof of the tool shed in an obvious homage to *Looney Tunes* (and a gag Dante first staged in his 1976 directorial debut, *Hollywood Boulevard*). There's the address number 669 that changes to 666 when Ray and Art knock on the Klopeks' front door. There's a glimpse of Tobe Hooper's *The Texas Chainsaw Massacre 2* (1986) which then cuts to a snowy TV as the camera pans over to a bed in a nod to *Poltergeist* (1982). There's a box of *Gremlins* cereal during breakfast. There's Ricky Butler (Corey Feldman) waxing on about the 1979 horror flick *The Sentinel.* There's a book about demonology written by Julian Karswell, a character in Jacques Tourneur's 1957 film *Night of the Demon*. There's the requisite appearances from Dante regulars Dick Miller and Robert Picardo as two garbage men. There's a quick cameo from a sled labelled 'Rosebud' in the Klopeks' basement in tribute to Orson Welles's *Citizen Kane* (1941). Then there's the devilish dream sequence that plays like a real-life Tex Avery cartoon in which Ray imagines himself strapped to a large outdoor barbecue grill by the Klopeks, while Art shows up as a demented ice cream shop clerk peddling "blood shakes".

"I like fantasy movies, so there's always a fantasy element in there, whether it deserves to be in there or not," Dante mused. "Not that I'm comparing it to (Hitchcock's 1945 feature) *Spellbound,* but the dream sequence used to be longer and it had some pretty cool things in it, but it really did stop the story so we had to take them out."

As he would be for his next two films - 1990's *Gremlins 2: The New Batch* and 1993's *Matinee* - Dante was, for the most part, allowed to make *The 'Burbs* without tinkering from Universal Pictures or his producers at Imagine Entertainment. But one key change from Olsen's original script was the ending, which resulted in several different options once Hanks was attached as star.

Sketch by Graham Humphreys

Sketch by Graham Humphreys

"The original ending was Tom Hanks's character discovers that (the Klopeks) are indeed crazy and the picture ends with him going off in an ambulance to be killed," Dante explained. "But once we hired Tom, they said, 'Well, you can't kill Tom Hanks. So you've got to have another ending.' That means we had to explain all the stuff they were doing in the basement, which was never written into the original script. Now we had to actually explain what they were doing, which I think diminishes it a bit."

"We shot three different endings. One of the endings is when Henry Gibson's character gets caught and he goes on and on about why the 'burbs drive people crazy, and that was on the original DVD release as an extra. There was another ending where inside the trunk it wasn't just a bunch of skulls, but the two garbage men (Miller and Picardo). In another ending, it was cheerleaders. But the ending we used I think is fine — it was sort of a compromise."

Yet in the film's penultimate shot – just before the camera zooms back out from the Mayfield Place mayhem into a bookending shot of the Universal logo – Dante manages to get in the final word as Ricky Butler breaks the fourth wall and speaks directly to the camera, saying: "God, I love this street." It's a gag as familiar as Dick Miller cameo in a Dante film and it dates back to the director's affection for a nearly-forgotten 1941 Universal comedy-musical called *Hellzapoppin'* directed by H.C. Potter and starring slapstick comedians Ole Olsen and Chic Johnson. (Ironically enough, the forgotten gem also featured a supporting role from Shemp Howard of Three Stooges' fame.)

"The audience is reminded constantly that they are watching a movie, and similar comic stylings have found their way into my own work," Dante once told *The Telegraph*.

There's no denying *The 'Burbs* is a manufactured movie as it unfolds on the screen... but it's a place worth revisiting if only for the non-judgmental point-of-view and understanding of human nature that Dante brings to it.

***This essay originally appeared in the Arrow Video edition of* The 'Burbs.**

A BATTLE WITHOUT END

Tom Mes on *Battle Royale*

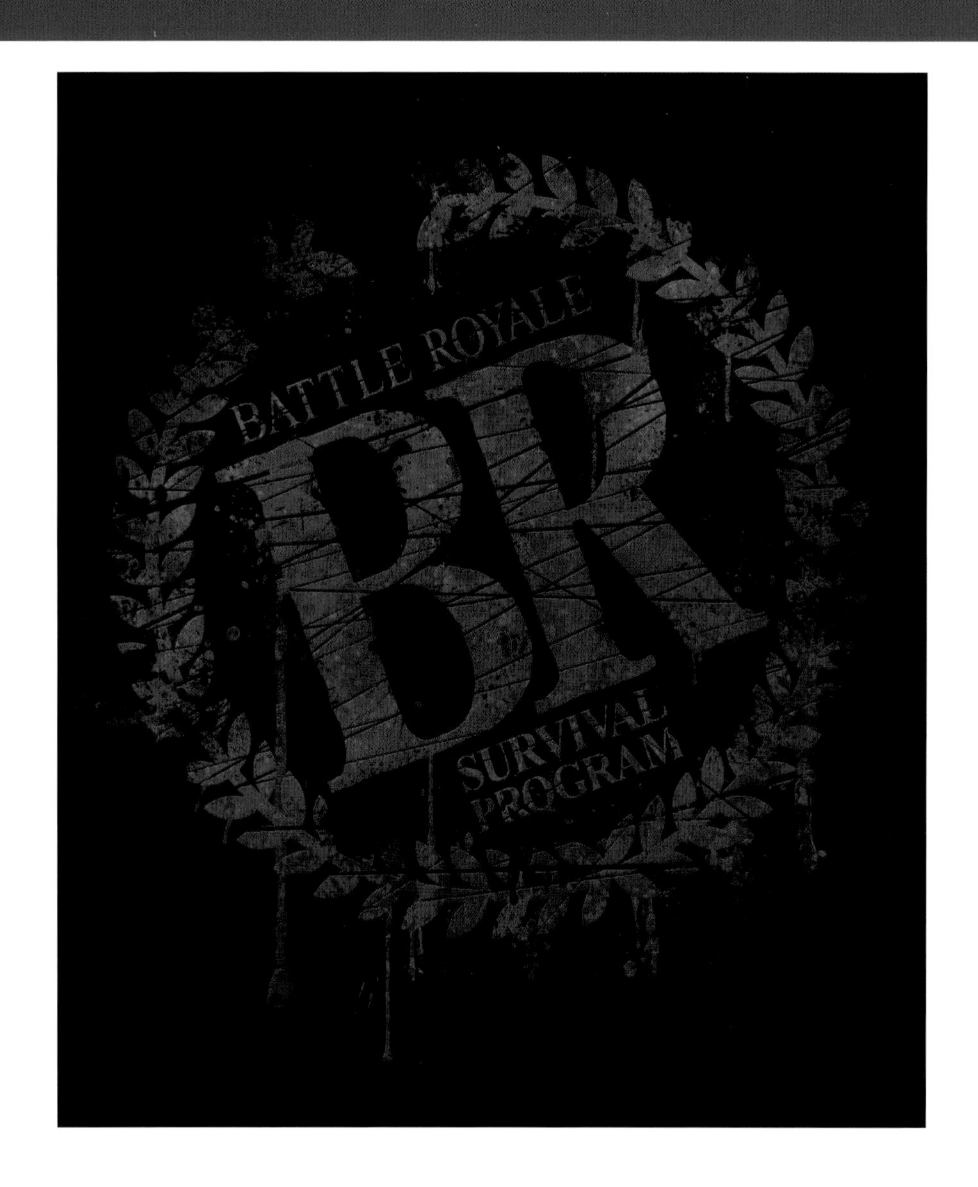

Japanese filmmaker Kinji Fukasaku (1930-2003) used cinema to rewrite the history of his country. His signature film, the 1973 gangster epic *Battles Without Honour and Humanity* (*Jingi naki tatakai*), tells of the rise of the modern yakuza, from the chaotic days immediately following Japan's defeat in World War II to the dawn of the seventies and the economic miracle. Its story and characters were inspired by events that were true, but hardly of the sort that make it into the history books. Yet the film laid bare the backroom dealings, under-the-table kickbacks and alleyway assassinations that helped the country rise from its ashes and become an economic superpower.

Fukasaku lived through wartime as a teenager. In the final days of the Pacific War, he was sent to work in a munitions factory. The factory became a target for Allied bombing raids in which Fukasaku saw many friends his own age perish. He later recalled that he survived the bombing by taking cover under the dead bodies of his co-workers.

The young Fukasaku emerged from the war with a deep-seated distrust of authority. When he attained his position in the director's chair in the early 1960s, he let his camera take aim at the officially sanctioned account of Japan's post-war reconstruction. Films like *If You Were Young: Rage* (*Kimi ga wakamono nara*, 1970), *Under the Flag of the Rising Sun* (*Gunki hatameku motoni*, 1972) and *Graveyard of Honour* (*Jingi no hakaba*, 1975) showed what went on behind the headlines of newspapers and between the lines of history books: strikes, corruption, maddening bureaucracy, violence.

Adapted from Koushun Tamaki's 1999 novel of the same, *Battle Royale* (2000) was Kinji Fukasaku's sixtieth and final film (he succumbed to cancer in the first days of shooting the 2003 sequel *Battle Royal II: Requiem*), and it had one marked difference from all Fukasaku features that came before: instead of telling an alternative history, it posits an alternative future.

The future, of course, is never written, so to speak of an 'alternative' future is a contradiction in terms. In the case of *Battle Royale*, though, what is shown is a future that deviates from the one that politicians like to paint us in their electoral promises: that future of harmony, security and growth in which we would so much like to believe when we cast our votes. Instead, the film stares unflinchingly at what the acts of these decision makers could very realistically lead to. As Fukasaku phrased the premise: "Where are these politics taking us?" In *Battle Royale*, the country has

Battle Royale

officially sanctioned the extermination of its own youth. A pre-emptive measure that is, as pre-emptive measures tend to be, massively out of proportion to the problem it is supposed to tackle, that of juvenile delinquency. Here is a future society that rather sees its children die than turn into criminals.

Battle Royale features a cast of soon-to-be young stars murdering each other (nearly all the main actors, and some of the minor ones, went on to achieve star status in Japan thanks to the success of the film). More than a tale of *Ten Little Indians*, however, the narrative focuses on how each individual teenager deals with this live-or-die situation. Scythe-wielding vixen Mitsuko (Kou Shibasaki) calmly applies her make-up while a PA system lists the names of all her classmates that died the previous day. Takako (Chiaki Kuriyama, later of Tarantino's *Kill Bill: Volume 1* [2003]) can, in this lawless environment, deal with harassment by sticking a knife in her unwanted suitor. Shuya (Tatsuya Fujiwara) emerges as protector of the put-upon Noriko (Aki Maeda), who was bullied for being the favourite of teacher Kitano (Beat Takeshi) – the same teacher who is now the man orchestrating this brutal, governmentally sanctioned massacre.

Knowing the director's wartime experiences, it's not hard to see where the main inspiration for Fukasaku's approach to the material came from. The situation painted in *Battle Royale* is one that is almost impossible to imagine for anyone who grew up in a peaceful world; and how we would react even more so. This is not the case for Fukasaku, who did see his friends die and who survived by pure luck where they perished.

The director's empathy for his young characters is remarkable, all the more for the 55-year age gap between them. There is not a trace of the pedantic 'I can tell you didn't experience the war' attitude with which a generation attempted to alleviate their shared trauma by laying it on the shoulders of their children and grandchildren. Fukasaku has always taken the side of the downtrodden against those in power.

For *Battle Royale*, the director's son Kenta, then in his late twenties, served as the bridge across the generation gap. Kenta Fukasaku wrote the screenplay, bringing to the table an understanding of these kids' predicament of having to grow up in a world in which all of society's securities have vanished. When Japan's economic bubble burst in the early 1990s, the country's social fabric came apart. The phenomenon of a job for life, which was such an integral feature of the economic miracle, virtually disappeared overnight. As a result, the whole educational system that groomed the nation's youth for this one goal lost its meaning. An entire generation was left with a future like a gaping black hole.

"At the dawn of the millennium, the nation collapsed. At 15% unemployment, 10 million were out of work. 800,000 students boycotted school and juvenile crime rates soared. Adults had lost all confidence, and now fearing the youth they eventually passed the Millennium Education Reform Act." *Battle Royale*'s opening words don't describe a future dystopia, but the unravelling social fabric of 1990s Japan. Today, more than a decade after the film was made, it is still as valid and topical as it was upon its release. Case in point: China has now officially usurped the position of the world's second-largest economy, held for decades by Japan. A belief is currently taking hold among the Japanese who are just now starting families: that by the time their children graduate from university, they will need to move to China to find a job.

It is a paradox that a father-son team should be responsible for making a film about parents who have lost faith in their children and vice versa. "Go Shuya! You can do it Shuya!" is the final message from the protagonist's father – their pathetic futility only emphasised for having been scribbled on a roll of toilet paper. Mitsuko's drunk mother tells her daughter to always fend for herself, "or you will end up like mommy" – words no sooner spoken than realised: the toddler pushes her mother's creepy new boyfriend down the stairs, killing him instantly.

Lack of confidence was hardly an issue between the two generations of Fukasaku. Kenta had already assisted his father on several films before tackling the screenplay for *Battle Royale*. He boldly took over the reins on *Battle Royale II* after his father lost the battle with cancer and has since forged a career as a director in his own right, including genre exercises *Yo-Yo Girl Cop* (*Sukeban Deka: Kôdo nêmu = Asamiya Saki*, 2006) and *X-Cross* (*XX (ekusu kurosu): makyô densetsu*, 2007)

Battle Royale's volatile cocktail of violence and razor-sharp social commentary landed the film in hot water even before its release. Members of parliament called for a ban. The film was released with an R-15 rating, prompting Kinji Fukasaku to call upon 14 and 15-year-olds (the same age group depicted in the film) to storm the theatres. Distributor Toei refused to have the film released in North America, fearing legal problems in the wake of Columbine and other high-school killings.

In spite of all this, *Battle Royale* became a phenomenon both at home and around the world, playing a capital role in reawakening interest in Asian genre cinema. Since its release it has spawned a special edition, a sequel, a 3D re-release and remains as topical as ever. The battle continues.

This essay originally appeared in the Arrow Video edition of **Battle Royale.**

CULT
DIRECTORS

CONTRACT KILLER

Jasper Sharp on Seijun Suzuki

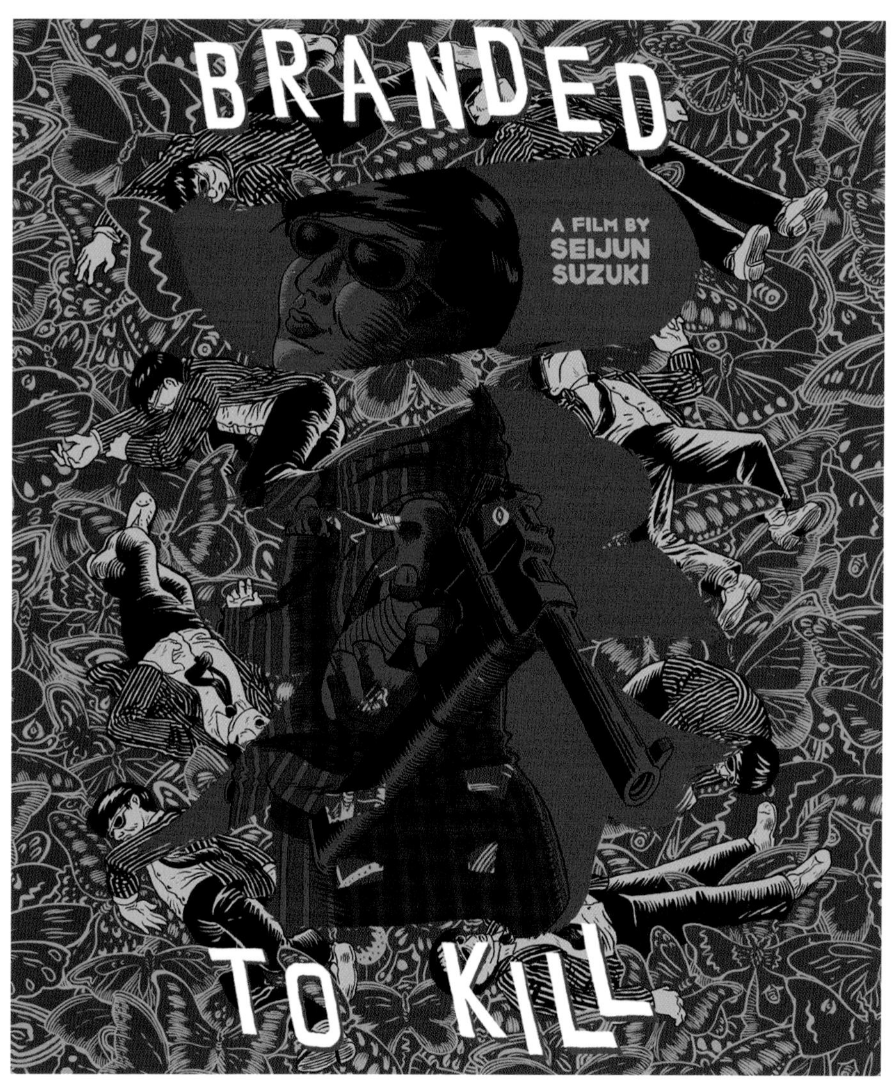

Artwork by Ian MacEwan

The process by which the reputations of certain filmmakers rise or fall over the years is a fascinating one, as too is the way in which some films acquire a patina of respectability with the passing of time. Now seen as an undisputed classic of Japanese cinema, the truth is that few outside of a small coterie of local cinéphiles and critics cared much for *Branded to Kill* (*Koroshi no rakuin*) upon its initial release on 15 June 1967, least of all Kyûsaku Hori, the president of the Nikkatsu studio that produced it, who famously fired its director Seijun Suzuki claiming that his films didn't make sense and didn't make money.

The slighted Suzuki, a Nikkatsu employee since 1954, was not going to take things lying down. Hori's subsequent blocking of a planned retrospective of his works organised by Kazuko Kawakita (daughter of the famed husband and wife team of Nagamasa and Kashiko Kawakita who had played such an instrumental role introducing Japanese cinema to the West from the late 1920s onwards) was the last straw, and Suzuki sued the company for unfair dismissal. Support from fellow filmmakers was strong, but this lawsuit against his former employers had the ultimate effect of making Suzuki *persona non grata* with those in the industry who might otherwise have funded future projects.

The critic Shigehiko Hasumi once claimed that Japanese cinema in the 1970s was "characterised more by Suzuki's absence than by Kurosawa's". The legendary director of *Seven Samurai* (*Shichinin no samurai*, 1954) made two films in this decade: the independently-produced *Dodesukaden* (1970), amazingly Kurosawa's first colour film, was a resounding commercial flop that drove the exasperated filmmaker to the brink of suicide, while his return to more familiar epic territory with the Siberian-shot Sovscope 70 production *Dersu Uzala* (1975) was bankrolled by the Soviet Union, so can't really be described as Japanese.

Suzuki fared even worse, managing only one release, *Story of Sorrow and Sadness* (*Hishû monogatari*, 1977), released by Nikkatsu's rival studio Shochiku. Its portrait of a professional golfing model who experiences the flipside of fame when she attracts a crazed fan stalker heralded Suzuki's return, at least in terms of its exuberant use of colour – for which he had become renowned through works like *Youth of the Beast* (*Yajû no seishun*, 1963), *Kanto Wanderer* (*Kantô mushuku*, 1963) and *Tokyo Drifter* (*Tôkyô nagaremono*, 1966) – after having being saddled with the cheaper option of monochrome for *Branded to Kill*. In stylistic and narrative terms, however, *Story of Sorrow and Sadness* was even more off-the-wall than the film his former boss had dismissed as "incomprehensible", and even his champions in the critical establishment weren't able to persuade a cinema-going public increasingly swayed towards Hollywood that Suzuki was really what the domestic industry needed.

Fortunately the broadcast medium provided a window of opportunity throughout this period in the wilderness. Suzuki first turned to television in 1968 with the one-off drama *A Duel* (*Aru kettô*), an episode in the TBS series *Good Evening Dear Husband* (*Aisaikun konbanwa*), and TV commercials provided his main means of earning a living for several years following his firing from Nikkatsu. His two best-known small-screen works however are *A Mummy's Love* (*Miira no koi*, 1973), a characteristically oddball entry in Fuji TV's *Horror Unbalance Theatre* (*Kyôfu gekijô anbaransu*) series representing Suzuki's first stab at the horror genre (and most probably Japan's first ever mummy movie), and *Fang in the Hole* (*Ana no kiba*, 1979), an instalment of Fuji's *Sunday Horror* (*Nichiyôbi kyôfu*) series, in which a murdered gangster returns from the grave to haunt his lover. The unrestrained nudity and bloodshed of the latter in particular are indicative of the wild anything-goes approach of 1970s Japanese TV, while both demonstrate how, despite obvious budgetary shortcomings, the uniquely eccentric vision of a filmmaker renowned for his expressive use of colour and scope refused to be hemmed in by the 4:3 ratio – a fact well-worth bearing in mind when Suzuki's hour finally arrived with his return to critical acclaim, *Zigeunerweisen* (*Tsigoineruwaizen*, 1980), which was filmed in this standard Academy aspect ratio.

Before looking at *Branded to Kill* in more detail, it is worth further considering Hasumi's notion that Suzuki was somehow more crucial to the national film culture of this time than Kurosawa, a director famed for his role in bringing the country's cinema to an international audience and the first filmmaker from Japan to have a book devoted to him in the English language, Donald Richie's *The Films of Akira Kurosawa*, published back in 1965.

At this stage, it is fair to say that the golden age represented by Kurosawa was already well over – 1965 was the year in which *Red Beard* (*Akahige*) was released, the director's final collaboration with Toshirô Mifune and his last for his studio, Toho. Suzuki's, however, was in full swing. The mid-60s represented the last great gasp of the traditional studio system, an era in which the production-line levels of output persisted (487 Japanese films were

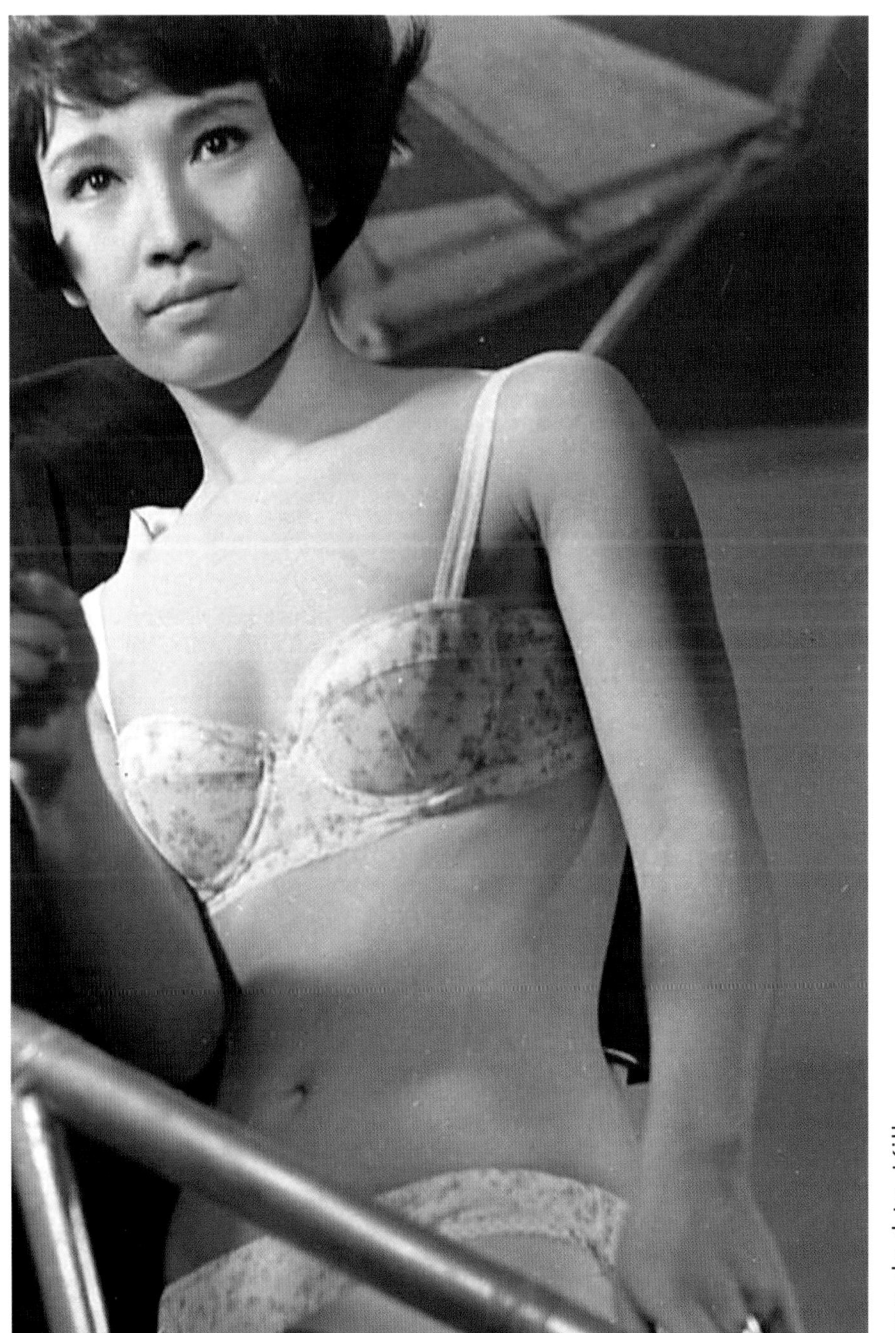

Branded to Kill

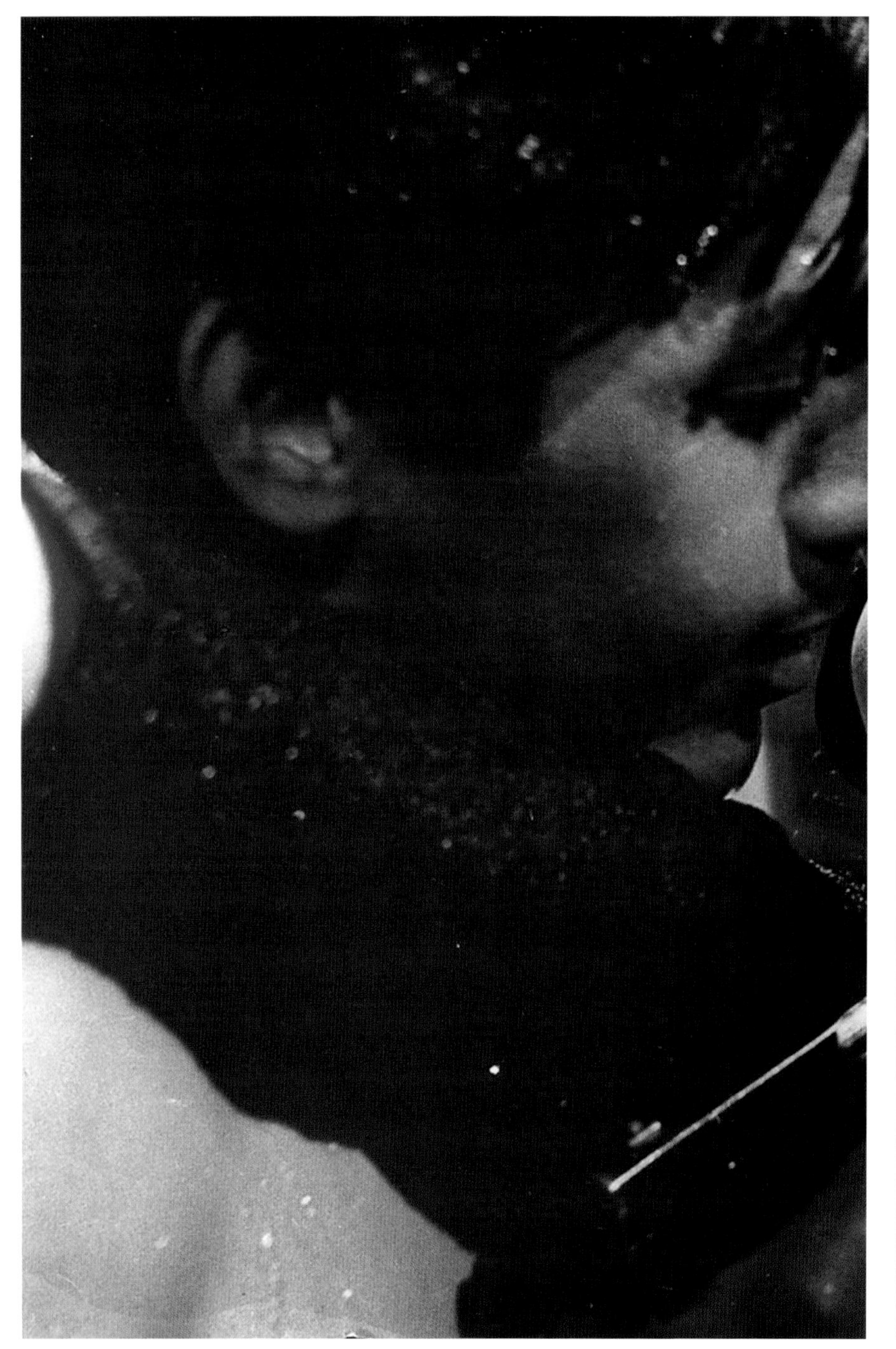

60
日活 殺しの烙印 映倫

released in 1965) but in which the studios did not have enough resources to give specialist treatment to would-be auteurs; to take the same financial risks, for example, that Toho had done with *Seven Samurai* (1954), the most expensive film of the period, and one which had taken over a year to produce.

Sure, throughout the decade there were the various studio tent-poles, although these tended to be driven by their stars or special effects, not the name of the director on the poster. The bulk of Nikkatsu's output consisted of programme pictures turned out at a conveyor-belt rate of some half dozen a month to feed the rapidly changing schedules of the exhibition outlets within its distribution chain. Provided one didn't stick one's head too far above the parapet, such an environment was conducive to and tolerant of a certain level of experimentation for directors like Suzuki, who directed forty films during his tenure at Nikkatsu, following his debut with *Harbour Toast: Victory Is in Our Grasp* (*Minato no kanpai: Shôri o wagate ni*, 1956). This is almost double the number realised by Kurosawa during a period at Toho lasting twice as long.

This studio system epitomised by Nikkatsu was fracturing circa 1967, however, with corners cut, directly-operated venues closed and the contracts of stars and directors ruthlessly severed over the following years in order to fend off the crisis brought about by falling attendances across the whole spectrum of Japanese cinema. The Nikkatsu that had produced Suzuki's previous films was a very different beast from that which went on to produce *Blind Woman's Curse* (*Kaidan nobori-ryû*, 1970) and the *Stray Cat Rock* films (*Nora neko rokku*, 1970-71) and which would commit itself fully to an erotic Roman Porno line in November 1971. *Branded to Kill* was released on the cusp of this change.

Hasumi points out that by taking his employers to court and thereby fighting the studio system, Suzuki "was mythologised and turned into a symbol of the season of rebellion" among local cinéphiles during the heated political climate of the era, which anticipated the events of May 1968 in France that led to the cancellation of that year's Cannes Film Festival partway through. (Suzuki was only informed of his dismissal by phone on April 1968, while working on *Good Evening Dear Husband*; he sued Nikkatsu in June of that year.)

Nevertheless, the fact is that no one outside Japan would have batted so much as an eyelid at the time. Seijun Suzuki's name meant nothing to foreign journalists (a few of his films, such as *Gate of Flesh*, had been released to the European exploitation circuit, but were never celebrated at more highbrow international events), and it seems highly likely that if Suzuki's career had ended with the *Branded to Kill* farrago, his name would be as well remembered overseas today as such contemporaries at Nikkatsu as Toshio Masuda, Buichi Saitô, Tan Ida and Umetsugu Inoue, similar purveyors of populist pulp that was generally a lot more profitable than Suzuki's films.

It was during his 1980s renaissance that Western viewers first came to enjoy the pleasures of Seijun Suzuki's idiosyncratic brand of cinema, somewhat perversely through a work that, while regarded as among his finest back in his home country, is relatively little seen or discussed overseas compared with the earlier studio-bound part of his oeuvre. Produced through his independent Cinema Placet company, the surreal ghost story *Zigeunerweisen* was the first in Suzuki's stylish Taisho Trilogy of arthouse movies that continued with *Heat-Haze Theatre* (*Kagerô-za*, 1981) and *Yumeji* (1991) – so-called because they were all set during Japan's Taisho era (1912–1926), in which Eastern and Western fashions, mores and political ideas commingled, creating a heady cultural brew that resulted in an inevitable nationalist backlash, exacerbated by the deteriorating economic situation following the Great Kanto earthquake of 1923 – incidentally the year of Suzuki's birth.

Zigeunerweisen gave Suzuki his first real international exposure when it was awarded a Special Jury Mention at the Berlin Film Festival in 1981, leading to his first overseas retrospective in 1984 at Pesaro Film Festival. From these appearances on foreign radars, the Suzuki legend began to grow, and ironically the studio-shot back catalogue of the man charged with losing Nikkatsu so much money when he worked there probably earns more for the company nowadays from overseas retrospectives and DVD releases than that of any of his contemporaries.

So the question is, how do we position *Branded to Kill* within Suzuki's oeuvre and within the broader situation of Japanese film history at large? Misguided by the small sample of films produced by Nikkatsu at the time that have made it to Western eyes, many have claimed that Suzuki's swansong for the company somehow went against the grain of its roster of predominantly gangster and delinquent-youths-on-the-loose flicks, that it was somehow intended as a cheeky subversion of the formulaic nature of such genre films.

A closer look at Nikkatsu's releases across the decade reveals an output that was incredibly eclectic and threw up just as many cinematic quirks as the typical Suzuki film. It was certainly not as unswervingly masculine as some have suggested: there were also more female-oriented lines of musicals, romances, literary adaptations and exotic overseas adventures alongside the more macho mash-ups of Western-inspired action genres, which included Takashi Nomura's 'Sukiyaki Western' *Fast-draw Guy* (*Hayauchi yarô*, 1961) and Tan Ida's swashbuckling tale of adventure on the high seas, *Pirate Ship: Tiger of the Sea* (*Kaizoku-sen: Umi no tora*, 1964) – both of which, incidentally, feature *Branded to Kill*'s Jô Shishido, the face of many a Suzuki title, whose collagen-enhanced physiognomy was a crucial component of his iconic, larger-than-life onscreen presence.

By comparison, work by Suzuki such as *Gate of Flesh* (*Nikutai no mon*, 1964), an adaption of Taijirô Tamura's groundbreaking novel about a guild of prostitutes set during the occupation, its thematic companion piece *Story of a Prostitute* (*Shunpuden*, 1965), another Tamura adaptation about a military "comfort woman" serving alongside the troops in a remote outpost in Manchuria during the war, and *Fighting Elegy* (*Kenka erejii*, 1966), a high school-set allegory for the rise of Japanese militarism scripted by New Wave luminary Kaneto Shindô, were rather less frivolous in their ambitions and all the better regarded by local critics for this.

That said, such films represented but one aspect of Suzuki's considerable output, which also included titles like *Fighting Delinquents* (*Kutabare gurentai*, 1960), *The Flower and the Angry Waves* (*Hana to dotô*, 1963), *Detective Bureau 23: Go to Hell, Bastards!* (*Tantei jimusho 23: Kutabare akutôdomo*, 1963) and *Tattooed Life* (*Irezumi ichidai*, 1965), portraits of outlaw life of a more generic nature, yet rendered in a sprightly style that was anything but generic.

Still, none of these latter titles look in any way out of alignment with other releases by the company. The defining features of Nikkatsu's films were that they were pitched at a young cosmopolitan audience open to what was going on in the rest of the world. Most downplayed their Japanese origins (in stark contrast to, say, the *yakuza* films released by Toei), embracing the fashions, music and iconographies of Europe and America in a manner that earned them the tag-line '*mukokuseki*', meaning borderless, or of no fixed cultural identity.

One need only need look at Takashi Nomura's *A Colt is My Passport* (*Koruto wa ore no pasupôto*), a

36

日Ⓚ活 殺しの烙印 映倫

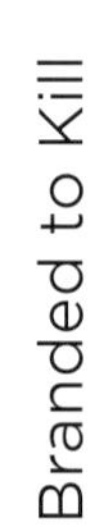
Branded to Kill

film noir-styled story of two hitmen on the run from the mob that looks (and sounds) as like it might have been directed by Sergio Leone, to see that, in terms of conception at least, *Branded to Kill* isn't quite as "out there" as has been suggested. Another Shishido starring vehicle, released a few months before Suzuki's, on 4 February 1967, its portrait of loner outlaws unfolds within a similar no-man's-land of industrial wastelands, anonymous tower blocks, landfill sites and other liminal spaces captured in moody chiaroscuro monochrome and expansive NikkatsuScope widescreen to create a unique and disorienting mood.

That said, *Branded to Kill* still presents quite an extraordinary experience. Opening with the sharp crack of gunfire beneath the Nikkatsu logo before the lilting theme tune kicks in to accompany the credits, from the offset the viewer is immersed in a world that can only be described as pure cinema. Its tale of Shishido's hitman, Gorô Hanada, and his attempts to rise to top-dog position in the underworld ranking of contract killers is pared down to mythic abstraction, its diegetic world the absolute distillation of the *mukokuseki* ethos.

Kazue Nagatsuka's cinematography renders the strong lines and rigid geometry of the modernist interiors of Hanada's own apartment space or the various smoky dive bars in which he skulks in a similarly oblique fashion to Raoul Coutard's work on Jean-Luc Godard's *Alphaville* (1965), conjuring up a completely otherworldly atmosphere through the expressive use of spotlighting, reflections, and low-key illumination, all heightened by the images of falling rain or shower water that add a noisy shimmer to this monochrome graphic minimalism. The everyday spaces of Tokyo have never looked so alien nor so alienating, with potential death lying in every shadow.

At the beginning of the story, Hanada is number three in an organised crime hierarchy in which it is never clear who is employer or fellow employee. Who and where, for example, is the *maboroshi* (phantom) number 1? Could it be, perhaps, the wife (Mariko Ogawa) who flirts openly with a colleague while Hanada's nose hovers over the steaming rice cooker that provides fuel for his killing commitments? Or the exotic but deadly beauty played by the half-Indian actress Annu Mari, whose lair is adorned with rows of Lepidoptera specimens pinned to her walls and who commissions the botched assignment that throws Hanada's life into jeopardy?

The film's ceaseless visual invention often strays

over into the realm of the ludicrous. There's a cartoon logic to some of the killings, as Hanada cold-bloodedly slays an unseen victim from another room by inserting his pistol into a drainpipe, rises to take a pot-shot through an open window while riding an inflatable weather balloon, or secretes himself within the mechanism of an elaborate advertising hoarding in the shape of a giant cigarette lighter.

"Time and place are nonsense," Suzuki once famously said of his films, and one could well describe the film as the cinematic equivalent of a 1960s Pop Art collage, as some have done. With the baroque framing and editing ellipses increasingly echoing the confused frame of mind of a protagonist kept as much in the dark as the viewer, we might even question whether what we are witnessing is nothing more than a washed-up assassin's paranoid fever dream. (How many times do we see Hanada swigging from his hip flask to steady his hand as the stakes get higher?)

Characters pop up with little in the way of introduction, only to disappear again without warning, while Suzuki abstains from clearly signalling flashbacks and other temporal changes for what they, further adding to the hallucinatory dream logic. None of this appears to make any sense at all, and it seems obvious why Hori, the president of a company facing an uncertain financial future, might dismiss this febrile vision as incomprehensible.

But within the butterfly-effect maelstrom of the narrative, some form of meaning does come across. We might rationalise the film as an abstract meditation on the absurd extremes of life as a freelance gun-for-hire in the increasingly anonymous, corporate and competitive world of a rapidly modernising Tokyo, or even more specifically, as analogous to Suzuki's own precarious position within the Nikkatsu hierarchy of its contracted directors.

What is perhaps interesting is how Suzuki's film coincided with two other existential treatises on the lives of professional criminals that popped up simultaneously elsewhere – namely John Boorman's *Point Blank* (released in the US on 30 August 1967) and Jean-Pierre Melville's *Le Samouraï* (which premiered in France on 25 October 1967) – all appearing so closely together in their distinct parts of the globe that there can be absolutely no question of mutual influence. Clearly there was something heady in the air in 1967 linking East and West.

But ultimately *Branded to Kill* is of a style all of its own. It operates simultaneously as a singularly nonconformist yet technically-polished mood piece and as a sophisticated cinematic Rorschach that can be savoured again and again, with every further viewing revealing previously unnoticed aspects and individual meanings. Nonsense it may be, but it is intelligent, stylish and deliriously enjoyable nonsense, nonetheless.

***This essay originally appeared in the Arrow Video edition of* Branded to Kill.**

NON-SENSORY INFORMATION

Caelum Vatnsdal on David Cronenberg

Artwork by Gilles Vrancx

When I was in my early teens, I visited Canada's capital city of Ottawa and made a little pilgrimage to the National Archives. I'd heard they had copies of, and might even be willing to show, the very earliest work of David Cronenberg, then and now my favourite filmmaker. Of course at that time, the mid-1980s, it was impossible to see them any other way, save perhaps a retrospective festival going for the really deep cuts. No such festival ever came through Winnipeg, though.

Cronenberg first flickered onto my radar when the exploding head from *Scanners* (1981) became a hotly debated topic on the nightly news across Canada by virtue of its violently un-Canadian audaciousness. The director who'd conceived it was at once praised for his daring and condemned for his vulgarity, and you could tell that pundits on both sides were a little afraid of him. The exploding head, meanwhile, was shown over and over again, and Cronenberg instantly became my hero. My devotion rapidly matured into a need to see everything else this director had ever made, no matter how early or uncharacteristic it appeared to be. So I went to the Archives, and within a few moments of arriving found myself installed in a small white room containing a chair, a table, a television, a pro-grade video player, and four video tapes: altogether a very Cronenbergian situation. I checked my belly, but there was no slit, not yet.

I popped the tape marked *Transfer* into the absurdly complicated VCR: may as well start at the beginning. Three hours later, I was trudging back up Wellington Street, pondering. They were the first art films I'd ever seen, and they'd baffled me utterly. But they were not made for 14-year-olds; they were made for intelligent but undemanding *avant-garde* audiences of college age. This seems a mighty specific demographic to shoot for, but in and around the University of Toronto in the late 1960s, representatives were in no short supply.

If the movies were not made for 14-year-olds, neither were they made for 44-year-olds. They're adolescent works, undeniably, but remarkable ones at any age. While they admittedly speak to a sensibility more broadly discovered in the 20-year-old, they document both a filmmaker learning his craft and an artist finding his subject, and any Cronenberg fan should not feel duty-bound to watch them, but privileged.

In 1966 Cronenberg, keen-minded and omnivorous in his interests, was a student at the University of Toronto. He was dissatisfied with his science courses and turning toward literature. He'd enjoyed movies for many years, but lacked the reverent mania for them found in Martin Scorsese or John Landis, or many other directors of that generation. Still, he watched and was captivated by the great waves of foreign film running through the local cinemas – Federico Fellini, Ingmar Bergman, Akira Kurosawa, Jean-Luc Godard, the usual suspects – and when he saw a film called *Winter Kept Us Warm* (1965), made by David Secter in and around the U of T campus, he was stunned by its implications. If a local guy like Secter had made a movie, Cronenberg realised, then, he could too. The latent filmmaker put aside his literary ambitions and began hanging around a local equipment house, where he befriended its materteral, gin-swilling owner, Janet Good, and learned as much as he could about building, loading and running 16mm and 35mm movie cameras from the gearheads who also frequented the place.

Cronenberg had in fact shot film before, though strictly smaller-gauge stuff. His first experience with a movie camera had come on August 13, 1960, when young Dave, aged 17 and clutching his new 8mm camera, went to the Harewood Acres speed circuit in Southern Ontario to shoot an amateur race held by the Sports Car Club of Toronto. He was filming as CBC television producer Ted Pope's Triumph TR3 was tapped from behind by another car, went out of control, and rolled over three times. Pope's vehicle was not outfitted with roll bars, nor was there anywhere for him to duck down; he was killed on the spot. "And *this* was my first footage," Cronenberg told an interviewer many years later, shaking his head in disbelief at the memory.

With this experience under his belt, and Good's boozy counsel, and his own precocious confidence and rabid autodidactism, Cronenberg felt he could handle making a movie of his own. The experimental film era, meanwhile, was in full flower. Various international New Waves had demonstrated that newer, more portable equipment could be used by almost anyone to make a film, and the results were screened on university campuses across North America.

It was tremendously exciting to Cronenberg, and he wanted in. He conceived of an idea and wrote a short script expanding on it, and then in January of 1966, in a snowy field somewhere near Toronto, Cronenberg shot his first movie, *Transfer*. Presaging Frank Oz's *What About Bob?* (1991) by over 20 years, it's the story of a vacationing psychiatrist dogged for further therapy by his most persistent patient, and finally harrowed to the point of acquiescence. The avant-garde aspect is provided mainly by the location: a snowy, desolate field dressed here and there with furniture. Along with the poor sound recording and chilly-looking actors, this setting also helps give the film a particularly Canadian aura.

Further evidence that *Transfer* is a student film comes with its first shot: a man pouring a glass of grape Crush and then brushing his teeth with it. This stands as Cronenberg's first fiction-film shot, and though never again would he compose so antic an image, it bolsters his assertion that all his pictures are fundamentally comedies. There is insect imagery in the dialogue ("You came to me, a dark butterfly, probing, gently probing...") and some forbidding architecture in the background, making it, ultimately, all of a piece with Cronenberg's oeuvre. As a bonus, you can faintly hear the tyro director calling "Cut!" at the tail of the final shot.

From the Drain, shot in July of 1966, moved the action indoors, allowing Cronenberg to play around with lighting for the first time; as evidenced by the one extant production photo, this meant pointing two undiffused 300 watt lights directly at the action. The action, however, is limited: two men, one of them Mort Ritts from *Transfer*, the other Cronenberg's friend Stephen Nosko, sit in a bathtub in a dim and cramped bathroom, which may or may not be part of the Disabled War Veterans' Recreation Centre. Nosko, a veteran of "The War", has some form of PTSD and a deathly, soon-to-be-validated fear of tendrils. Ritts, who affects an outrageous camp act for some reason, pretends to be a fellow veteran and grouses about his tub-mate before revealing that he himself is the centre's Recreation Director, and the patient his special case. Cronenberg's very first special effects scene, a stop-motion drain tendril, interrupts this cosy scenario and spells doom for the nerdy veteran. "It's obvious," Cronenberg told interviewers William Beard and Piers Handling, overstating the case slightly, "that somewhere along the line there is a plot to get rid of these veterans so they won't talk about what they know."

From the Drain, like *Transfer*, displays a profound fear of psychiatry and a mistrust of analysis, and implies a wish on the part of its director never to be analysed himself. It's no real surprise that Cronenberg tried for years to suppress the films. "I guess they have an academic interest," he admitted to Chris Rodley, "but artistically they're so bad." Cronenberg is hardly the world's most committed censor, however, and his wormy little progeny have long escaped their creators' orifice.

But anyway they aren't bad, just early; and Cronenberg certainly was not at the time dispirited by his work. In fact, he was charged up and excited by the public screenings, at which his films ran amongst dozens of others just like them. Even a notice in the *Globe & Mail* which accused him of stealing *Transfer* from Mike Nichols and Elaine May, was not enough to get him down. ("It was nice to be compared with them," he said.) The thrill of showing work to a crowd, an intoxicating feeling for any filmmaker, energised Cronenberg's filmmaking ambitions, and he began preparing something longer and much more complicated.

The first thing he decided on was moving to a larger canvas and shooting the movie on 35mm stock instead of the 16mm he'd been working with. The problem here was that he couldn't afford to do both that and to record synchronised sound. The natural solution was to populate his story with telepaths who never had to open their mouths. (As a lay student of biology, Cronenberg is nothing if not adaptable.) He wrote reams of narration made entirely of mock-technical buzzwords, then, through the late summer and fall of 1968, filmed his friends and various U of T theatre people wandering around the campus. His primarily subject was an "elegant gay scholar", Ron Mlodzik, a fascinating, spacey creature whose otherworldliness is let down only by his given name. (He should be called, perhaps, Fettenbaum Mlodzik.)

The story takes place in the unimprovably-monikered Canadian Institute for Erotic Enquiry, where psychics are undergoing testing at the hands of a Dr. Luther Stringfellow. (Stringfellow is only the first in a long series of Cronenbergian scientist-Gods with synthetic-sounding names and a notable lack of laboratory ethics.) After many silent stretches and striking monochrome images, and shots of Mlodzik wearing a cape and wrinkling his nose at things, *Stereo*, like the later *Shivers* (1975), features a descent (ascension?) into polysexual bacchanal. The narration (there are three narrators, all effective, but of whom Mlodzik gives the most confident readings) delivers a baffling stream of theories; and finally the monologues, summoning an aptitude that extends beyond diegetic boundaries, conclude that it will be quite a while before any conclusions can be reached from this information.

The film provides a key disclosure: input received telepathically has more impact than things apprehended by the usual set of senses. Otherwise it's mainly gobbledygook, but is visually compelling the whole way through. An empath hangs upside down in a doorway, silhouetted and crowned in her own long hair; bodies lie naked and splayed in concrete bunkers; Mlodzik twirls an umbrella in the sun or peeks down a pit-like stairwell. As had been the case with the shorts, Cronenberg was his own cinematographer, not realising the position was usually held by someone other than the director. But between *From the Drain* and *Stereo*, his camerawork improved dramatically. It wasn't just the move from 16mm to 35mm, but a great leap forward in framing and lighting sophistication. Influence had clearly been taken from Kubrick (another director easily qualified to act as his own DP), and it fit the film perfectly.

In June of 1969, the sixty-three minute *Stereo* premiered at the National Arts Centre in Ottawa, only a few weeks after the grand new building was opened. It was a prestigious screening (and no doubt a bewildered audience), but did not augur any popular success to come. In the fall of 1969, Toronto's cavernous Uptown Cinema closed while its owner, Nat Taylor (who had produced Canada's first horror movie, *The Mask*, a decade earlier) created one of the world's first multiplexes by dividing it into five smaller venues. The rear part of the theatre became the Backstage 1 & 2, and the word in Toronto film circles was that these two smaller cinemas would show art films. Sometime after the theatre's Christmas Day re-opening, Cronenberg took *Stereo* down and ran it for the manager, but after a minute had gone by with no sound apparently forthcoming, the manager walked out.

Cronenberg didn't let this bother him because he was already deep into production on another short feature, *Crimes of the Future*. Again he was shooting on 35mm, but this time in colour: the better to show off the nail polish worn by some of the almost exclusively male cast members. Ron Mlodzik starred again, this time as Adrian Tripod, the director of the House of Skin. Tripod wanders a modernist buildingscape, sporadically murmuring a report on the state of society following a cosmetics-related pandemic unleashed by the mad dermatologist Antoine Rouge; he visits organisations complementary to his own (The Institute for Neo-Venereal Disease, The Oceanic Podiatry Group); and occasionally pauses to lick his glasses, or dispassionately observe a man hunting goldfish with a croquet mallet. At one point he unexpectedly encounters a hoser dressed in jeans and a plaid shirt, in case we've forgotten this is a Canadian movie. Cronenberg again sacrificed synchronised sound, but this time gussied up his audio track with electronic bleeps, percussive clunks and chirping birds. The end result ran the same awkward length as *Stereo*: 63 minutes.

Viewed with Cronenberg's subsequent work in mind, *Crimes of the Future* is a totipotent catalogue of Greatest Hits to come: a protean blob with gills and webbed feet, but also startlingly recognisable features. Disease with a purpose, self-willed transformation, the body bio-politic, the flowing goo and the poured-concrete Toronto architecture, it's all there. This was ideation as art, and, according to Ivan Reitman, would have been a commercial hit had Cronenberg resisted his fancier inclinations and played it as a straight science-fiction thriller. (He more or less did that later on with *Scanners*, and proved Reitman correct.)

These two mid-length films did little for the emergent filmmaker's career, but this seems to have been part of the plan. His production company name, after all, was Emergent Films, indicating he well knew where he was situated in the larger scheme of film production, and that, whatever reception these renegade works faced, he had future crimes planned. It would be five long and often frustrating years before he managed the big step forward he'd been striving for since he'd first picked up a camera, and the going would be slow for a while after that. But in the dozen years between *Crimes of the Future* and his first studio release, *Videodrome* (1983), David Cronenberg would make a profound impression on Canadian film and on genre cinema, and would manage to make an adjective of his own name. 'Cronenbergian', though to dullards merely a synonym for 'weird', would come to mean something you couldn't describe, but you sure knew when you saw it.

My own reaction to this concentration of prelapsarian Cronenbergia was to return home and make a movie of my own, *Life of Pain*, in which a bespectacled teenager wanders a poured-concrete landscape, mumbles impenetrable cod-philosophy on the soundtrack, and, yes, licks the inside of his glasses. That the intellectual mopishness of *Crimes of the Future* rather than the exploding heads of *Scanners* or *Videodrome* was the aspect of my cinematic hero I chose to emulate says less about me than about the strange reservoir Cronenberg tapped into so early in his filmmaking. It represented primal, immutable truths, not about society or biology or what it means to be human, or anyway not just about those things, but about the necessary, often humiliating, stations along the road to artistic maturity.

Art filmmaking of such devotional purity may have seemed to me merely something that had to be got over before progressing to the real business of sex parasites and armpit vampires, and maybe it was that way for Cronenberg too. But deep down there was much more. In an interview published in *Rolling Stone* around the time *Naked Lunch* (1991) was released, Cronenberg described his *modus operandi* as "really just [doing] whatever the fuck I want". With *Transfer*, *From the Drain, Stereo* and *Crimes of the Future*, long before he had any industry capital to spend, or an audience, or a budget, or a reason beyond chutzpah to award himself the possessory credit 'A David Cronenberg Film' (as he did on both the mid-length pictures), Cronenberg was already doing whatever the fuck he wanted, and that, in the end, might be the greatest lesson these movies have to offer.

***This essay originally appeared in the Arrow Video edition of* Videodrome.**

FRIVOLOUS TINTO

David Flint on Tinto Brass

Artwork by The Red Dress

By the time that *Frivolous Lola*, aka *Monella*, emerged in 1998, Tinto Brass was the Last Man Standing of Italy's once vibrant sexploitation industry. All his rivals had either retired, died, moved on or shifted their attentions to hardcore, and even that business was beginning to flounder. The 35mm porno film productions that Joe D'Amato, Luca Damiano, Mario Salieri and others had passed their peak, having benefitted a few years earlier from the new wave of American adult movie making that saw a brief return to shooting on film, a new emphasis on quality and a ready international market for these Italian costume epics – long before the porn parody explosion that we have had in recent years, D'Amato and Damiano were making the likes of *Tarzan X* and *X Hamlet* (both 1995). However, a shift in tastes – not to mention the fact that, for all their gloss, the Italian films were simply not very good – saw public interest start to diminish by the end of the decade. The high profile global distribution enjoyed by these directors began to decline and they started to seem as dated within the hardcore world as they had in the softcore. Their time, it seems, was up. Within a year of *Frivolous Lola* being released, D'Amato would die of a heart attack, aged 62, and that effectively signalled the end of the Italian (s)exploitation industry.

Yet Brass seemed able to shrug off the commercial pressures and the changes that had first killed the Italian sexploitation industry and then seen its hardcore successor grind to a halt. For reasons unknown, Brass proved to be the great survivor. He made four films in the first decade of the new millennium – only one fewer than his 1980s and 1990s output. Not bad for a man who entered his seventies during the decade.

But it's perhaps not entirely surprising that Brass was unaffected by the changes that took out most of his rivals. Brass was never really a part of the Italian exploitation scene, after all. When the industry was at its peak in the 1970s and early 80s, Brass seemed a man apart – having entered the film industry with politically flavoured films in the 1960s (films that ran the gamut from drama to comedy to *giallo*-esque thriller), Brass's entrance to the world of sexploitation came with *Salon Kitty* in 1975, a kinky, contentious mix of Nazi exploitation, softcore sex, outrage and politics that caused international controversy in a way that cheeky comedies starring Gloria Guida or Edwige Fenech could only dream of. Not only did the film spawn the short-lived, outrageous Italian Nazisploitation genre of 1976 – a genre that a few years later would be at the forefront of the British video nasties controversy (cf. *SS Experiment Camp/ Lager SSadis Kastrat Kommandantur* [1976], *The*

Beast in Heat/La bestia in calore, *Gestapo's Last Orgy/L'utlima orgia del III Reich* [both 1977]) and even today seems at the very edges of acceptability – but it also led to Brass being handed the directing job on *Caligula*, the infamous Gore Vidal-Bob Guccione collaboration that would drag on for years with Vidal walking away from the film in anger at Brass's changes to his story, Brass disowning it after Guccione shot additional hardcore scenes featuring Penthouse Pets (having been aghast at how "unattractive" the women Brass was filming were!) and cast members lining up to condemn the final movie when it finally appeared in 1980.

With such high profile and controversial movies to his name, it's unsurprising then that Brass was never a part of the Italian sexploitation mainstream, ignoring its trends and tendency to imitate box office hits. In the three years plus that Brass struggled with *Caligula* (either shooting it or dealing with legal wrangles), D'Amato shot several films, including a number of entries in the increasingly bizarre *Black Emanuelle* (*Emanuelle nera*) series. Having started as a straightforward imitation of the 1974 global smash hit *Emmanuelle*, the series took ever weirder turns under D'Amato, including the cross-genre effort *Emanuelle and the Last Cannibals* (*Emanuelle e gli ultimi cannibali*; which combed two popular sub-genres of the era!), the grim *Emanuelle Around the World* (*Emanuelle: Perché violenza alle donne?*; translated as E*manuelle Against Violence to Women*) and the outrageous *Emanuelle in America* (all 1977), which mixed fake snuff movies and pseudo-bestiality with hardcore inserts.

D'Amato wasn't alone in grinding out outrageous Italian sexploitation movies during the 1970s – for a nation that had declared *Last Tango in Paris* (*Ultimo tango a Parigi*, 1972) to be obscene in 1976 (insisting that all copies be destroyed and handing director Bernardo Bertolucci a four-month suspended prison sentence), Italy seemed oddly at ease with extreme sex and violence. As well as the shocking Nazisploitation films, Italian filmmakers specialised in violent cop movies and *giallo* thrillers, erotic dramas and sex comedies, gory zombie and cannibal films, sex-and-violence documentaries inspired by *Mondo cane* (1962) and, from the end of the decade, hardcore porn. Often, the same directors would move between all these genres, blurring the lines between them. For fans of exploitation cinema, Italian movies of the 1970s and early 80s represent some sort of glorious period of excess – a period that was over all too quickly. By the middle of the 1980s, the number of low-budget sex and horror films being made in Italy had dwindled and their outrageousness been curtailed somewhat.

Yet it was just as the Italian exploitation movie seemed to be on its last legs that Brass found his own erotic style. Regardless of their controversial content, both *Salon Kitty* and *Caligula* had been ostensibly 'serious' cinema – major productions that were far removed from the low budget quickies of people like D'Amato, Mario Landi, Bruno Mattei and the like. Even *The Key* (*La chiave*), made in 1983, was seen as something more than simply a sexploitation film at the time... Although we can look at it now as essentially being Brass's Year Zero – a new beginning that set out the style that Brass would increasingly refine over the next two decades.

This style is full of trademark touches, some more obvious than others. Often working in collaboration with his wife Carla Cipriani, Brass tended to adapt literary erotica – either openly or otherwise. *The Key*, *Miranda* (1985), *Capriccio* (1987), *Snack Bar Budapest* (1988), *Paprika* (1991) and *The Voyeur* (*L'uomo che guarda*, 1994) all began as novels. And more or less all his films from this second period take a joyful, liberated view of sexuality – usually (as is the case with *Frivolous Lola*) with sexually open, happy, unrepressed young women having to slowly bring around their backward, hypocritical partners – it's a thumb to the nose for Catholic morality (and Brass, an atheist, delights in exposing the sexual desires of priests, like the cycle-seat-sniffing pair in *Frivolous Lola*) and a light-hearted celebration of sex that is welcome in these times of moral austerity. Watching Brass films today, we are struck by the sheer joy of sex that they celebrate – as I write this, Britain is in the grip of a full blown moral panic about sexualisation and online porn, with demands for increased censorship of everything from Page 3 to the entire internet, and the world of carefree sexuality featured in Brass's work seems a universe away, sadly.

Brass, of course, loves the female body. His ass fetish is well known, but he has a genuine adoration for women – their sexuality and their naturalness. He's as obsessed with pubic (and armpit) hair in this film as with breasts and buttocks. And he also has a fixation with voyeurism, self-reflection (most of his films see the lead actresses examining themselves in mirrors and exploring their own bodies) and public sex – as well as having a seemingly obligatory urination scene in each film.

With many of his films being period pieces, the Brass oeuvre increasingly seems like a nostalgic look at a time of more innocent sexuality – and

Frivolous Lola

Cheeky

this is especially the case with *Frivolous Lola*. It's unlikely that the 1950s were anything like this in reality, but Brass creates a charming alternate world, helped partly by a smart soundtrack that mixes Pino Donaggio's score with rock 'n' roll numbers (and the delicious Euro pop theme song) and mostly by Anna Ammirati in the lead role, who is delightful to watch – her natural charm and casual sexiness making her one of the more impressive leads in a Brass film. Fans of Italian cult cinema will be glad to see Serena Grandi (veteran star of *Miranda* and assorted Italian sex and horror movies) while British viewers will be amused by the presence of Patrick Mower, star of *The Devil Rides Out* (1968), *Cry of the Banshee* (1970) and more recently, soap opera *Emmerdale* (1972-).

It's highly questionable whether or not we'll ever see another Brass film. He is, after all, in his eighties now and reportedly in poor health, suffering an intracranial haemorrhage in 2010. That same year, he announced a 3D remake of *Caligula* – we may now never see the film and honestly, that might not be a bad thing. But if we have seen the last work from Brass, then we shouldn't be too upset. He's already provided us with a fine body of work, unique in style. Like Russ Meyer, Brass showed that you can make sophisticated, stylish and original erotica by staying true to your own desires. If more filmmakers would heed that lesson, there might yet be hope for the genre.

***This essay originally appeared in the Arrow Video edition of* Frivolous Lola.**

THE PRINCIPAL OF NUKE 'EM HIGH, PRESIDENT OF TROMA

David Hayles on Lloyd Kaufman

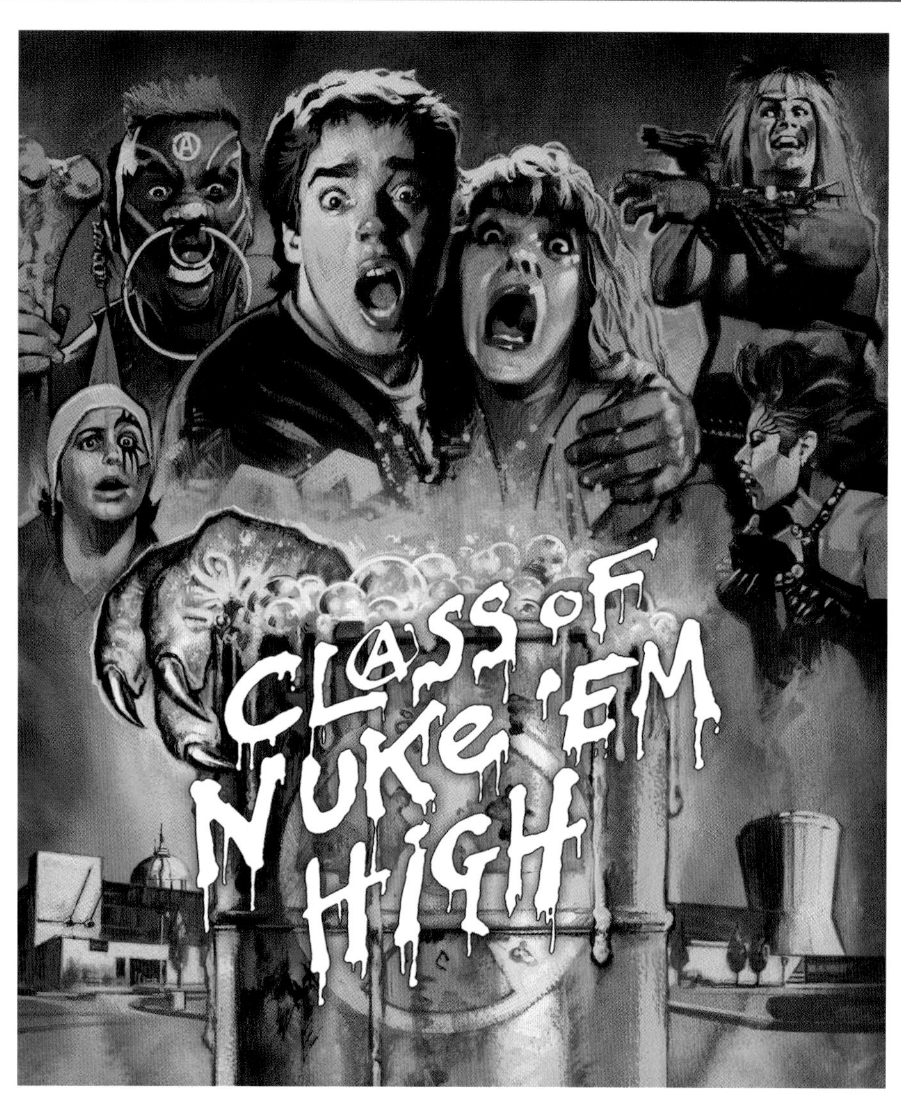

Artwork by Graham Humphreys

Lloyd Kaufman – the co-founder of Troma Entertainment, the irrepressible cinematic vulgarian, producer of such films as *The Toxic Avenger* (1984), *Igor and the Lunatics* (1985) and *Sgt. Kabukiman N.Y.P.D.* (1990) – is sitting at a table in the bar of London's Groucho club. He is smartly dressed, in a suit, with neatly combed hair, and twinkling eyes that belie his age. The eyes are the giveaway; they sparkle with mischief, otherwise he might be mistaken for a chartered accountant on his lunch break. He is talking to another man in a suit, blond-haired, in his mid-thirties, with cold sores round his lips. The man is gesticulating wildly, and Kaufman is politely intent on the conversation. I approach the table, and introduce myself. I am carrying Toxic Avenger's green rubber head in a plastic carrier bag.

It is the summer of 1996, and I am there to interview Kaufman, who is launching the Troma brand on the United Kingdom: a series of VHS videos of the Troma favourites – *The Toxic Avenger, Class of Nuke 'em High* (1986) and so on – as well as a limited cinema release for the company's latest film, *Tromeo and Juliet*, Kaufman's truly nutty and irreverent take on Shakespeare's most famous play. Troma's version, which features the lead character, Tromeo, masturbating to internet pornography (which, in 1996, is not something you see every day) will play for one week at the Prince Charles Cinema on Leicester Square). Channel 4 will also shortly begin broadcasting Troma TV, a late night barrage of sex and violence the likes of which insomniacs the length and breadth of the country have never seen. Nobody knows if the British public is ready for an all-out onslaught of all things Troma, but Kaufman is a firm believer in throwing everything at the screen and seeing what sticks. What usually sticks are acres of guts, geysers of blood, bouncing bosoms, distended eyeballs and severed limbs, scored with cheap rock 'n' roll soundtracks and punctuated with shamelessly crude dialogue.

The Troma formula is thus: take one part 1950s beach party film, mix in with a monster movie, add a smattering of leather-jacketed middle-aged punks with their hair sprayed pink, drizzle with copious amounts of green goo, sprinkle words like *Bloody*, *Rabid* or *Lust* into the title, have the hero transform into a mutant and the heroine take her clothes off, and vomit onto the public. Repeat ad nauseam for five decades and counting.

Kaufman introduces me to his coffee companion, who, as it turns out, is a British film producer (or, at least, would-be film producer) who is pitching an idea to the low budget horror comedy impresario.

"What's the film called?" I ask the fellow.

"*Dracula HIV Positive and Hating It*," the man says.

I almost ask what it's about.

Kaufman chuckles gleefully. "It's a wonderful idea, wonderful."

The would-be producer leaves, and I show Kaufman the Toxic Avenger head that I picked up earlier from Troma's London offices, a ramshackle space in the basement of a building off Oxford Street, piled high with Troma VHS stock, badges ('Toxie for Mayor'), stickers, T-shirts and props.

"Ah, there he is, Toxie," Kaufman says as if greeting an old friend, beaming at the disembodied head staring up at him from inside the plastic bag.

After chatting for a while, about Troma (what else?), we go upstairs to an empty room so I can take some photographs for the article. My friend Zeb has arrived, who I asked to don the Toxie mask for the pictures. He was wearing, as was his wont, a tweed cape and a deerstalker hat.

"Great!" Kaufman says, playing up to the camera, as Zeb, as Toxie, puts his hands to Kaufman's neck as if to strangle him. "*Sherlock Toxie. The Toxic Detective*. A British Toxic Avenger movie. I can see it now: Toxie at Bucking-ham Palace," he goes on, elongating that word in the peculiar way that Americans do. Toxie's drooping left eyeball pops out of the rubber mask onto the floor. Zeb scrabbles around on the carpet to retrieve it.

"Why don't you stand on that chair, Lloyd," I suggest, "and it can look like Toxie is holding you off the ground by your throat."

"Sure, sure," Kaufman says, obliging. "Wait, wait! Where's his mop? Toxie has to have a mop." He jumps off the chair and charges out the room, coming back minutes later brandishing a janitor's mop he has retrieved from downstairs.

Afterwards, over dinner at Pizza Express, I ask Kaufman what sort of films he enjoys, and his answer surprises. "Most recently I saw *Nixon*," he says, directed by his old Yale classmate Oliver Stone, "and I thought it was perfect. It was, to me, the best example of what can be achieved in the medium of cinema."

With Kaufman, what you see is most definitely not what you get. An Ivy League graduate, he is intelligent, charming company, and seemingly without a hint of malice: on the face of it, the man least likely to be in charge of an outlaw outfit that peddles some of the most repulsive and borderline insane cinematic mush ever to have been smeared across the silver screen and to have cluttered the video shop shelves. He has written, directed and produced dozens of films, and acted in around two hundred (he usually has a blink-and-you'll-miss-it cameo as a drunk or a stoned hippy). He is a constant promoter of Troma, which he believes is the only truly independent film company in the United States, and, during the course of the afternoon, only becomes riled when discussing the monopoly the film studios have over distribution. He never passes up an opportunity to remind one that, like a latter-day Roger Corman, he gave many struggling actors and filmmakers, if not their big break, at least a chance to practice their craft. Who can forget Kevin Costner in *Malibu Hot Summer* in 1981 (aka *Sizzle Beach USA*); the aforementioned Oliver Stone worked on Kaufman's first film *The Battle of Love's Return* (1971); and in due course, Eli Roth and James Gunn would have Troma to thank for helping them on their path to becoming horror directors.

Kaufman not only sees himself as the proud father to these cinematic talents, but is also unduly fond of his roster of Troma characters, of which Toxie is the figurehead, peering out as he does from the Troma logo. He is thrilled that the Toxic Avenger was turned into a cartoon series, *Toxic Crusaders*, in 1991, failing to see the irony of the inappropriateness of the star of a series of X-rated films featuring exploding heads, dripping flesh and plentiful amounts of naked women, becoming a kids cartoon replete with an environmental message.

It's easy to regard Troma Entertainment with scorn – and let's face it, some of the Troma films don't even deserve that – but never let it be said that Troma films do not have a social, even political, undertow. You might scoff, but isn't Buddy Giovinazzo's *Combat Shock* (1984) a morality tale about the devastating effects of Vietnam War on the psyche of the combatant? Isn't *Mother's Day* (1980) a commentary on the dangers of maternal smothering? Can *Class of Nuke 'em High* be taken as a knockabout gross-out sci-fi comedy, or as a prescient reaction to the Chernobyl disaster that occurred six months before the film was released? That film, which spawned two sequels, acts as a companion piece to the similarly themed *Toxic Avenger* series. It is a veritable high water mark in the

Troma canon, a cross between US kids' sitcom *Saved by the Bell* and David Cronenberg, best summarised by its plot keywords on IMDb: female frontal nudity, eye gouging, gay slur, choke hold, violence, deeply disturbed person, death spasm, rampage, nerd, bare breasts, nuclear waste, cheerleading squad, evil teen, dope, flatulence, science runs amok, splatter, spoof, death and yanked off bikini top. It would make a good dictionary definition of Troma.

So, did Kaufman ever make *Sherlock Toxie*? Not as of yet. And what *of Dracula, HIV Positive and Hating It*? No sign of it with that particular title, although a couple of years later Troma released a straight-to-bargain-bucket film called *Sucker: the Vampire* (1998), about the lead singer of a rock band, who is actually a vampire, who contracts AIDS. It's not Troma's finest hour, but then who's counting? And what of Troma Entertainment now? They're still releasing films and selling Blu-rays and DVDs online through the Troma store website. A glossy remake of *Mother's Day* came out in 2010, while a Hollywood version of *The Toxic Avenger* is said to be in the works. You can even buy a Toxie mask for $60. But for the real Troma connoisseur, for $649.95 you can buy a 'cinema quality' Toxie mask, described thus: "This officially licensed Toxic Avenger mask captures the lumpy, malformed majesty of Melvin the monster hero down to every disgusting detail and features a drooping realistic silicone left eye". Mop not included.

***This essay originally appeared in the Arrow Video edition of* Class of Nuke 'em High**

Class of Nuke 'em High

CIVILISATION VERSUS THE PRIMITIVES

Mike Sutton on Wes Craven

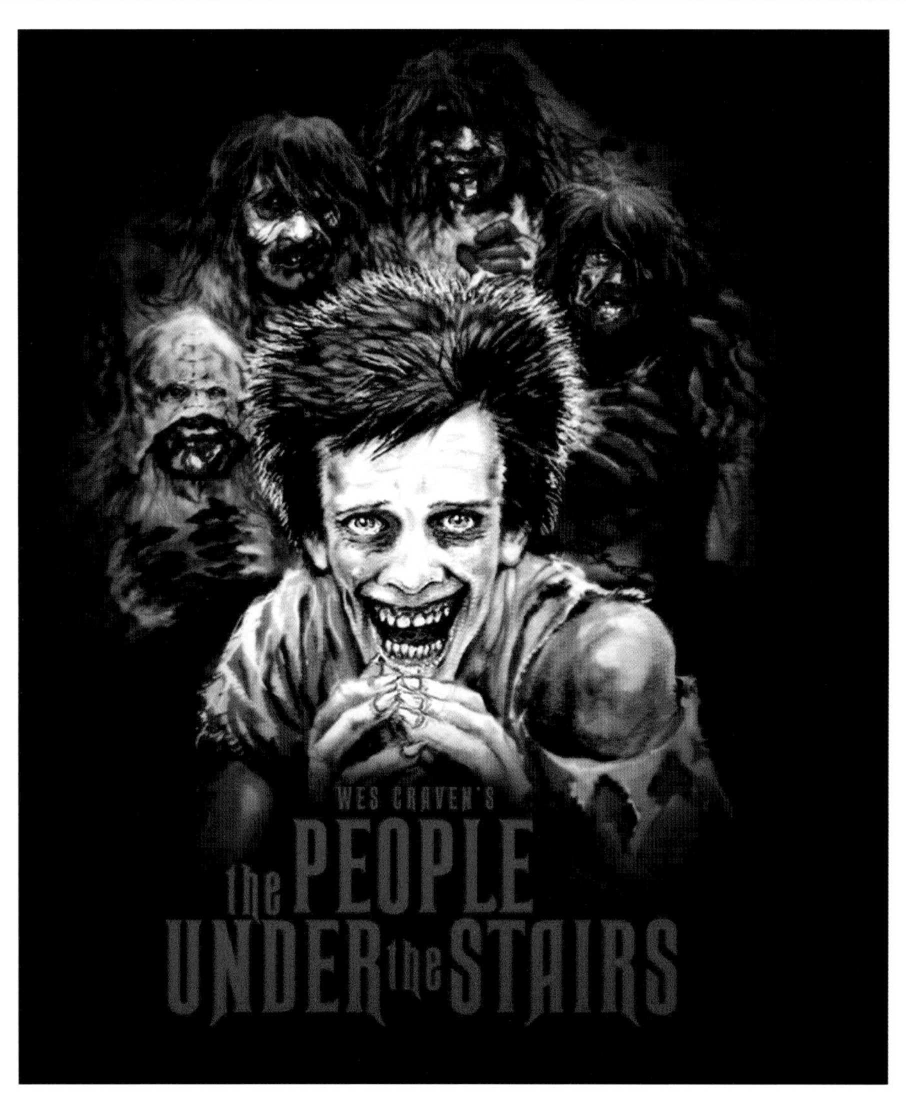

Artwork by Stephen R. Bisette

Wes Craven made at least four iconic horror films. Not bad for someone who didn't see a movie until he was 17 due to a strict Protestant upbringing, let alone one who spent the first part of his career as a Professor of Humanities. Unhappy with academia, he moved to New York and, after teaching high school, dropped out to become a messenger in a post-production company. It was here that he learned the craft of editing and eventually hooked up with Sean S. Cunningham, a budding filmmaker. With Craven acting as associate producer, they made a no-budget softcore flower-child picture called *Together* (1971), best known as the film debut of Marilyn Chambers.

The success of the film led to an offer to make a horror film on a budget of between fifty and a hundred thousand dollars.[1] Thus, Craven received his first credit as writer-director on *The Last House on the Left* (1972). The two men have always maintained that the aim of the film was to show the true, horrible nature of death as opposed to the Hollywood cliché. Certainly, the resulting film is brutal but whether it gets at any fundamental truth about violence is a moot point. Much of it remains edgy and shocking. In particular, some of the performances, particularly David Hess playing a thug named Krug who organises the rape and murder of two young girls, have a vicious and startling intensity which is unusual and upsetting. The story is based upon Ingmar Bergman's *The Virgin Spring* (*Jungfrukällan*, 1960) and follows the same formal structure – a middle class girl is tempted into very mildly aberrant behaviour by a lower class acquaintance and the result is her brutal defloration, mutilation and death. The killers seek shelter in the nearest house, which just happens to belong to their victim's parents who accidentally discover the truth. The civilised products of the middle-class subsequently seek revenge in the most direct and violent manner possible.

For most seasoned horror viewers, the shock value of *The Last House on the Left* has probably declined due to the occasionally amateurish style, some banal dialogue, and the unfortunate interpolation of comic relief policemen. But the central murder sequence is still one of the unforgettable scenes of extreme cinema – it was allegedly as gruelling to film as it is to watch. Craven and Cunningham's inexperience certainly adds an edge of roughness which more experienced filmmakers may well have blunted. The final scenes of the parents' revenge has not dated as well, largely because the middle-class family is not as well defined or played as the Krug cabal. However, in 1972 it was sufficiently extreme

1 - The figure depends on whom you believe. The original intention was to make the film for $40,000 and pocket $10,000.

to cause controversy in several countries, although it actually received generally good reviews in the USA. In the UK it was refused a certificate and then effectively banned as a 'video nasty', not emerging until 2003 in a cut form. It has only been generally available uncut in the UK since 2008.[2]

Nowadays, such a *succès de scandal* would spark a brilliant career, but Craven wound up working in the porn business. He edited several hardcore films as well as directing *The Fireworks Woman* (1975) under the pseudonym of Abe Snake. (He also appears briefly in the picture.) His second break came when that film's producer, Peter Locke, offered him the chance to make another horror film, *The Hills Have Eyes* (1977). This is much more polished than anything Craven had previously made but it was still violent enough to provoke comment, although it was not cut by the British censor – the difference this time was probably the amount of black humour. The set-up is brutally simple. An extended family is on a vacation trip to California. The father, Big Bob decides to take a detour through the desert, ignoring the protests of his family and the dire warnings of a gas station owner. Soon, the family is stranded, not realising that another family is already there and watching them. This other family, a group of cannibals led by the patriarch Jupiter, begin an onslaught which begins at sunset and lasts through a freezing desert night into the next morning. Only by throwing off the trappings of civilisation can the family, being culled one by one, find a way to survive.

The two families battle and gradually become mirrors of each other. At first, our sympathies are straightforwardly with the all-American family. But Craven complicates matters. The cannibal father Jupiter isn't much more obnoxious than Big Bob, albeit more partial to human flesh; his group begin as stereotyped killers and gradually gain character and, most importantly, humour. The central scene where Jupiter eats Big Bob while ranting at his corpse offers us one very suggestive line – "Don't you come here pushing your life in my face". Why, the film asks, do we think we have the monopoly on morality and why is our 'civilisation' the only one which we are capable of understanding? If we blunder blindly into a situation which we don't understand with a culture we aren't even interested in understanding, why should we be surprised that

---

2 - I'm indebted to a 2009 interview between Wes Craven and Randy Lofficier, and the featurette 'Celluloid Crime of the Century' on the UK Metrodome DVD of the film.

we come a cropper? The parallels with American history are obvious. By the end of the film, the extremes to which the 'normal' family have gone to wipe out the 'primitive' family are as vicious as anything which is done to them.[3]

Both of these horror films deal with two interlinked themes. Firstly, the point of contact between 'civilisation', however that might be defined, and some kind of outside force which is diametrically opposed. In *The Last House on the Left* we have Krug and his followers, brutal to the point of being some kind of primal force, becoming involved with the bourgeois respectability of the Collingwood family, while in *The Hills Have Eyes* the All-American happy family meets the primitive hill dwellers led by Jupiter who vocally resent them. Secondly, the knife edge upon which civilisation rests between order and anarchy. Time and again, 'respectable' people in Craven's films are forced to do horrendous things simply in order to stay alive. Alternatively, the horrendous thing they do, in the name of justice, causes the trouble in the first place.

You can see this latter variation in *A Nightmare on Elm Street* (1984) where Freddy Krueger, the monster unloosed on a suburban neighbourhood, is created by the very middle-classes whom he seeks to destroy. He was, at one time, in their midst but already the 'other', a predator whose outward appearance as a family hid his proclivities for the kidnap and murder of his neighbours' children. Upon discovering his crimes, the parents cornered him and burnt him to death. There's a powerful sense here of the sins of the past returning to haunt the present, something which Craven also investigates in *The Hills Have Eyes* when we discover the hidden story behind the cannibals. Of course, it's important to remember that in the first *Elm Street*, Freddy is a horrendous, scary child killer with whom we have no sympathy but Craven seems to be saying that not even the worst in our society deserves a lynching. Freddy is also, like villains in horror from Bram Stoker's *Dracula* (1897) onwards, a vigorous, liberating force within the stifling conformity of the middle-class community of adults and fiercely conformist high-school teenagers. He represents everything that society represses – just like Krug and Jupiter, he reminds us just how close to savagery we all are. There's a great and terrible irony that Freddy, a killer of the innocent, became a horror hero, complete with quips and ingenious ways of killing

3 - Kim Newman comments on Craven's penchant for contrasting families in *Nightmare Movies* (2011)

unsympathetic and largely anonymous teen victims.

Craven became very uncomfortable with this version of the character. His involvement in the first five sequels was, needless to say, minimal. But in 1994, he returned to Freddy in *New Nightmare* and made him scary again, an ancient supernatural force who gains his power from the stories he inspires. This film, while excellent, is significant largely for what it heralded. For the postmodern approach which Craven adopted – having Heather Langenkamp and John Saxon, actors from the first film, playing themselves and featuring Robert Englund as both himself and Freddy – was a huge influence on his fourth horror film for the ages, *Scream* (1996), a decidedly self-referential horror comedy which exploits the clichés of the slasher genre to devastating effect.

Using a traditional slasher plot – a mysterious killer terrorises then murders a group of high school kids – writer Kevin Williamson and director Craven brew up a deliciously entertaining concoction of genre references, unexpected twists, black comedy and genuine scares. Both the killer and the kids are sophisticated, they know all the rules of the genre and one of them, a film geek, explains them to us. But much of the joy of the film is how it takes the rules and turns them on their heads, particularly in an extended denouement which, in its perverse ingenuity, looks beyond the slasher movie to the *giallo* and might even have warmed the heart of Agatha Christie. It's a film full of affection for horror, even adding a new icon to the movie murderer shelf in the form of the Ghost Face mask.

While Craven's four great genre works will be, quite rightly, endlessly discussed and appreciated, it would be wrong to ignore his other films as these are often just as interesting in their own way and add a considerable amount to some of his favourite themes and ideas.

After *The Hills Have Eyes* Craven worked on the bland *Stranger in Our House* (1978, aka *Summer of Fear*), a TV film which is notable for being his first 35mm production. Far more interesting is *Deadly Blessing* (1981), a film set around an enclosed religious order called the Hittites, a fictional order inspired by various Anabaptist groups, who are led by a restrained but decidedly unnerving Ernest Borgnine. They live in splendid isolation, refuse to use modern technology and deny their members the right to leave or contact the outside world. It transpires that one of their members has rebelled, gone to college and met an outsider before returning to become a farmer. When he is killed, his wife is forced to cope on her own and battle the ignorance of her neighbours who blame her for stealing one of their own. They despise her as an "incubus".

The basic idea is a strong one; a group of repressed, fiercely religious people have so suppressed their baser feelings that they eventually erupt in violent mayhem. Indeed, some of it is played out rather well, the repression of the Hittites mirrored in the character of Louise, played by the veteran actress Lois Nettleton, a woman whose deep-rooted hatred of men has caused her to make some drastic decisions about the raising of her child. The strongest scenes of the film feature the frighteningly credible rituals of the Hittites. Oddly enough, these sequences are far more effective than the well achieved but predictable genre stuff, suggesting that Craven is more interested in the social context. Symptomatic of the problem with the film that a potentially classic scene – the heroine being menaced by a snake while she's in the bath – is slightly neutered by the fact that she's obviously still wearing her pants.[4] It is only fair to note, however, that Craven conjures up a wonderful final scene which is all the more entertaining for being either illogical or wonderfully suggestive, depending on personal taste. The hint that the Hittites might have been right all along is typical of Craven's own black humour.

Deadly Blessing did well at the box office and led to *Swamp Thing* (1982), a slightly underrated film, which suffered from its low budget and the studio insistence on a PG certificate in the US. It wasn't a commercial success but led the way to *Elm Street* which was itself followed by another flop, *Deadly Friend* (1986). The less said about this effort the better, but it's caught in an identity crisis between being a Disneyesque teenager movie, a dark romance, and a gory romp. It provides some campy fun but it was a troubled production and the compromises show.

Regardless, Craven subsequently got the chance to make two of his most interesting films. In 1988 came *The Serpent and the Rainbow*, very loosely based on the academic book by Wade Davis, an anthropologist who went to Haiti and discovered various local customs surrounding the legend of voodoo. Craven adds crazy dream sequences, shock moments, a thoroughly supernatural explanation, and some fascinating local colour. He also creates a potent vision of a country in chaos where the secret police's idea of interrogation is to ram a nail through a suspect's scrotum. It was a troubled production, filmed largely in the Dominican Republic after the

4 - How obvious this is depends on which version of the film you watch: the undergarments were visible in the full-screen VHS and TV versions, but were (correctly) cropped out in the theatrical and widescreen DVD/Blu-ray versions.

Deadly Blessing

Haitians proved difficult to get on with, and deserves a wider audience. It echoes Craven's theme of the shifting dichotomy between primitive and civilised, epitomised in one fantastic moment when, during a swanky dinner party, a society wife is possessed by a magician and begins eating a wine glass.

Four years later, following the incoherent *Shocker* (1989), Craven made *The People Under the Stairs* (1991), something of a cult favourite which represents his own brand of blacker-than-black comedy. It tells the story of the haves and the have-nots of America through the prism of Fool Williams, a 13-year-old who breaks into his landlords' house in search of treasure. What he doesn't realise is that the landlords, the Robesons, are insane and have a basement full of cannibalistic children who were adopted then rejected when they failed to live up to extreme 'three wise monkeys' expectations. Only one girl is allowed into the main part of the house and she has survived purely through absolute obedience to her captors.

The metaphor of respectability masking primal brutality is clear enough but what's also interesting is the direct link that the film makes between money and insanity. The Robesons, we discover, are actually siblings who are the product of generations of inbreeding and became rich through corrupt real estate practices. The more money they make, the more decadent and demented they become. The children they imprison eventually destroy them in a neat, somewhat H.G. Wellsian turn of events whereby the oppressed devour their oppressors. There's also another favourite Craven theme: the sins of the fathers are to be laid upon the children. It's an often funny, occasionally creepy picture which has a distinct fairy-tale feel about it, right up to the happy-and-richer-ever-after ending. Craven's affinity for comedy is one of the more rarely discussed aspects of his oeuvre but it has emerged in such unlikely surroundings as a Disney television movie (1986's *Casebusters*), a segment in the 2006 anthology film *Paris, je t'aime,* and a peculiar and not entirely effective Eddie Murphy vehicle *Vampire in Brooklyn* (1995), which suffers from the obvious tension between director and star.

The *Scream* films occupied Craven for much of the latter part of his career, although he did direct a straight drama entitled *Music of the Heart* (1999), which earned Meryl Streep an Oscar nomination, and a very efficient thriller called *Red Eye* (2005). But when he died in August 2015, it was his four classic films which received most of the attention and it is those, along with two or three others, for which he will be remembered.

NO MORE MYSTERIOSO: HORROR'S GREAT SOCIOLOGIST

John Kenneth Muir on George A. Romero

Artwork by Rick Melton

If the late Wes Craven is remembered as the horror genre's great psychologist – an artist intent on peering into the dreams and psyches of the human animal – then it is appropriate, perhaps, to term director George A. Romero the genre's dominant sociologist. As any review of his canon makes plain, Romero's films gaze deeply at matters of social order, social disorder and social change. His most famous cycle of films, the *Dead* movies, revolves specifically around these issues. Initially, Romero conceived of *Night of the Living Dead* (1968) in an unpublished story called 'Anubis'. Notably, it features a bookend structure, commencing with a lone zombie chased over a hill, pursued by armed human soldiers. The story climaxes with a deliberate reversal. "We see it is an army of zombies, chasing a human with an injured, bleeding leg," Romero told Paul Gagne in *The Zombies that Ate Pittsburgh* in 1987.

What's at stake in 'Anubis' – and, indeed, in the *Dead* cycle – is social change, the bailiwick of sociology. Those at the top of the system in the *Dead* films may fall to its bottom, but the system itself remains largely unchanged. The new social order looks different, certainly, but at heart it is the same social structure as before, just with different beneficiaries. The hill is still there. The two armies remain as well.

Night of the Living Dead (1968) is often lauded by horror scholars for its treatment of racial and gender issues. However, the film more aptly concerns the volatile social change of the year 1968. This was a span of non-stop crisis. In Vietnam, the American Embassy was overwhelmed during the Tet Offensive. On the home front, riots about racial inequality flared up nationwide, and leaders such as Martin Luther King, Jr. and Robert Kennedy were assassinated. Then, in late August of 1968, anti-war protesters at the Democratic National Convention clashed with the Illinois National Guard and Chicago Police Dept. On TV, it appeared that two armies were warring on American streets. Worse, it was virtually impossible to distinguish the good guys from the bad guys. Who was wrong? Who was right? Where were the heroes?

Night of the Living Dead symbolically expressed this idea of a standing social order collapsing before a mob that, suspiciously, looks just like the TV audience, but seems guided by irrational, incomprehensible, and violent impulses. One can thus detect how the ghouls of *Night*, dressed like your average neighbour, represent this disorganised army on the march, tearing down social order, forging change, and for the silent majority, inciting terror.

Day of the Dead

The remaining *Dead* films similarly revolve around social matters. What occurs when America experiences, in the words of President Carter, a "crisis of confidence"? Carter and Romero envisioned in the late seventies how the shift in America's economy from being 'need-based' to 'desire-based' was forging materialistic zombies out of everyday citizens. Set in a shopping mall, *Dawn of the Dead* (1978) revealed human survivors ignoring the zombies (who have since grown in number) and instead focusing on hedonism and on the things they can own. Drugged by their own materialistic impulses, they simply neglect the real problem.

Day of the Dead (1985) presented the zombies firmly in control of society while the last vestiges of human authority – science and the military – fall. But the film is important in term of embodying the shifting social order because it also showcased a zombie revolutionary, Bub (Howard Sherman), who can metaphorically lead that army over that hill from 'Anubis'. In the closing scenes, Bub, packing a pistol, leads a posse of zombies after the military leader. And he wins, too. The zombies are now in charge. The social order has flipped.

Land of the Dead (2005) concerned itself with the "idea of living with terrorism", according to Romero in a *New York Times* interview. But who, precisely, are the terrorists? The film opens with idyllic views of a sort of Every Town, U.S.A., as its zombie inhabitants live peacefully. They stroll in the park and even enjoy marching band music until an outside terrorist force – humans scavenging for resources – destroys that peace.

While *Diary of the Dead* (2007) was a found-footage movie recounting the onset of the zombie apocalypse, Romero's final *Dead* film thus far, *Survival of the Dead* (2009), very explicitly addressed the Iraq War and the ways that people can be manipulated into fighting for a cause that is not their own. The film features an Ahmed Chalabi-like exile from Plum Island (Kenneth Welsh), who, with false intelligence, basically, promises American soldiers safety and security if only they depose a dictator (Richard Fitzpatrick) and re-install him in his rightful place as ruler. The soldiers take the bait, and become enmeshed in a war that is not their own, and which does nothing to enhance anyone's safety and security. The film's Western veneer, with cowboy zombies duking it out against the backdrop of a full-moon, deliberately echoed the swaggering foreign policy of the 2000s, which talked of terrorists "wanted dead or alive" and "smoked" out of their caves.

Romero's cinematic masterworks not only offer keen social commentary and suggest his most important qualities as a sociologist - curiosity, keen observational skills and the gadfly's desire to comment on social injustice or hypocrisy - they actually reground the very concept of horror itself. In this case, such grounding might adequately be described as the sociologist's ability to apply logic and reason to a situation that appears to be lacking such qualities. If horror is generally surreal, absurdist, irrational and romantic in nature, Romero's films attempts to rewrite the genre within the grounded realms of reason and science.

Gazing across his film catalogue, one can detect how Romero consistently subtracts romantic or glamorous interpretations of monsters from his narratives. In an interview at *Wired.com* in 2010, Romero explained why *Night of the Living Dead* proved such a success with audiences: he removed "the mysterioso stuff of voodoo" and instead made his flesh-eating monsters "the neighbours". In an interview with *NPR* in 2014 he re-stated his premise, this time noting that he took zombies out of the realm of "exotica". Why did he ground them in this fashion? Perhaps because Romero maintains that there is "nothing scarier than neighbours". Again, that's a sociologist's perspective, isn't it?

Although there are scattered cinematic antecedents to Romero's flesh-eating zombies in the genre, older zombie films, by contrast, strongly feature elements of the supernatural, of voodoo. Films such as *White Zombie* (1932) and *I Walked with a Zombie* (1943) focus on not merely on the walking dead, but the puppetmasters who resurrect them for sinister purposes. Romero casts aside the "exotic" (and indeed, non-Western or foreign) concept of zombie. Instead of representing viewpoints exploring American ethnocentrism, Romero's zombies explicitly involve matters, as noted above, of social order, disorder, and change.

Repeatedly throughout Romero's films, one detects this approach in practice. Romero knowingly removes his monsters from the realm of the Romantic or Gothic, and places them, instead, squarely in the domain of the human. In a career that stretches back to the '60s, the director has translated such classic monsters as zombies, witches, and vampires to this terrain. Romero has done so because as an observer of human behaviour and institutions, he sees us as the real threat, the real monsters. "In my work, it's usually the humans that are the worst," he told NPR.

Romero's first horror film after *Night of the Living Dead*, *Hungry Wives* (1972, aka *Jack's Wife* and

Season of the Witch) followed a similar pattern. The film revolves around a middle-aged housewife, Joan (Jan White), a suburbanite who is bored with her life. In her dreams, she imagines herself being led around by her husband (Bill Thunhurst) on a leash. At a party, however, she learns that her neighbour Marion (Virginia Greenwald) has recently become a witch.

Before long, Joan dabbles in the occult too, and conducts a spell which brings an amorous college professor (Ray Lane) to her bed. Soon, Joan joins Marion's coven, and self-identifies as a witch, but the movie's ultimate point is that being a witch is no more a satisfying label than is wife or mother. Joan has merely traded one for another. The supernatural nature of witchcraft is dismissed in the film, though Joan's spell appears to work as intended. "Voodoo only works because you believe it works. Your mind does the work," suggests one character in the film.

The Crazies (1973) was an even more "exotica"-free zombie story than *Night of the Living Dead*. In this case, the violent, discontented mob representing social change is not physically or biologically dead, merely rendered insane and murderous by a biological agent called Trixie. The zombies aren't even really zombies anymore; they are products of human,

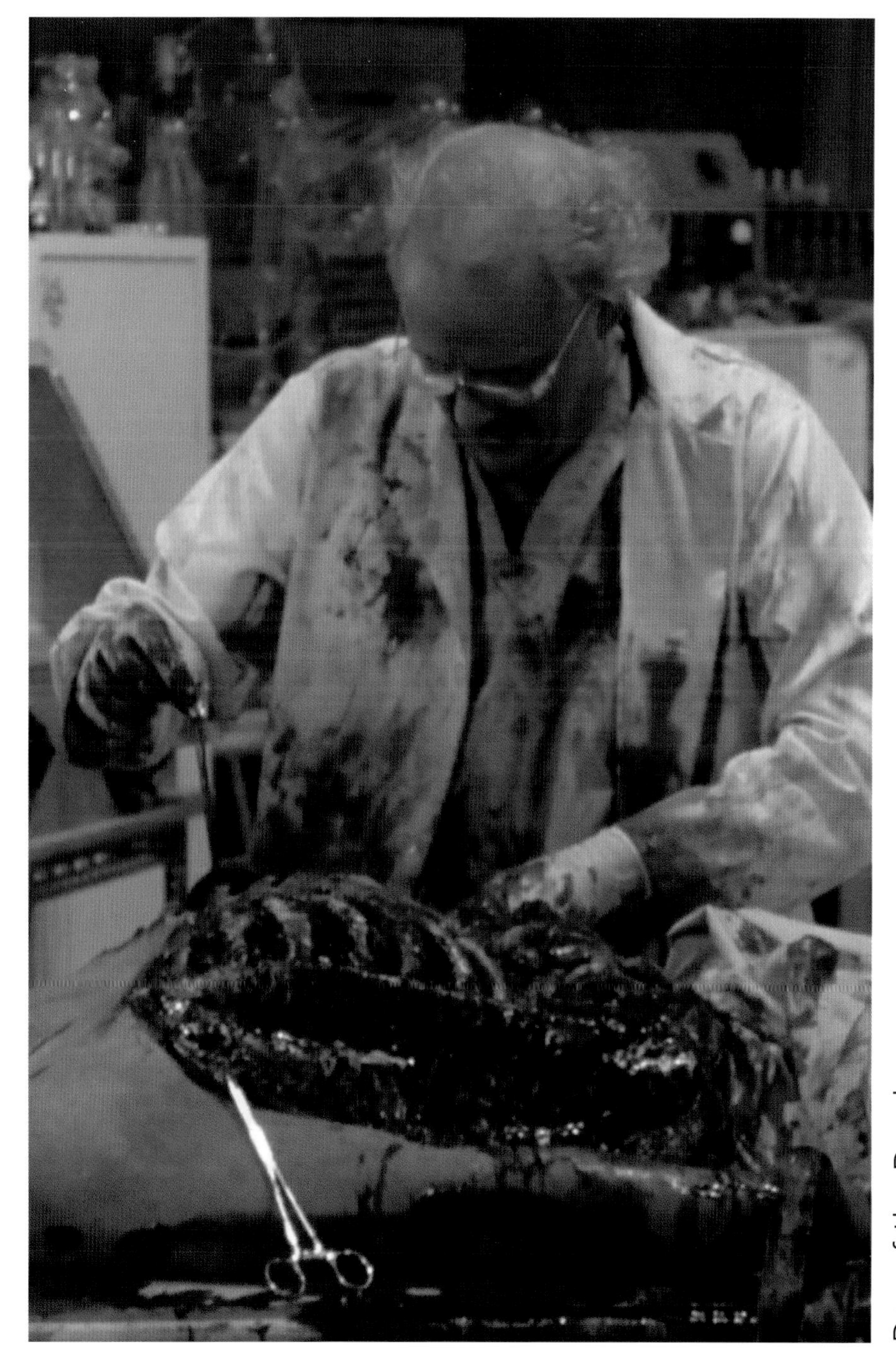
Day of the Dead

military, and governmental incompetence. *Martin* (1977) was similarly grounded. The film depicts the life of a troubled teen, Martin (John Amplas), who believes himself to be a vampire. Importantly, Martin is not like the famous vampires of the silver screen. To drink the blood of his victims, for example, he must drug his victims with tranquillisers, and then slit their wrists with a razor blade. Martin may be a vampire in practice, but he exists in the grounded world of Pittsburgh, and boasts none of the 'magic' powers that horror movies typically ascribe to creatures of the night. The "mysterioso" has been bled from the genre. Martin, in the words of Romero in *The Michigan Daily* in 1978, is just a kid "with a hang-up".

In this context, *Creepshow* (1982) may seem anomalous in Romero's canon, since it involved the supernatural, and the EC Comics notion of cosmic-scales-of-justice-righted by supernatural forces. Yet the film was structured visually like a comic-book, thus signalling that viewers are not to take it as real, but rather as a translation of another fictional form. It also made a social argument about the validity of horror comics in America circa the 1950s; the very era of EC. Specifically, comics were derided in that era as a bad influence, especially for young boys. The stereotyped image of a comic-book lover – forever imprinted in the imaginations of Romero's generation – came from the Charles Atlas advertisement about the "90-pound weakling". In *Creepshow,* Romero gets his revenge on that stereotype in the person of a reader's disapproving father. A young boy and comic fan orders from the magazine a voodoo doll that he can use to punish his dad for throwing out his favourite issue of *Creepshow*. Although the movie may not qualify as a typical Romero re-grounding of the genre, it is about social change. The 90-pound weakling of the 1950s is all grown-up, now making his own movies... and fashioning his own image of acceptable masculinity.

Even *Monkey Shines* (1988) is "rooted in plausibility", according to critic Ed Blank of the *Pittsburgh Press*. The monster here, a monkey called Ella, is the victim of not voodoo curses, but altered instincts and impulses. She serves as a dark repository for the lead character's animal nature and Id. So once more, Romero the sociologist rips the "exotica" from the horror format so he can tell his audience something important about man, and the social institutions of man. And as Romero reported in *Cinema Blend* in 2014: "I really think that's the purpose of horror."

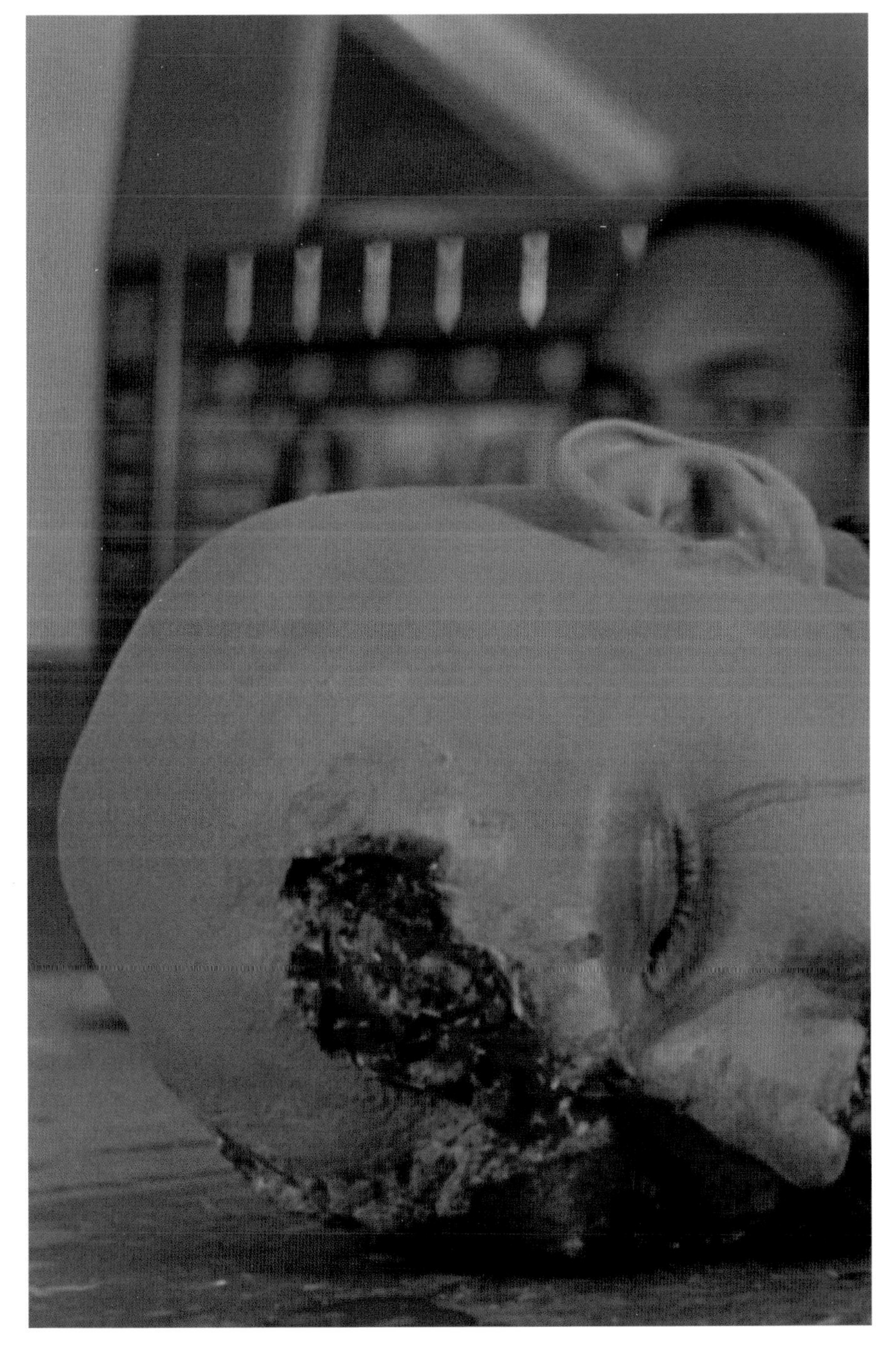

CULT ACTORS

COMEDY AND KARLOFF

Vic Pratt on Boris Karloff

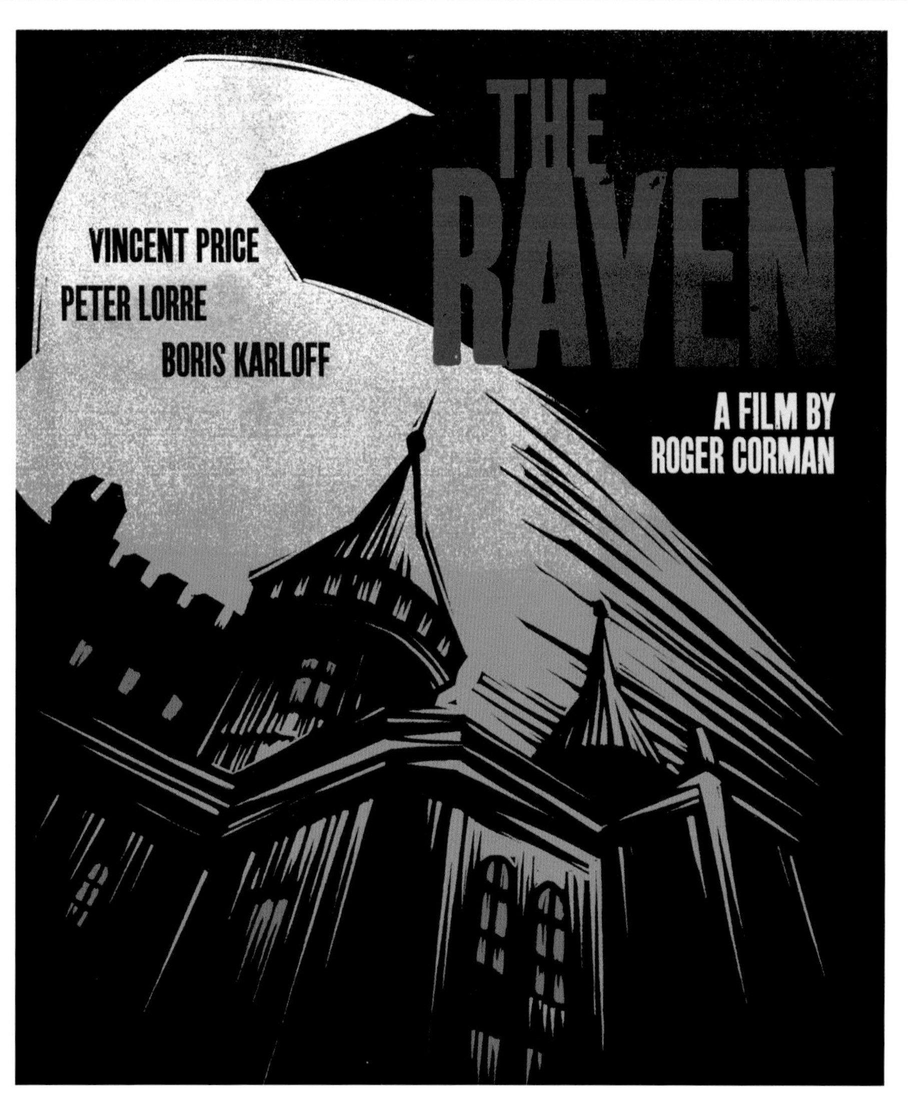

Artwork by Vladimir Zimakov

Four films into the Poe cycle, and poised to begin work on the next, Roger Corman feared that recent additions to the series – though still doing well at the box office – were beginning to look slightly similar. He was ready to do something just a little bit different, and the refreshing result was *The Raven*. It successfully rejuvenated the series once more with two key ingredients: comedy and Boris Karloff.

Karloff's career needed a shot in the arm just as much as the series. Boris was still busy, increasingly on television these days, but some of his recent small-screen parts lacked distinction. It was certainly time for another meaty film role. Corman's film provided Karloff with exactly the kind of restorative showcase for his talents that he needed.

Karloff had done a screen version of *The Raven* before, of course, back in the golden age of Hollywood horror – starring alongside his old rival for the title King of Horror, Bela Lugosi. Their gruesome 1935 Universal classic had seen Boris – playing a fugitive murderer on the run – horribly disfigured by Bela's crazed Poe-obsessed surgeon, the latter the proud possessor of a basement filled with custom-built torture devices. So perturbed was the British censor by the sadistic thrills contained within this grisly entertainment, that five minutes of footage were snipped out before the impressionable public were allowed to see it. But more irksome for Karloff than the scissoring might have been the niggling suspicion that, on this particular occasion at least, Lugosi had upstaged him.

The second time around, it all ended up very differently, and doubtless to Boris's quiet satisfaction. Despite a top drawer cast of splendid horror stars, all excellent, the 1963 version is unquestionably Karloff's film. And despite the claims made on a scream-filled giveaway record promoting the feature, on which an excitable chap – perhaps from the American International Pictures press department – seemed to suggest *The Raven* was abundant with "the shrieking of mutilated victims", there was nothing at all to frighten the censor in Corman's latest. In fact, there is nothing more horrible in this thoroughly jovial entertainment than the mental pictures conjured up by Jack Nicholson's reminiscences of the titular bird: "The raven we used shit endlessly over everybody and everything. It just shit endlessly. My whole right shoulder was constantly covered with raven shit." That, indeed, sounds like the stuff of nightmares.

Here the Poe series took a new offbeat humorous direction, after Corman and writer Richard Matheson – enlisted to pen the script – shared an inspired brainwave. Matheson was of the opinion that it was pretty ludicrous to attempt a full-length feature based on Poe's slight poem – almost laughable, in fact. Meanwhile, at the back of Corman's mind was his recollection of the terrific comic chemistry shared by Vincent Price and Peter Lorre. Their exploits in an episode in a previous series entry, the portmanteau *Tales of Terror* (1962), had provoked at least as many laughs as thrills. Why not, Corman and Matheson decided, make *The Raven* an all-out horror comedy? Inspired, and using the poem as a springboard, Matheson went on an outrageous flight of fancy, pouring out the pages of his fanciful, farcical terror tale on a portable typewriter in a holiday motel.

Price and Lorre were enlisted once again; and, with the addition of Boris Karloff, Corman had assembled, in the grand words of that aforementioned promo record, "the great triumvirate of terror... greater than Dracula, Werewolf and Frankenstein together." This may perhaps have been overstating it slightly, but one thing was for certain: all three of these gifted actors had a genuine flair for comedy. Karloff was an old hand at humour. Playing the pantomime villain, he had appeared onscreen with Danny Kaye, for example, and on various occasions with those slick vaudevillians Bud Abbott and Lou Costello; not to mention his hugely successful, critically acclaimed stage run starring in the black comedy *Arsenic and Old Lace*. Peter Lorre – who'd featured in Frank Capra's film of that same hit play, though Karloff hadn't – had long ago appeared with Boris in such movie mirth-fests as *You'll Find Out* (1940, which also featured Bela, incidentally) and *The Boogie Man Will Get You* (1942). Price, the slightly sprightlier young buck of the group by comparison with his co-stars, was perceived by now primarily as man-of-the-moment when it came to screen horror, but certainly couldn't be accused of taking his work too seriously. Indeed, he'd confessed to having trouble keeping a straight face when shooting highly serious films like *The Fly* (1958). Having enjoyed his skit in *Tales of Terror,* he eagerly embraced this extended opportunity to play the clown.

The Raven, though, was not exactly your standard-issue Hollywood horror comedy. Unusually, there was no wisecracking scaredy-cat comedian on hand to be frightened by Karloff, Price and Lorre – instead, they put the frighteners on each other. Subtlety is the keynote, and as the colourfully spooky title sequence ushers us into the opening scenes, casual viewers could be forgiven for not noticing at first that it's a comedy at all. But even if you don't catch on when you hear the just-so-slightly overwrought organ flourishes on the soundtrack, or twig that all is not as serious as it seems when Price's Craven bumps into his telescope in almost slapstick fashion, never fear. The clincher comes when Craven, having admitted the raven at his window, ornately wonders out loud whether he shall ever hold again that radiant maiden whom the angels call Lenore. "How the hell should I know?" the bird pipes up unexpectedly by way of answer. "What am I – a fortune teller?" It's a great comic moment – a marvellous magic trick that signals the modern, offbeat direction *The Raven* is to take.

The time was right. With his hep horror comedy, Corman rode the zeitgeist again, skilfully capitalising on the fact that Karloff, Price and Lorre were now being discovered by a new generation of film fans. They, and the other horror stars, were regularly celebrated in Forrest Ackerman's flourishing fan mag *Famous Monsters of Filmland;* significant to the success of the magazine was the fact that their bounteous back catalogues were finally being dug out of the vaults, and returned to circulation, thanks to the wonders of television syndication. *The Raven* must surely have had a special appeal not only for the drive-in crowd, but also for all those new aficionados who stayed up to catch creepy old Universal classics - presented by their favourite 'Horror Host' – on late night television. Spoofing horror was all the rage, too. Just the previous year, Bobby 'Boris' Pickett had recorded *The Monster Mash*, a hit novelty beat number which showcased his Karloff impression; '63 saw *Mad Magazine's* 1950s comic strip version of *The Raven* poem, by Will Elder, reprinted in paperback; and in 1964, Charles Addams' enduringly popular *New Yorker* cartoon series *The Addams Family* would transfer to television. In 1965, Karloff would even end up singing *The Monster Mash* himself on television pop show *Shindig!* Groovy old Boris. Horror – with a self-referential, post-modern twist – was happening.

Slickly styled, *The Raven* was filled with deadpan quips and imbued with a cheerful awareness of the limitations of the film's modest budget. It could almost have been Corman's version of a *Mad Magazine* parody of a Corman horror picture. This was a comedy for literate, intelligent audiences already aware of the conventions of horror cinema, not just for the kiddies. But thanks to the understanding touch of Corman and Matheson, this was more than merely a quick cash-in on those monster men of yesteryear. This was also a warm and affectionate celebration of the life and work of some still much underrated genre actors. And what's more, best of all, it looks like everybody involved had a ball making it.

Price seems to be enjoying himself immensely in the opening scenes, concocting the cure to Bedlo's feathery condition, and the viewer can't help but share his joy. Off-camera, of course, Vincent was something of a gourmet, and, later on, he enlightened bored British housewives as to the mysterious intricacies of 'Continental' cooking, with his remarkable 1971 television series *Cooking Price-Wise.* How, then, could you not be enraptured at the sight of him rustling up a revolting recipe for bird-like Bedlo, especially when he delicately flicks his whisk at the simmering cauldron of jellied spiders as if he were preparing a soufflé? His disgust at the "entrails of troubled horse" discovered in the potion-pantry seems quite genuine.

The Price-Lorre double act really gets going when Lorre's Bedlo, returned to human form at last, seeks outdoor attire. He tries on Craven's splendidly impractical cloaks, direct from the horror B-Picture costume-cupboard, while velvet-voiced Price presides like a salesman at a gentlemen's outfitters. "The sleeves are a little long," Price's Craven purrs politely, affecting concern, as diminutive Bedlo is engulfed by a garment. "Yes, but I can hold them," mutters Lorre. "It'll keep you warm," Price suggests hopefully. Further funny business ensues as Lorre chooses a hat. There's also much to enjoy in Lorre's anguished relationship with his well-meaning, overly tactile son, Rexford (Nicholson). Hats, cloaks, family relationships: it's all splendid stuff, and all wonderfully irrelevant to the story. But something more substantial *is* on the way.

It comes after a frantic coach ride across the cliffs, as we enter the ominously shadowy castle that is Scarabus's lair. What Karloff crucially brings to the proceedings is gravity, weight, and darkness. His evil sorcerer is the perfect counterbalance to the levity of Lorre and Price. Corman has spoken of the "incredible clash" of acting styles practised by Karloff and Lorre, with the older star flummoxed by Lorre's improvisational method. But Karloff's solid, old-school performance style certainly paid dividends. As soon as he appears on screen, the film takes on greater substance, greater depth; and we are aware that we are in the presence of the true King of Horror. *The Raven* is of course an ensemble piece. But Karloff brings something extra to the table – that strange duality, that mixture of light and darkness, genius and madness, at which he excelled. His Scarabus is simultaneously wonderfully funny and genuinely menacing.

Karloff is not simply playing a comic turn – it's a fully-fleshed out characterisation. The evil power of his sorcerer, initially hidden beneath a veneer of geniality and polite false modesty, is immediately apparent; concisely communicated to the viewer, simply by small gestures of his hands, or a momentary glittering of the eyes beneath those bushy brows. And as the narrative progresses, his air of geniality is gradually discarded, and he becomes increasingly sinister. A delightfully dark relationship with Lenore – his "precious viper" – is fascinatingly hinted at. He knows his fickle mistress is no good, but he wants to hang on to her anyway, simply so Craven can't have her; and he looks forward with quiet delight to the thought of torturing Craven's daughter with a red-hot poker. Scarabus, it is clear, is a thoroughly evil man. But he's charming too, and you can't help liking him.

If Karloff dominates the proceedings in the middle part of the film, Price reasserts himself somewhat in the climactic final sequence, which must be one of the strangest encounters between rival sorcerers ever committed to celluloid. As they play their tricks, with coloured lights and confetti, in high-backed chairs before a roaring fire, the young 'uns watching respectfully from the balcony, Price and Karloff seem less like wizards, and more like two beloved uncles performing their party pieces at a family get-together. The charm lies in the fact that we, as viewers, are part of the family; as Price flies through the air (his chair hoisted on a camera crane) and waves, like Rexford we almost want to wave back. No matter that some of the spectacles seem a little less spectacular than they might; just being in the presence of these legends as they play out their pantomime is more than enough. We share their sense of fun, and revel in this celebration of the screen presence of Karloff and Price. We are being entertained by two generations of screen-horror royalty, both of whom warmly and indelibly impress their personalities upon the proceedings without the need to say a word. What could be more magical than that?

The Raven was another box office success for Corman; and Karloff's connection with the director continued. His talent for humour would be further utilised (if under-utilised) in *The Comedy of Terrors*; while for *The Terror* (both 1963), in a series of speedily shot scenes grabbed in a couple of days to make the most of *The Raven's* lush sets before they were packed away, Karloff sensibly played it straight, the calm at the eye of the hurricane. There are those that might describe *The Terror* as a bit of a dog's dinner, but it is testament to Karloff's skill to lift whatever he appeared in, that he *still* got good notices for it, with the reviewer at the *Kine Weekly* pausing from the obligatory grumbling to note that "Boris Karloff as the Baron is of course always worth seeing." Even if, by the time the film was finally cobbled together, nobody knew any longer what the hell was going on.

The important thing was that Karloff's work with Corman allowed him to reassert himself both as noble old-school trouper of an earlier age of horror, and, at the same time, a charismatic contemporary presence in hip American movies for the college crowd. *The Raven* especially had given Karloff the chance to remind everybody of his skill and versatility as an actor; and there were further excellent performances still to come: in Michael Reeves' *The Sorcerers* (1967), shot back in England, and Corman protégé Peter Bogdanovich's *Targets* (1967).

When *The Raven* inevitably ends with the castle burning down in a huge fire (and, no, you're not imagining it – you did see some of those shots of flaming timbers in previous Corman movies), Karloff delivers one of the funniest lines in the picture, and one that also wonderfully reflects his awareness of his own mortality. Sitting shamefaced in the rubble with vain Lenore, his defeated Scarabus intones sadly: "I'm afraid I just don't have it anymore." Physically, perhaps, as Boris became increasingly frail, this was true; but in acting terms, quite the opposite was the case. Surrounded by a splendid cast, armed with a juicy script, and championed by a director who understood what made the horror veteran great, Karloff remained impressively able to deliver the goods. Despite Scarabus's lament, *The Raven* proved he still had it, all right.

***This essay originally appeared in the Arrow Video edition of* The Raven.**

WEIRDER THAN FORBIDDEN ZONE

David Hayles on Hervé Villechaize

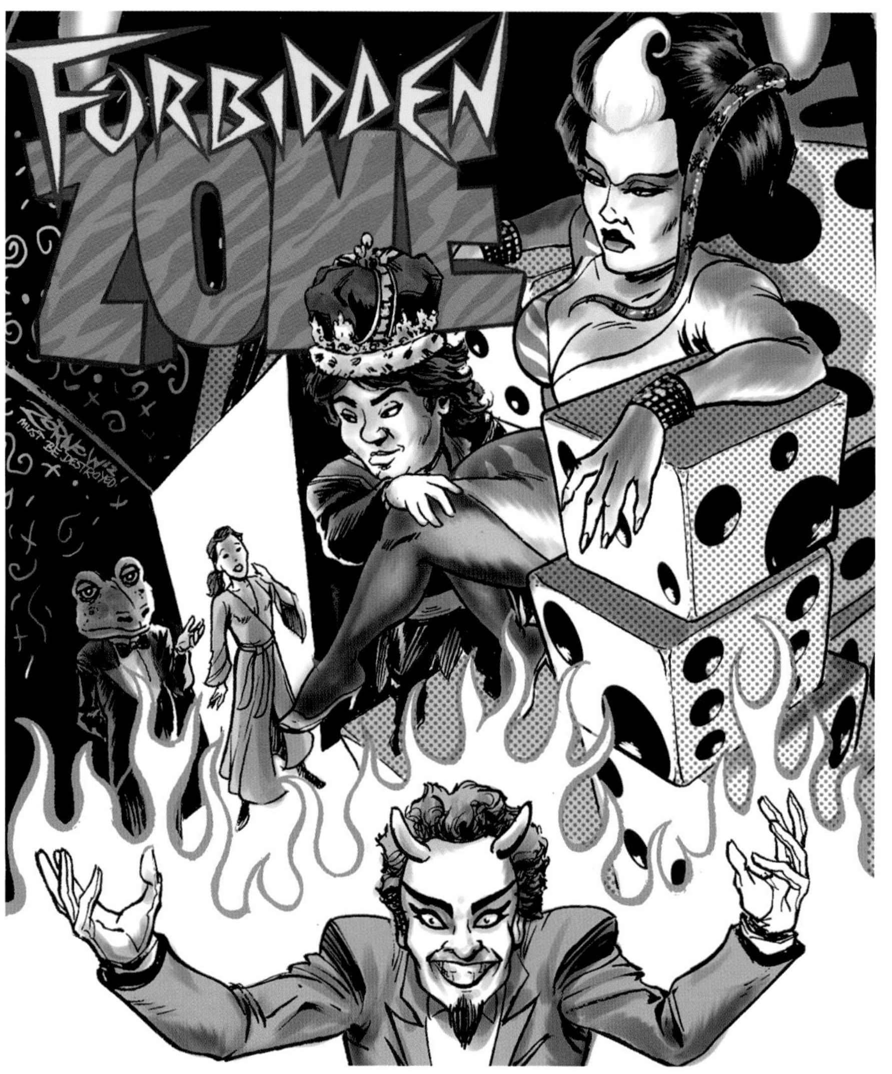

Artwork by Jeff Zornow

"Have you ever had a dream with a dwarf in it? Do you know anyone who's had a dream with a dwarf in it? No! I don't even have dreams with dwarves in them. The only place I've seen dwarves in dreams is in stupid movies like this! 'Oh make it weird, put a dwarf in it!' Everyone will go 'Whoa, this must be a fuckin' dream, there's a fuckin' dwarf in it!' Well I'm sick of it! You can take this dream sequence and stick it up your ass!"

Peter Dinklage as Tito, *Living in Oblivion* (1995)

In the short 74-minute runtime of *Forbidden Zone* (1980), director Richard Elfman managed to cram into his marvellously nutty musical fantasy elements of Dante's *Inferno* (1320), Lewis Carroll's *Alice's Adventures in Wonderland* (1865), Kenneth Grahame's *The Wind in the Willows* (1908), German Expressionistic classic *The Cabinet of Dr. Caligari* (1920), early talkie *The Jazz Singer* (1927), Tod Browning's *Freaks* (1932), James Whale's *Bride of Frankenstein* (1935), Nathanael West's *The Day of the Locust* and MGM's adaptation of *The Wizard of Oz* (both 1939), Curt McDowell's *Thundercrack!* (1975), David Lynch's *Eraserhead* (1978), Busby Berkeley, the Marx Brothers, the Three Stooges, Betty Boop, Flash Gordon, the Addams Family, Ed Wood, Fritz the Cat and Pee-wee Herman. He did all that and managed to nab Hervé Villechaize, the dwarf from *Fantasy Island* (1977-84), still riding high on the success of that show, to play Fausto, King of the Sixth Dimension. The strangest thing is that out of all the film's characters – a demented queen, a transgender school teacher, a human chandelier, a constantly topless princess, a schoolboy old enough to be his own grandfather, a frog-headed servant – Fausto seems to be about the most normal.

On the face of it, by the time Villechaize appeared in *Forbidden Zone*, life was sweet for the three-foot-and-one-inch French actor. He'd carved out a successful niche as the go-to guy for 'people of restricted height' roles, appearing opposite James Bond in *The Man with the Golden Gun* (1974), and was a household name thanks to his part as Tattoo in *Fantasy Island*. He was living in California and married to a gorgeous model. But the truth was, Villechaize was unhappy. A little over ten years after the release of *Forbidden Zone*, the actor would be dead.

Villechaize moved to the USA from his native Paris in the 1960s to pursue a career as a painter. It was while earning a living as a photographer that Villechaize fell into acting. He met the director of the avant-garde film *Chappaqua* (1966), which featured appearances by William Burroughs and Allen Ginsberg, and was offered a part. His early acting career from thereon was typical – he was shipped in to add to the necessary weirdness to the dream sequences and netherworlds of a couple of B-rate 1970s horror films. In the 1973 obscurity, *Malatesta's Carnival of Blood*, he played Bobo, a dwarf amid a freakshow of cannibals, transvestites and caped ghouls terrorising the owners of a run-down fairground. And in *Seizure* (1974), Oliver Stone's first film as director, he was Spider, one of the three characters (along with Martine Beswick and a 'giant') that terrorise a horror novelist's dreams. ("You can never run from it - you can never hide from it – the breath-stopping panic of *Seizure* – rated PG," went the original radio ad.) When these little-seen films were finally issued on DVD, in 2003 and 2007 respectively, Villechaize, credited fifth in both upon their original release, was now top-billed on the video sleeves. "Don't be fooled - Hervé is NOT the star!" writes a disgruntled Amazon customer about their purchase of the *Seizure* DVD. But who can blame the distributors? Thanks to *The Man with the Golden Gun* and *Fantasy Island*, he had since become world famous.

Villechaize played the white tuxedoed sidekick to Ricardo Montalban, who runs the dream-fulfilling holiday resort, in *Fantasy Island*. Each episode opened with a new planeload of passengers arriving to live out their wildest fantasies. "Every Saturday night," wrote a Florida newspaper in 1980, after the show had become an established prime time staple, "millions of television viewers sit down and watch a little man less than four feet tall run up into a belfry, ring the bell three times, and excitedly announce 'the plane, the plane'." Rather like Villechaize's character in *Forbidden Zone* (sample quote: "I loved to feel your nipples harden when I caress them with my fingertips"), Tattoo was a randy fellow. As was, apparently, Villechaize in real life. Apparently, his dressing room door bore the legend "Sex Instructor - First Lesson Free". And he had no qualms about being able to pleasure a 'normal sized' female. "It would be a pretty poor lumberjack who couldn't climb a tree that had fallen down," he once said. (Incidentally, contrary to rumour, Villechaize did not star in a porno film; *Forbidden Zone* is the closest he came to an X-rating. It is the actor Luis de Jesus, who was actually a couple of inches taller than Villechaize, who appeared in the 1980 sex film *Ultra Flesh* as Midget 1 under the pseudonym Mr. Short Stud. De Jesus died in 1988 of a heart attack.)

During *Fantasy Island*'s seven-season run Villechaize was the toast of television. He was earning good money, married to the young model Camille Hagen, and living on a ranch in the San Fernando Valley. But things soon started to turn sour. He suffered ridicule at the hands of the tabloids for his marriage to the striking, tall Hagen (his first marriage had collapsed a few years earlier after the strain of public scrutiny). He had to travel with a bodyguard and kept a gun at home, because, as his co-star Montalban noted, "There are sick people in this world." (Firearms, it seems, would be Villechaize's un-doing – he once pulled a gun on his agent in a Hollywood restaurant.) His health was suffering too, and Villechaize attended a dwarfism research centre in a bid to prolong his life. He felt his work was wearing him out: "I shouldn't be as active as I am. I have to take three steps to an average person's one," he said in 1980.

Then, after appearing in 131 episodes of *Fantasy Island*, Villechaize left the show following a pay dispute, only for it to fold a year later. His second marriage ended amid claims he fired a gun at her, his health deteriorated and, due to complications with his dwarfism, he suffered near constant pain. The actor became despondent, and started drinking heavily. In 1985 he got sentenced to a year's probation for illegally carrying a handgun. He was plagued with legal problems, and while he still got sporadic film and TV roles, they were nothing to compare with *Fantasy Island*, and he often had to turn down work because of his health. And to compound matters, he nearly died from pneumonia in 1992. In 1993, citing his ongoing health problems, he decided to take his own life.

Suicide notes are doomed to be pored over by the bereaved, and the prurient, for reasons and explanations, with multiple possible interpretations hanging off every word in an attempt to divine why someone should choose to end it all. Villechaize's is no exception. In it he talks about the pain he has suffered for most all of his adult life – physical, psychological, both? "I have to do what's right. At 6 years old I knew there was no place for me. [...] Never one knew my pain – for 40 years – or more. Have to do it outside less mess." And with that, he went out onto the patio of his North Hollywood home and shot himself in the chest. He was 50 years old.

***This essay originally appeared in the Arrow Video edition of* Forbidden Zone.**

THE IMPORTANCE OF BEING VINCENT

David Del Valle on Vincent Price

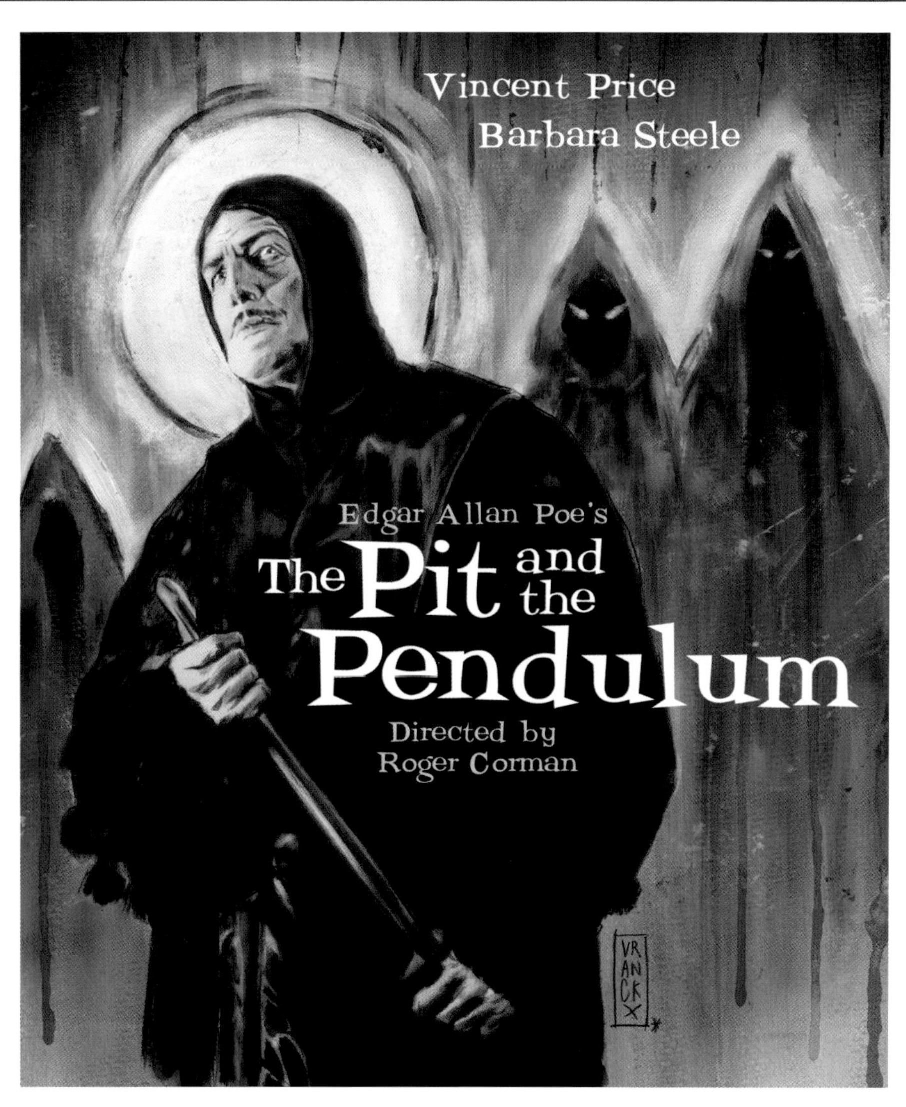

Artwork by Gilles Vranckx

When Vincent Price finally agreed to sit down with me to tape what would become *Vincent Price: The Sinister Image* (1987), I promised him faithfully that he would have an interview that would address only his film career as the reigning horror icon of my generation. He joked afterwards that if any of his fans wanted to know about his horror films he would just give them our show. It is wonderful to know that, before he passed away in 1993, he had some idea as to just how much he was loved by his fans around the world, and that love continues to this day. I am convinced that one of the reasons his films endure is because of Vincent's superb sense of humour regarding his image as an actor. I also believe that he is now appreciated for his acting skills and the talent he always possessed, but rarely (if ever) got the proper respect for. This is why he loved *Theatre of Blood* (1973), in which he played a vengeful actor killing off his critics one by one, so much.

The night Vincent died, the local television station here in Hollywood ran the famous scene from *Pit and the Pendulum* (1961) with John Kerr strapped to an altar as the titular torture device swings ever-nearer. In the minds of the public he was the big screen embodiment of Edgar Allan Poe, yet he could have been a famous art historian rather than a movie star with a penchant for the macabre. Dazzled by the stage as a young man, the feeling never left him. Horror films may have prevented him from doing more serious work on Broadway, but Vincent was destined for greatness and the path he chose served him well. I know that, were he still around today, he'd be pleased so much of his work is still out there for fans to appreciate, especially the Poe films made with Roger Corman.

House of Usher (1960) was the first of this now legendary cycle as well as a continuation of Vincent's good fortune with films that have the word *House* in their title. Both *House of Wax* (1953) and *House on Haunted Hill* (1959) helped create the persona that playing Roderick Usher would solidify and, in doing so, make Vincent the legitimate successor to Boris Karloff as the king of the horror genre. The film seemed to be a gamble for all concerned at American International Pictures (AIP). When Samuel Z. Arkoff greenlit the project Corman assured him that the true monster in this film would be the house itself and only a truly baroque actor like Price could knock such a project out of the park – and that is exactly what he did. His performance as Roderick Usher is masterful in every detail; by bleaching his hair and removing his iconic facial hair he "created a character that had not been seen in the cinema since the days of Conrad Veidt, [...] so pale and withdrawn that the sunlight never ever touched his flesh." *House of Usher* was done for the modest sum of $270,000 with a cast of four and sets on which production designer Daniel Haller worked miracles, giving the film a lavish look that became the signature for the seven Poe adaptations that would follow. Richard Matheson weaved a spidery script that was tailor-made for Price and since Matheson was also a film buff he wisely referenced Vincent's earlier excursion into Poe territory with *Dragonwyck* (1946), a Gothic melodrama Price did for 20th Century Fox where all the elements of the Poe film were brought together for the first time pre-Corman: the haunted aristocrat with the dead or dying wife living a hermit-like existence in a vast mansion or castle; all these things were there in the character of Nicolas Van Ryn. The very moment we see Vincent standing by the portrait of his dead wife while wondering if that harpsichord music he heard was played by a ghost, we are already well within what would follow in Matheson's script for the next of Corman's Poe pictures.

House of Usher proved to be a summer box office hit and made enough money to ensure a need at AIP for a follow-up. With Corman unable to film *The Masque of the Red Death* within his allocated budget, he chose the only logical alternative: Poe's wildly popular short fiction *The Pit and the Pendulum* (first published in 1842). This time Matheson outdid himself creating a script influenced - as was everyone else in films after its release in 1960 - by Alfred Hitchcock's *Psycho*. Price's character, Nicholas Medina, is the ultimate tortured nobleman; hypersensitive like Usher, yet soft and totally in touch with his feminine side to the point of madness. In this case he tends to slip into the persona of his late father, Sebastian, a sadist and one of few times in his career where Vincent actually plays a monster. (He is terrifying as a Norman Bates with a daddy complex.) The sheer physical presence of co-star and horror diva Barbara Steele helps *Pit and the Pendulum* stand out from the rest of the series since these two play off each other like no-one else in the genre. It is our loss that these two icons never made another film together because they were literally the male and female versions of each other's screen persona. (Barbara recalled that, during their time together on set, Vincent wore pink socks under his silk robes: "Just a little kink of mine, darling," he told her.)

So overwhelming was Price's performance that it overshadowed almost all that followed in the actor's long career. When Vincent and I recorded *The Sinister*

Image, we sat in front of a monitor and watched the famous scene which had played on television the night of his death. He held his head in his hands in mock despair and apologised, "That was way over the top, David, and very hokey." I instantly reassured him that this was the kind of bravura acting which had made him a horror star and he simply smiled. "Whatever, dear boy. If you really enjoyed it then I did my job."

Pit and the Pendulum set the tone for the rest of the Poe films that would be shot on California backlots or Carmel seascapes with sets saved and revamped by Haller and photographed by Floyd Crosby. The music by the always-underrated Les Baxter made these films look and sound so special that they made a strong case for the American horror film at a time when the UK's Hammer studios seemed to dominate the world market.

The cycle's sixth entry, *The Haunted Palace* (1964), was unique insofar as it was not really a Poe film at all, but rather the first big screen adaptation of an H.P. Lovecraft fiction. The film allowed Vincent to work with Lon Chaney Jr. in one of his last good feature film roles. As he recalled of its making: "I really enjoy the acting process; you know – leaving yourself in the makeup chair, and then stepping into these fantasy roles. In playing the warlock I had some real help from our makeup man, Ted Coodley, who created a green skin tone which also hardened my face a bit especially around the eyes and mouth. This allowed me to develop the character, who was ruthless and cruel. Poor Lon Chaney had to stay in that makeup chair throughout filming. I remember the young woman [Cathie Merchant] who played my mistress in the film causing me no end of amusement. She had this great buxom figure to begin with, but the wardrobe heightened her already ample cleavage giving her more room than the Rocky Mountains, and every time that I would glance in her direction my eyes would head down that mountain along with my concentration. She proved to be a great sport. I kidded her once as she remarked that she had no dialogue. So I told her with what she had going for her there was very little that needed to be said, which made her laugh. I will always remember these films with great pleasure, even though they were hard work, we all had such a good time making them."

The Masque of the Red Death (1964) is considered by many to be perhaps the finest of all the Poe films. It may well be one of the finest horror films ever made considering the quality in front and behind the camera, including the gifted Nicolas Roeg as director of photography. Price, playing Prince Prospero, gives a subtle (for him) performance, showing yet again just what a consummate performer he really was. Co-star Hazel Court, a 'scream queen' of the first order, recalled: "I loved making this film so much because we had such marvellous people on both sides of the camera. We were having such a good time until word reached the set that the President had been shot. Roger closed the set for the day and we all went home. Vincent told me he never felt so far from home as he did on that day."

The Abominable Dr. Phibes (1971) was a very special film since it represented the actor at the zenith of his career, both as horror icon and a longstanding villain of the big screen, dating back to his contract days at Universal and 20th Century Fox. The character of Anton Phibes certainly owes a tip of the hat to scarred genius Professor Henry Jarrod from *House of Wax*, at least in visage at any rate. Promoted as Vincent's "one hundredth film", it was not, but it did encapsulate the actors' life at AIP and for that it is a crown jewel in both Vincent's career as well as AIP's remarkable catalogue.

Witchfinder General (1968) is so highly regarded by fans and critics alike that is hard to say anything against it - and simply it as a masterpiece,

Theatre of Blood

I personally don't believe it is. While I admire Vincent for enduring a tough shoot with a young director, Michael Reeves, who had less than four credits to his name and whom he would refer to as "that goddamn boy genius", I think one needs to step back and realise that it is an historical drama and not a horror film. Having said that, it contains one of Price's most restrained performances, making one wonder just what kind of film *The Oblong Box* (1969) might have been under Reeves direction (he died at the age of 25 following a misadventure with prescription drugs).

I first met Vincent shortly after he'd finished work on *Witchfinder General*. "I just did this film in England," he told me, "which is the place to make this kind of picture because they do it all so well. I worked with an exciting young talent who I believe is really going places as a director. I am looking forward to working with this young man again soon." Nothing in the conversation could have prepared one for three decades of speculation as to what really happened on set between Price and Reeves.

All of these films – with a special nod to *Theatre of Blood* – represent Vincent Price at the top of his game and, through each performance, you may notice a wink or a nod as he moves his head and throws his voice. That "goddamn boy genius" might not have approved, but for the audience there is no such problem since Vincent is now regarded as a larger than life star driven by his need to be liked by everybody that came into his orbit. And on that score I think we can say he succeeded beyond his wildest imagination. This, my friends, is the importance of being Vincent...

UNCHAINED MELODY

Tom Mes on Meiko Kaji

Artwork by Jack Pemberton

"Meiko Kaji's strongest point is her eyes, her stare. They are literally the eyes of the netherworld: powerful, glamorous and dark."

Kazuo Koike

What we know of Meiko Kaji is but a sampling from a long and diverse career. Yet she will perhaps forever be remembered for her roles as Nami Matsushima, aka the Scorpion, and as Yuki Kashima, aka Lady Snowblood. She portrayed these deadly women with equal parts grace and determination, her lean face, red lips and sharp but delicate nose visible between curtains of black hair. And, of course, those eyes. That stare. It was all in the eyes. These characters didn't rely on words to express their anger, their resentment, their grudge; the eyes said it all. That defiant piercing stare, thrusting outward like the jab of a knife or the swish of a blade, able to impale whoever was unlucky enough to tread into their field of vision.

These qualities, however, belong to Kaji the actress. They are part of that elusive quality called charisma. Take any other film she was in, from any other period and any other genre, and you will find the same brooding sense of defiance, the same innate desire for independence.

This defiance marks even her career choices. Kaji never did what others told her to do. The peak of her popularity coincided with a phase in Japanese film history in which moral guidelines were swiftly losing currency. The degree of sexual and violent imagery increased drastically, in a desperate attempt to lure people away from their brand new television sets and back into the cinemas. Kaji left the studio where she started her career, Nikkatsu, because it was a little too eager to embrace this newfound promiscuity. She ended up at rival Toei, only to find that it was quickly heading in the same direction. Where Nikkatsu dreamed up the concept of Roman Porno – professionally made softcore pornography – Toei went a step further by mixing skin flick with violent action, giving birth to what has been retroactively, and somewhat clumsily, referred to as 'Pinky Violence'. These films may have been full of tough female protagonists kicking, slashing, and shooting male butt, the leading ladies were nevertheless expected to disrobe at the most inopportune times, preferably while doing the kicking. The message was clear: You can slice and dice as many guys as you want, as long you submit to the male gaze in the end.

One of the first questions Meiko Kaji was asked at her casting interview for the *Female Convict Scorpion* series was: "Could you play in the nude?" She almost stormed out of the office, not to return until she had imposed her own interpretation of the character. Kaji has always had an amount of disregard for career planning that will strike many as foolish. At the peak of her popularity in the wake of the *Female Prisoner Scorpion* and *Lady Snowblood* films, she voluntarily accepted smaller supporting roles in films by major directors over tailor-made star vehicles. She would continue to do so whenever she found a second-tier character more challenging than any of the lead parts she was offered. Kaji has had more than one opportunity to grow into a real star, a silver screen diva, but status never interested her. She was and remains an actress first and foremost, and she has always abided by Konstantin Stanislavsky's rule of thumb that there are no major or minor roles, only major and minor actors.

The Nikkatsu Years

In Japanese, the term *ojo-sama* signifies a well-bred young lady. One who is polite, courteous, chaste, and modest to the point of self-effacing; all the qualities of *yamato nadeshiko*, or ideal Japanese womanhood. Foreigners may not be familiar with the terms, but they will know the type: around the world, it is the stereotypical image of the Japanese woman.

Nikkatsu initially did its best to make Kaji in that image, but soon saw the error of its ways. By her own admission, Kaji – or rather Masako Ota, the name with which she was born in Tokyo's Kanda ward on March 24, 1947 – was always the headstrong type, who refused to conform to the image of the ideal young lady. Though she was an introverted child, she had a knack for sports, particularly basketball, and occasionally modelled in teen-oriented magazines. The leading ladies at Nikkatsu during that decade typically either played what Mark Schilling has described as "angels in kimono or fashionable modern girls". Whatever their style of dress, their characters were inevitably of the pure-hearted type. Ota was initially groomed to follow in their footsteps. From her wordless debut appearance as a seamstress in 1965's *Sad Song of Parting* (*Kanashiki wakare no uta*) to her first lead role in *Taiyo ga Daisuki* [translation: I Love the Sun] the following year, she too played pure girls. The latter film even won her the tag of Nikkatsu's "brightest hope", but it wouldn't be long before the top brass began to see that Ota's talents lay elsewhere. Before the year was up, she had moved from making youth dramas to working with the studio's action specialists.

One director who saw her potential, and would become instrumental in this turnaround, was Yasuharu Hasebe, a former assistant to Seijun Suzuki who had only just been promoted to the coveted director's chair. At this make-or-break moment, Hasebe cast Ota as the girlfriend of one of the studio's biggest stars, Akira Kobayashi, in the excellent *Retaliation* (*Shima wa moratta*, 1968), a decision that would later prompt Kaji to call him "the most important director in my career". *Retaliation* is a hard-boiled yakuza caper that is sometimes reminiscent of Suzuki (the blood-drenched finale set in a blindingly white, tiled room), at other times foreshadows Kinji Fukasaku (plenty of guerrilla-style handheld shots), and even at moments recalls Yasujirô Ozu (interior dialogue scenes done with a fixed camera at medium height).

Retaliation was typical for a tougher approach to the genre that was then beginning to rear its head. Times were getting difficult for the film business now that television sets had found their place in most family homes and people preferred to stay at home for their daily dose of entertainment. The old filmmaking formulas were no longer a guarantee of success and new approaches were encouraged, including a harder-edged, more violent type of action film. Ota looked much more at home playing a cat-fighting juvenile delinquent in Yuji Tanno's *Zankoku onna rinchi* (1969) [translation: Cruel Woman Lynching] than as all the pure-hearted high-schoolers she played in her first four years at Nikkatsu. To mark the transition, the studio suggested that Masako Ota assume a new screen name. And so, in 1969 she became Meiko Kaji.

These developments culminated in the *Stray Cat Rock* (*Nora-neko rokku*, 1970-71) series, five films filled with delinquents, street gangs and bikers kicking up a storm in the streets of contemporary urban Japan. Their anti-authoritarian tone and contemporary setting fit Kaji well. Once more it was Hasebe - who directed three of the five episodes - who spotted her potential, allowing the sassy woman who usually strutted around the Nikkatsu lot in tight jeans and leather boots to play characters that weren't very far removed from her real-life persona. Kaji had emerged from kimonos and puppy fat; the transformation was now truly complete.

The series proved to be a last stand for Nikkatsu. In a last ditch attempt to save its own hide, the studio decided to scale down production and to produce only softcore pornography. The exodus of talent that followed did not go unnoticed by other studios, and soon enough Kaji received a phone call from Toei, which had to contend with the early retirement of its top female star, Junko Fuji. Toei saw in Kaji the ideal replacement: Fuji's biggest successes had been as lone avengers that were as stoic and deadly as they were sophisticated and beautiful. Toei felt that the young Nikkatsu actress fit the mould.

Grudge Songs

Toei had acquired the rights to the manga series *Female Prisoner Scorpion* (*Joshu Sasori*), the story of a young woman serving a long-term jail sentence after having been made a scapegoat. With its female protagonist, ample nudity, foul-mouthed dialogue, and scenes of grievous bodily harm, this bawdy tale seemed to be precisely the kind of thing that Kaji had left Nikkatsu for. Her mood began to change when she read Toru Shinohara's original manga and found herself enjoying it. Her conception of the central character was to eliminate most of her lines of dialogue and render Nami Matsushima quasi-mute, someone whose actions speak for her: she is the Scorpion, and her sting is swift and deadly.

Female Prisoner 701: Scorpion (*Joshû 701-gô: Sasori*, 1972), and the two sequels – *Female Prisoner Scorpion: Jailhouse 41* (*Joshû sasori: Dai-41 zakkyo-bô*) and *Female Prisoner Scorpion: Beast Stable* (*Joshû sasori: Kemono-beya*) – that followed the same year, were hugely successful. Toei had every intention of continuing it for several more instalments, but director Shunya Itô felt that his job was done. Kaji received a similar proposition and decided to continue with the character, although her original intention had been to make only one *Female Prisoner Scorpion* film and then move on to more dramatic and diverse acting work than the outlaw parts in which she was consistently typecast. Nevertheless she stuck with the part, succeeding in gradually rendering Sasori more human. There are moments in the third film, particularly in her flight through the sewer tunnels, where she is at her most fragile. This development would continue into Kaji's final performance as the character, in *Female Prisoner Scorpion: Grudge Song* (*Joshû sasori: 701-gô urami-bushi*, 1973), directed by her old Nikkatsu cohort Hasebe. Still, *Grudge Song* ends on a note that leaves no doubt that we are dealing with the Scorpion and no one but the Scorpion. With her revenge on the man who seemed to be her saviour but who ended up betraying her like all the others, Nami Matsushima is buried forever and the Scorpion lives on, black-clad and knife in hand, ready to sting whoever wrongs her.

Another Nikkatsu old boy, *Stray Cat Rock: Wild Jumbo* (*Nora-neko rokku: Wairudo janbo*, 1970) and *Stray Cat Rock: Beat '71* (*Nora-neko rokku: Bôsô shudan '71*, 1971) director Toshiya Fujita, knew that Kaji had initially turned down *Female Prisoner Scorpion* when he offered her the lead role in his new project, *Lady Snowblood* (*Shurayukihime*, 1973). It was another comic book adaptation about a deadly female avenger. The actress, however, had fond memories of Fujita and liked the prospect of working with him again. After she had read, and thoroughly enjoyed, the manga by writer Kazuo Koike and artist Kazuo Kamimura, Kaji accepted Fujita's offer. It is no coincidence that *Lady Snowblood* remains one of the actress's quintessential performances. She is perfect in the part, inhabiting it completely. She would go on to more challenging roles, stretch her boundaries as an actress further than many might have believed her capable, but there is no denying that, along with the Scorpion, Yuki Kashima was one of the roles in which she excelled. It was in the skin of these two characters that Kaji's innate, natural qualities came most strongly to the fore.

A Farewell to Outlaws

Nevertheless, *Lady Snowblood* marked the end of an era for Kaji. Since the beginning of her career she had been part and parcel of the production line mentality of the major studios: shaped and moulded; given an image. Her image had become that of the outlaw, a vengeful woman who fights oppression and rights the wrongs she has suffered. At the same time, she had been kept busy churning out product: films, TV series, hit singles, albums. By the middle of the 1970s, while her popularity was at its peak, she decided to shrug it all off.

Kaji found the way forward for herself as an actress in her first of three films with Kinji Fukasaku, *Battles Without Honour and Humanity: Hiroshima Death Match* (*Jingi naki tatakai Hiroshima shitô hen*, 1973). Though the dog-eat-dog atmosphere on set gave her stomach cramps, the experience made her decide that she was going to be an actress instead of an image. In 1974 she made a radical turnaround in her career: she left Toei, left her agent, and made her last film playing an outlaw character, Sadao Nakajima's *Jeans Blues: No Future* (*Jinzu burusu: Asu naki furaiha*). The decision kicked off her most fascinating period as an actress, exemplified by Kaji's three collaborations with Yasuzô Masumura, one of the great directors from the Daiei studio, responsible for caustic masterpieces like *Giants and Toys* (*Kyojin to gangu*, 1958) and *Red Angel* (*Akai tenshi*, 1966). Her performance in *Double Suicide in Sonezaki* (*Sonezaki shinju*, 1978), an adaptation of a Chikamatsu puppet play, won Kaji great acclaim.

Thanks in part to her volatile but fruitful working relationship with Masumura, she was at the peak of her powers as an actress by the time the 1980s rolled around.

However, there were precious few occasions to display her abilities on the big screen: the old studio system had collapsed and interesting projects were getting harder and harder to come by. Kaji retreated almost exclusively into television, only venturing back into big screen territory to work with venerable directors, such as Kon Ichikawa, Yoshitarô Nomura, Kôichi Saitô and Kaneto Shindô. Always her appearances were limited to supporting roles.

The trickle became a drought in the 1990s, a decade for which Kaji has only two big-screen credits to her name – one being a spin-off from the television series *Onihei hankachô* [translation: Onihei's Crime File], one of her longest-running commitments. Starting in 1989, this series revolves around a high-ranking Tokugawa-era investigator named Hiruzo. Kaji plays his confidante Omasa, who has carried a torch for this top cop since childhood but has been content to let her flame burn in secret. Remarkably, in the 27 years of the series' run, different actors have played Hiruzo, but Omasa has only been portrayed by Kaji. It was the character's femininity which made her so alluring; she is leagues removed from Nami the Scorpion and the even more sexless Lady Snowblood. Omasa, this bundle of feminine emotions, has proven to be Kaji's most enduring screen role in a 50-year career.

Stray Cat Rock - Machine Animal

A ONE-WOMAN ARMY

Cullen Gallagher on Pam Grier

Artwork by Gilles Vranckx

As far as opening scenes go, it's hard to find one as memorable and groundbreaking - and not to mention as downright electrifying and shocking - as the beginning of *Coffy* (1973). Posing as a junkie in need of a fix, Pam Grier agrees to trade her body to a drug dealer for some heroin. When they go back to his bedroom, she gives him a bigger surprise than he could have ever imagined.

"This is the end of your life you motherfucking dope pusher!"

With these eleven words - and the help of a sawn-off double-barrel shotgun that blows said dope pusher's head into oblivion - Grier irrevocably changed cinema history. Her character, Coffy, was a one-woman army. Nurse by day, vigilante by night, on a mission to single-handedly take down the dope, prostitution, and political corruption that was plaguing Los Angeles and responsible for turning her 11-year-old sister onto drugs. Equal parts strong, street smart, sexy, and sophisticated, Coffy was a quadruple threat. Had there ever been a more powerful screen heroine? Hell no.

Coffy premiered in 1973. Grier was a new type of star for a new era, and Coffy was a new type of character for a new type of movie. But while *Coffy* is very much a film of its time, it is also a reaction against the times. Like many exploitation films, it took advantage of certain tastes and trends of the time, playing into what was popular and in vogue, but it also challenged many of those same conventions. To see it merely as 'just another Blaxploitation film' is to overlook its radical and history-altering accomplishments.

The late-1960s and early-1970s was a time of great social upheaval in America and around the world, and Hollywood was not immune to these crises. Movies like *Bonnie and Clyde* (1967) and *The Wild Bunch* (1969) reflected the rising tide of violence, while *Midnight Cowboy* (1969) and *Carnal Knowledge* (1971) revealed new levels of sexual frankness. Meanwhile, there was the first wave of Blaxploitation cinema, a movement of both independent and studio-produced movies that prominently featured black characters. These films not only indicated a changing racial consciousness in America at the time, but were also an attempt for an industry in financial straits to cash-in on a large audience that had been alienated and ignored almost entirely since the beginning of cinema. Some of the earliest Blaxploitation films were *Cotton Comes to Harlem* (1970), *Shaft* and *Sweet Sweetback's Baadasssss Song* (both 1971), and *Blacula*, *Hammer*, *Slaughter*,

Super Fly and *Trouble Man* (all 1972). What these films shared in common, aside from their African-American protagonists, is that they were all male-oriented films. *Coffy* changed all of that.

The company behind *Coffy* was American International Pictures (AIP), created in 1954 by James H. Nicholson and Samuel Z. Arkoff. AIP's initial output catered to the low-brow double-bill tastes of teenagers: *It Conquered the World*, *Runaway Daughters* (both 1956), *I Was a Teenage Werewolf* (1957) and *High School Hellcats* (1958), to name just a few. And while all the movies followed what came to be known as the 'A.R.K.O.F.F. formula' – Action, Revolution, Killing, Oratory, Fantasy, and Fornication – AIP soon distinguished themselves from other fly-by-night B-companies through not only their endurance and prolific output, but also the actual quality of the films themselves (well, some of them). Amidst all of the drive-in sensationalism, there emerged a series of genuine masterpieces from then-emerging directors, including Roger Corman's Poe cycle (eight films between 1960 and 1965), Curtis Harrington's *Night Tide* (1961), Francis Ford Coppola's *Dementia 13* (both 1963), Sidney Lumet's *The Pawnbroker* (1964), Corman's *The Wild Angels* (1966), Leonard Kastle's *The Honeymoon Killers* (1969) and Martin Scorsese's *Boxcar Bertha* (1972). These weren't just background images to ignore while making out in a car, they were avant-garde pulp: a mixture of counter-cultural edginess, artistic ambition, formal elegance and forward-thinking cinematic innovation. This was cinema at the fringes of society, using exploitative attractions to reveal the ugly truth about the contemporary world. Dirty, cheap films for a dirty, cheap audience in a dirty, cheap world.

One of the producers behind the scenes at AIP was Larry Gordon. He was hoping to develop an ass-kicking female-focused film along the lines of *Shaft* called *Cleopatra Jones*. When that project wound up going to Warner Bros. instead (where it would be made in 1973 with Tamara Dobson, later Grier's roommate), Gordon wanted to strike back and beat the competition to the punch. He called on Jack Hill to create "a black woman revenge film". For the opening, Gordon wanted "this woman to just kill the shit out of two guys," Hill remembered during this release's accompanying commentary track. "That's what I had to work with and I created the story from that." In the end, Hill only had 18 days and $500,000 to complete the picture, he related in an interview in *Jack Hill: The Exploitation and Blaxploitation Master, Film by Film* (2009).

Hill was the perfect choice for the project that would come to be known as *Coffy* (a title he suggested). A classmate of Coppola's at UCLA, he got his start working as an assistant to Corman. From his first features as a director, Hill exhibited a strong sense of cultural commentary and feminist politics, as well as a compositional style whose fusion of classical elegance and in-your-face-delirium suggested Orson Welles. In *Mondo Keyhole* (1966, additional footage directed by John Lamb), about a rapist husband and his junk-addicted wife, Hill appropriated images ranging from Grant Wood's *American Gothic* (1930) to cheesecake photos to furniture advertisements, a visual clash of the perverse and the mundane that critiqued the ideology of modern society, in particular the objectification of women. Such is the double-edge of exploitation cinema, revealing the artifice of entertainment while still delivering batshit-crazy mayhem. Hill's feminist critiques are also present in *Blood Bath* (1966, additional material directed by Stephanie Rothman), in which a male artist murders the women he paints by dipping them in hot wax, quite literally objectifying their beauty. Other films, such as *Pit Stop* (1969), *The Big Doll House* (1971), *The Big Bird Cage* (1972), *Foxy Brown* (1974, in many ways a spiritual sequel to *Coffy*) and *Switchblade Sisters* (1975 aka *The Jezebels*), not only focused on female characters, but also broadened the scope of roles available to actresses, allowing them to be as tough, violent, wild, and adventurous as their male counterparts.

In Grier, Hill found the perfect embodiment of this modern, revolutionary heroine. Originally hired as a receptionist for AIP's offices in Los Angeles, Grier was encouraged to audition for a role in *The Big Doll House*, AIP's latest 'women in prison' picture to be shot on the cheap in the Philippines. The story was far from sophisticated: a group of prisoners in an all-female jail band together to fight the sadistic female warden and bust out of the joint. On the surface, the film was little more than an excuse for scantily clad bombshells to catfight and roll around in the mud for 90 minutes, but therein lay the subversive brilliance of exploitation cinema: that's exactly what *The Big Doll House* was, but that is also what separated it from the mass stupidity of mainstream cinema that gender-locked women into playing conservative and limiting roles. The prisoners weren't just breaking out of a jungle jail – they were breaking out of cultural confinement, too, tearing down the walls of cinema's own prison. Grier auditioned to play one of the prisoners (a lesbian who plays informant to the warden in order to satisfy her girlfriend's junk habit) and was given the role on the spot. "I had no concept of categories like A, B, or C movies. A movie was a movie, and I intended to deliver an A performance, no matter what anybody else did," Grier related in her 2010 memoir, *Foxy: My Life in Three Acts*. "Since I was playing a radical black woman, I could draw personally from my own anger and the anti-war rallies I'd observed at UCLA and in Colorado when I lived there. That kind of raw energy was real for me, and I worked hard to make sure none of it looked fake or manufactured."

Grier's performance won her instant adoration from AIP. From the moment she hit the screen, Grier wasn't an actor-in-training, she was a natural born star. She stayed in the Philippines for two more 'women in prison' pictures, including *The Big Bird Cage* and Gerardo de León's *Women in Cages* (1971). While these and other exploitation pictures would boost Grier's career, it wasn't until 1973 that she would achieve screen immortality.

"You want me to crawl, white motherfucker? You want to spit on me and make me crawl? I'm going to piss on your grave tomorrow."

In *Coffy*, Grier redefined what it meant to be a powerful black woman on screen (as well as a powerful woman, and – hell – a powerful person in general). What she did on screen in 1973 was radical – and would have been as impossible at any other time. Just four decades earlier, things were quite different for black actresses. In the 1930s, Theresa Harris was relegated to the background (and often in uncredited roles) at Warner Bros. Louise Beavers and Fredi Washington broke new ground as the mother and daughter pair in the original *Imitation of Life* (1934), and it was remarkable that Hattie McDaniel won the Oscar as Mammy in *Gone with the Wind* (1939). The 1940s and 1950s saw actresses such as Lena Horne and Dorothy Dandridge making bold strides forward, too, while the 1960s brought a new generation of black actresses to the screen, including Diahann Carroll (*Hurry Sundown*, 1967), Ruby Dee (*A Raisin in the Sun*, 1961), Abbey Lincoln (*Nothing But a Man*, 1964), Cicely Tyson (*The Heart is a Lonely Hunter*, 1968), and even Eartha Kitt as television's Catwoman (1966-68). Grier took things to a whole other level. Because *Coffy* was an independent exploitation film, she was allowed to be sexier, smarter, sassier and more individualistic than almost any woman in film history. Her performance has had such influence that it is easy to take for granted just how revolutionary Grier was at the time at the time, and you'd still be hard pressed to find any character on screen now to rival Coffy.

Just who is Coffy? That's her nickname, short for

Flower Child Coffin, a name that conjures up images of Spaghetti Western antihero Django, dragging around his coffin full of guns (in a way, she is like a Western gunslinger, out for revenge and dragging around her metaphorical coffin of social and personal wrongs that need righting). "Coffin" also reminds of Coffin Ed and Gravedigger Jones, Chester Himes's African-American revisionist hardboiled private eyes that not only diversified the racial landscape of crime fiction in the 1950s and 1960s, but also injected true grit, surreal violence, street realism, and a fantastic grandeur into noir that most certainly influenced the Blaxploitation films of the 1970s. Flower Child Coffin also represents the shattered idealism of the 1960s, the peace-loving person she wants to be but can't in the face of the politically corrupt, racist, sexist, and drug-and-poverty ridden world she inhabits. In *In the Heat of the Night* (1967), Sidney Poitier as Mr. Tibbs had to fight oppression from inside the boundaries of the system; in *Coffy*, Grier is like a renegade Mr. Tibbs, someone outside of the system who doesn't have to be nice and play by the rules.

As a heroine (or anti-heroine, as the case may be, considering how many conventions she defies), Coffy is an amalgamation of many different archetypes. She borrows the best, the most alluring, and the most badass characteristics from an array of predecessors, building on their styles while creating something undeniably her own. Whereas women in crime stories were often restricted to supporting roles (the secretary, the girlfriend, the wife, the victim), Coffy takes the lead role as the hardboiled action protagonist. More than just muscle, she's also part *femme fatale* – the dangerous woman of *film noir* who manipulates men with her intelligence, sexuality, and ambition, like Barbara Stanwyck in *Double Indemnity* (1944) or Peggy Cummins in *Gun Crazy* (1950). (Cummins' line, "I've been kicked around all my life, and from now on, I'm gonna start kicking back," almost sounds like it could have been written expressly for Grier). Coffy is also a working class warrior who, like Stanwyck in *Baby Face* (1933), uses her sexuality to infiltrate, dominate, and ultimately destroy, the patriarchal hegemony that is trying to keep her down. (In her memoir, Grier herself noted the similarity between her films and 1930s Pre-Code cinema: "The plots nearly always resembled old Warner Bros. melodramas, with dashes of MGM fashion glamour – via the street – thrown in. It was common for the persecuted female character, angry and less conflicted than her male counterpart, to destroy a white-based power structure that had caused pain and harm to herself and her family.") Coffy is also like the black angels of Cornell Woolrich's *noir* nightmares *The Bride Wore

Black (1940, filmed in 1968), *The Black Angel* (1943, filmed in 1946) and *Deadline at Dawn* (1944, filmed in 1946); the devoted lover who ventures into the shadows for revenge. With her espionage expertise, sexual prowess, and verbal wit, Coffy is also a bit like James Bond (though, unlike him, she doesn't need Q or his hi-tech gadgets, nor is she a walking-and-talking relic of sexism). And then there's her vigilante spirit, which pre-dates such iconic revenge flicks such as *Walking Tall* (1973), *Il cittadino si ribella* (*Street Law*), *Death Wish* (both 1974), *Taxi Driver* (1976), *I Spit On Your Grave* (1978 aka *Day of the Woman*) and *The Exterminator* (1980), among many others. And with her extreme willingness to blow her opposition away – as well as her signature farewell speeches – she's a 'Dirty' Harry Callahan for the radical left. What's significant about Coffy's lineage is that she is largely co-opting characteristics that belonged to male characters. By merging both the male detective figure with the femme fatale, Coffy reinvents – and revitalises – the *noir* genre for the post-Civil Rights generation.

"To me, what really stood out in the [Blaxploitation] genre was women of colour acting like heroes rather than depicting nannies or maids," Grier wrote in *Foxy*. "We were redefining heroes as schoolteachers, nurses, mothers, and street-smart women who were proud of who they were. They were far more aggressive and progressive than the Hollywood stereotypes. Despite the fact that many men and some women were not supportive of female equality like they are today, the roles all made sense to me. After all, these were the women with whom I grew up. I guess I was ahead of my time, because today, contemporary women are scantily dressed but are still dignified and very intelligent."

Grier's strong dramatic performance and mesmerising star quality, Hill's subversive brilliance, and the film's vibrant and infectious spirit, made *Coffy* a hit with audiences. Critics, however, were slow to realize the film's smartness. Instead, they saw more clichés and overlooked the cleverness. "Despite a good deal of lip service against the evils of drugs and the like, there's a maximum of footage devoted to exposing Miss Grier," A.H. Weiler cheekily reviewed in the *New York Times* when the film was initially released. "What happens? She kills them all off, including her two-timing lover. All of which leaves a viewer with the happy thought that she now can get back to nursing and away from films like *Coffy*." Meanwhile, *Variety* offered the backhanded, sexist compliment, "Grier, a statuesque actress with a body she doesn't hesitate to show, is strongly cast." Roger Ebert was dismissive of the film's professionalism, seeing it as a detriment rather than a strength: "*Coffy* is slightly more serious and a little more inventive than it needs to be." On the other hand, Ebert was one of the rare critics who was able to pick up on Grier's screen-shattering star persona. "She's beautiful, as I've already mentioned, but she also has a kind of physical life to her that is sometimes missing in beautiful actresses. She doesn't seem to be posing or doing the fashion-model bit; she gets into an action role and does it right." Still, he only gave the film "two stars." Such a humble beginning for a film that, forty-one years later, is an enduring classic.

Part of why the film holds up so well is that, like any great movie, it is an ensemble effort. Supporting Grier was a cast of cult cinema's finest, including longtime Hill collaborator, virtuoso character Sid Haig, who would ultimately appear in several films with Grier, including *The Big Bird Cage*, *The Big Doll House*, *Black Mama White Mama* (1973) and Quentin Tarantino's *Jackie Brown* (1997). Appearing as Coffy's boyfriend, a straight cop in a world of corruption, is William Elliott, who later starred in Henry Hathaway's final film, *Hangup* (1974, aka *Super Dude*). And no Blaxploitation film would be complete without a soulful score to capture the musical zeitgeist of the times. One can't imagine the great Blaxploitation films without their iconic scores: Isaac Hayes and *Shaft*, Curtis Mayfield and *Super Fly*, James Brown and *Black Caesar* (1974), or Marvin Gaye and *Trouble Man*. *Coffy*'s score was composed by Roy Ayers, the great jazz vibraphonist, who blended funky grooves with complex modernist harmonies. Like with those other films, Ayers's contribution is so magnificent that it stands on its own as one of the best soundtracks of the 1970s, but it is so fully integrated into the movie that one can't imagine watching *Coffy* without the music or listen to the album without seeing the film's images in your mind. In the end, however, it is Grier and her unstoppable aura that has ensured that *Coffy* will never be forgotten. It was a role that not only defined, but also redefined, an entire era of culture, celebrity, and cinema.

This essay originally appeared in the Arrow Video edition of* Coffy*.

CULT GENRES

[AND SUB-GENRES]

BLOOD AND BLACK GLOVES

Michael Mackenzie on the Giallo

Artwork by Graham Humphreys

Film historians David Bordwell and Kristin Thompson state that "a genre is easier to recognise than to define". Rarely has this seemed more relevant than when referring to the *giallo* – a sensual, stylish and luridly violent body of Italian murder-mystery films which, like the American *films noir* which preceded them by a few decades, responded to a unique set of sociocultural upheavals and were therefore influenced as much by the period in which they were produced as by generic conventions. The Italians have a specific term to describe this phenomenon: *filone*, meaning 'vein' or 'streamlet'. These faddish, often highly derivative genres each tended to enjoy a brief spell of immense popularity and prolificacy before fading into obscurity as quickly as they first appeared, their creative potential (and their audience's appetite for more of the same) exhausted. Throughout its long and colourful history, the Italian film industry has borne witness to the rise and fall of an almost mind-boggling number of *filoni*, ranging from Spaghetti Westerns to high-octane *poliziotteschi* crime thrillers to playful sex romps. There is something uniquely compelling about the *giallo*, however, that not only allows it to stand the test of time but also invites repeat viewings – the better to unpick their hidden meanings.

The word '*giallo*' is the Italian for 'yellow', and derives from the yellow jackets of the plethora of detective novels that began to saturate the Italian market in the late 1920s, among them translations of the works of authors as diverse as Arthur Conan Doyle, Raymond Chandler and Agatha Christie. The *giallo* film is something altogether different and more narrowly defined, emerging in the early 1960s and enjoying a brief spell of immense popularity in the early-to-mid 1970s. The conventions of these films have been well-established elsewhere and are iconic enough that even those without an intimate knowledge of the genre can recognise them: the black gloves, hat and trench coat that disguise the killer's identity and gender; the modern urban locales which provide a backdrop to the carnage that unfolds; the 'whodunit' investigative narratives with their high body counts and multitude of suspects and red herrings; the amateur detective who is often a foreign tourist in a major European city; the lush lounge scores by composers such as Ennio Morricone, Bruno Nicolai and Stelvio Cipriani; the allusions to animals in the titles, which often have little to do with the content of the films themselves... Critic Stephen Thrower defines the mood of the *giallo* as "one of moral decay and cynicism, with ever more convoluted plots emphasising morbid details in a Janus-faced world of paranoia and betrayal" – and that cuts straight to the central conceit of these films: everyone is guilty because everyone has something to hide.

The first 'true' *giallo* film is broadly agreed to be Mario Bava's 1963 effort *The Girl Who Knew Too Much* (*La ragazza che sapeva troppo*). Shot in striking black and white, its plot is - as its title implies - decidedly Hitchcockian, detailing the exploits of an American tourist, Nora Davis (Letícia Román), who, while visiting her sickly aunt in Rome, inadvertently witnesses a murder on the Spanish Steps and, in the face of police inactivity, turns amateur sleuth in order to track down the so-called "Alphabet Killer". Many of the early, prototypical *gialli* of the 1960s take their cues from this film, offering up a series of emotionally fragile women - many of them played by American star Carroll Baker - and revelling in their psychological torture, often with little to no explicit bloodshed. Of these, the quintessential example is arguably Romolo Guerrieri's *The Sweet Body of Deborah* (*Il dolce corpo di Deborah*, 1968), which details the increasing paranoia and mental instability of a wealthy American woman, Deborah (Baker), who is menaced by the vindictive ex-lover of her new husband's deceased wife. Others, like Lucio Fulci's *One on Top of the Other* (*Una sull'altra*, 1969), focus on morally and psychologically compromised male business professionals who fall into downward spirals as the wealth and privilege they hold dear are stripped away - often as a result of the machinations of a duplicitous femme fatale.

A year after the release of *The Girl Who Knew Too Much*, Bava returned to the *giallo*, bringing it closer to its final form with *Blood and Black Lace* (*Sei donne per l'assassino*, 1964). A lush, Technicolor extravaganza, the film introduces the rich primary colours, baroque architecture and ultramodern fashion that would come to define these films, and the notion of the *giallo* as a showcase for a series of graphic murder set-pieces - earning it the reputation for being "the first authentic body count movie".

With these two early *gialli*, Bava laid much of the groundwork for what would become the 'classical' *giallo*. However, it was not until 1970, when young first-time director Dario Argento gave the world *The Bird with the Crystal Plumage* (*L'uccello dalle piume di cristallo*), that the floodgates truly opened and the *giallo* boom was born. Forty-five years after its release, it remains a striking, innovative and masterfully constructed film. The plot is that of a model *giallo*, focusing on an American novelist, Sam Dalmas (Tony Musante), who, while bumming around Rome waiting for inspiration to strike, becomes involved in a fiendishly twisted murder mystery when he chances upon a beautiful woman

being attacked in an art gallery by a knife-wielding maniac. Through the amateur investigation that follows, Argento explores, in an oblique manner, concerns about globalisation, urbanisation and the changing dynamic between men and women – key themes which tapped into the sociocultural anxieties prevalent during this period and would go on to preoccupy the *giallo* as a whole.

The late 1960s and early 1970s were a time of immense social upheaval, and what arguably makes the films produced in this period so potent is the way in which they reflect tensions and anxieties lurking beneath the surface of society. To be clear, *gialli* rarely, if ever, comment directly on real world events, preferring instead to thrill their audiences with a potent mix of sensuality, globe-trotting adventurism and audacious set-pieces. However, they nonetheless allude, in a refracted manner, to the existential crisis that was engulfing Italy, and indeed the Western world at a whole, at this time. These films, produced for a primarily male audience, invariably view the various sociocultural anxieties with which they engage exclusively in terms of their effect on men. As a result, themes that are in theory not gender-specific, such as alienation within an increasingly homogenised urban metropolis, become specifically masculine concerns and are viewed through the prism of how they affect the films' male protagonists. While the main focus of any *giallo* tends to be the central mystery surrounding the identity of the killer, these films also explore, albeit indirectly, a plethora of less initially obvious problems which play out in parallel to and often overlap with the 'whodunit' narrative, all of which help to form the colourful and unpredictable backdrop against which these murder-mystery scenarios play out.

Similarly, rather than providing concrete solutions to these perceived problems, they instead contribute to an ongoing discourse about the changing nature of society. Attempts to characterise these films as either purely reactionary or purely progressive are, however, overly reductive. Indeed, one of the most striking aspects of the *gialli* is the way in which they simultaneously undermine and reinforce traditional gender values. The confused and often contradictory nature of the *giallo* articulates the confusion and contradictions of a sociocultural milieu in which the old assumptions about the way the world works can no longer be relied on. Regardless of whether the underlying feelings towards the social changes of the 1960s and 1970s were positive, negative or indifferent, the *gialli* capture them on celluloid in a way that is entertaining, idiosyncratic, ostentatious, and even thought-provoking.

Following the success of *The Bird with the Crystal Plumage*, the imitators soon came thick and fast. Over the next five years, virtually every jobbing director working in Italy turned their hand to at least one *giallo*. Some were merely content to churn out uninspired imitations, seemingly ticking off a checklist of elements: the black-gloved killer with a psychosexual motivation, an obscure reference to an animal in the title, and so on. Others succeeded in harnessing the *giallo*'s generic conventions to explore their own preoccupations and crafted distinctly different takes on the genre. It is a testament to the *giallo*'s malleability that houses entries as distinct as Aldo Lado's *Short Night of Glass Dolls* (*La corta notte delle bambole di vetro*, 1971), a disturbing political thriller set in Soviet Prague which serves as an allegory for the establishment's suppression of the aspirations of the young, and Fulci's *A Lizard in a Woman's Skin* (*Una lucertola con la pelle di donna*, 1971), a lurid *Repulsion*-esque psychodrama set in a decidedly post-Swinging London, lifting the lid on the hanky-panky going on behind the lace curtains of Belgravia and exposing a society at an ideological crossroads post-1968.

One filmmaker who succeeded in adding a distinctive spin to the *giallo* was Sergio Martino. In his first of five films made within the genre, *The Strange Vice of Mrs. Wardh* (*Lo strano vizio della Signora Wardh*, 1971), he combined two distinctive strands of the *giallo* — the violent, urban and typically male-centric body count thrillers popularised by *The Bird with the Crystal Plumage* and its imitators, and the more languorous, psychologically-driven female-centric films in the mould of *The Sweet Body of Deborah* — to create a hybrid which proved that the 'F-*gialli*' (female *gialli*) could be every bit as bloody and frenetic as their 'M-*gialli*' (male *gialli*) counterparts. *The Strange Vice of Mrs. Wardh* established the formula that Martino would go on to employ in his four subsequent entries in *giallo* canon, alongside a plethora of fellow filmmakers who leapt at the chance to craft narratives of their own about harangued, emotionally unstable female protagonists and their luridly violent mishaps. One director who succeeded in harnessing this format to his own end was Luciano Ercoli, who crafted a number of *gialli* as vehicles for his wife, actress Nieves Navarro (aka Susan Scott). Of these, the standout is *Death Walks at Midnight* (*La morte accarezza a mezzanotte*, 1972), in which Navarro stars as Valentina, a fashion model who believes she has witnessed a murder while under the influence of an experimental hallucinogenic. While most female *giallo* protagonists are shrinking violets in the mould of Edwige Fenech – the star of *The Strange Vice of Mrs. Wardh* and the actress who can most legitimately lay claim to the crown of *giallo* 'scream queen' – Navarro was made of sterner stuff, and her brash, forceful persona provides a welcome antidote to her less assertive counterparts, typically called upon to do little more than strip, scream and swoon (and not necessarily in that order).

By the mid-1970s, the *giallo* was in decline, with the genre having followed the same trajectory as the Spaghetti Western, the *peplum*, and countless other *filoni*. Tired of films about black-gloved killers slicing and dicing their way through the bourgeoisie, audiences sought out new pleasures at the box office, and transferred their allegiances to the *poliziotteschi*, which engaged more directly with contemporary concerns about political corruption and society on the brink of violent collapse, and to that perpetual staple of the industry, the *commedia all'italiana*. It seems somehow fitting that the *giallo* boom both began and ended with Argento, who in 1975 delivered what critic and author Julian Grainger calls "the final word on the subject": *Deep Red* (*Profondo rosso*), not only the last great *giallo* of the classical era but arguably also the greatest *giallo* ever created. While both Argento and other directors would subsequently return to the form and indeed use it to explore new territory with films like Argento's *Tenebrae* (*Tenebre*, 1982) and Alex Infascelli's *The Vanity Serum* (*Il siero della vanità*, 2004), there is a definite sense that, with *Deep Red*, Argento had succeeded in perfecting the form and said all there was to be said about it at that particular point in time.

The *giallo*'s legacy, however, lives on, and almost half a century later, they continue to beguile, enthral and disturb audiences with their striking visuals, mesmerising soundtracks, and convoluted narratives of paranoia, conspiracy, degradation and vice.

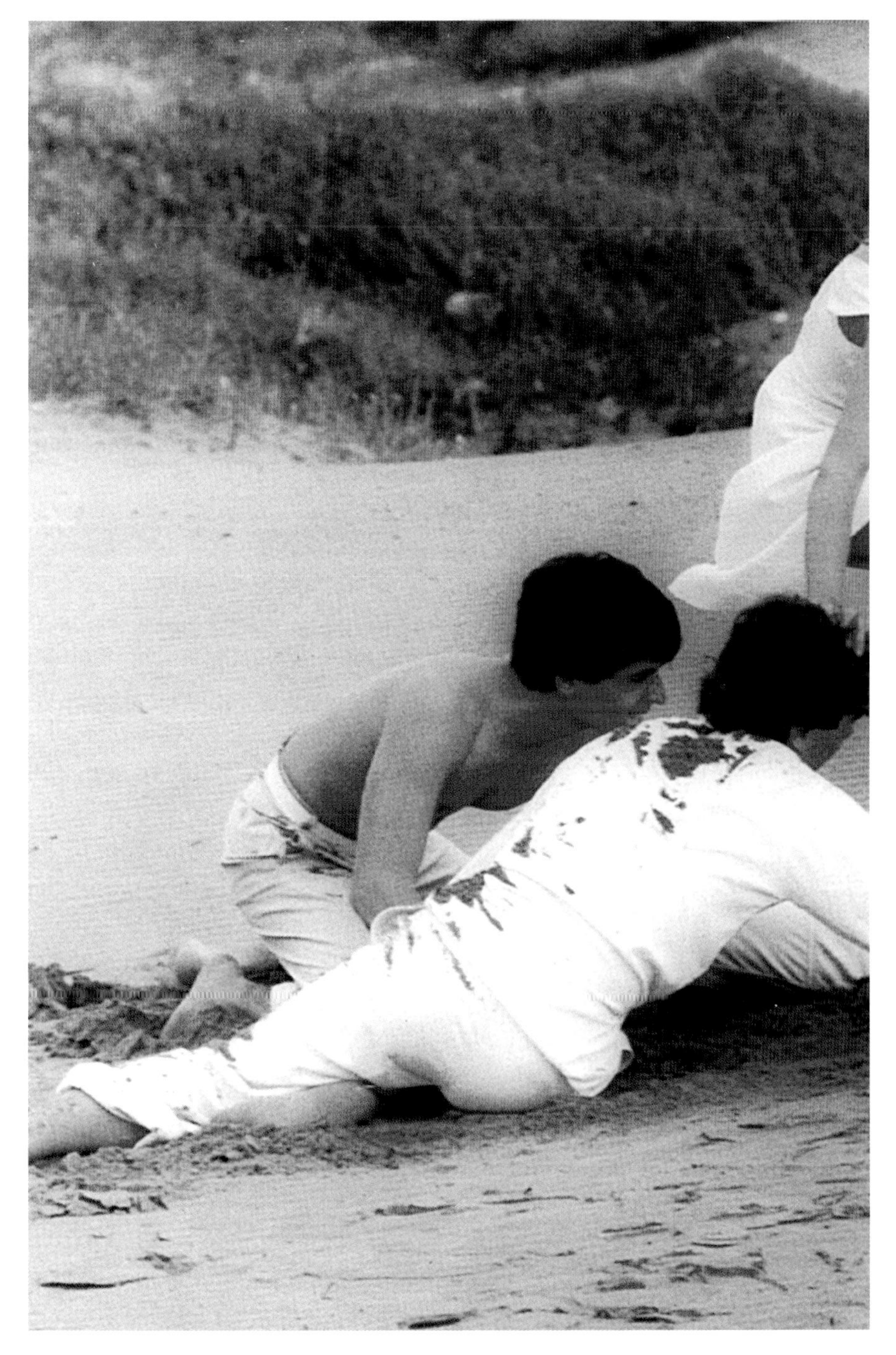

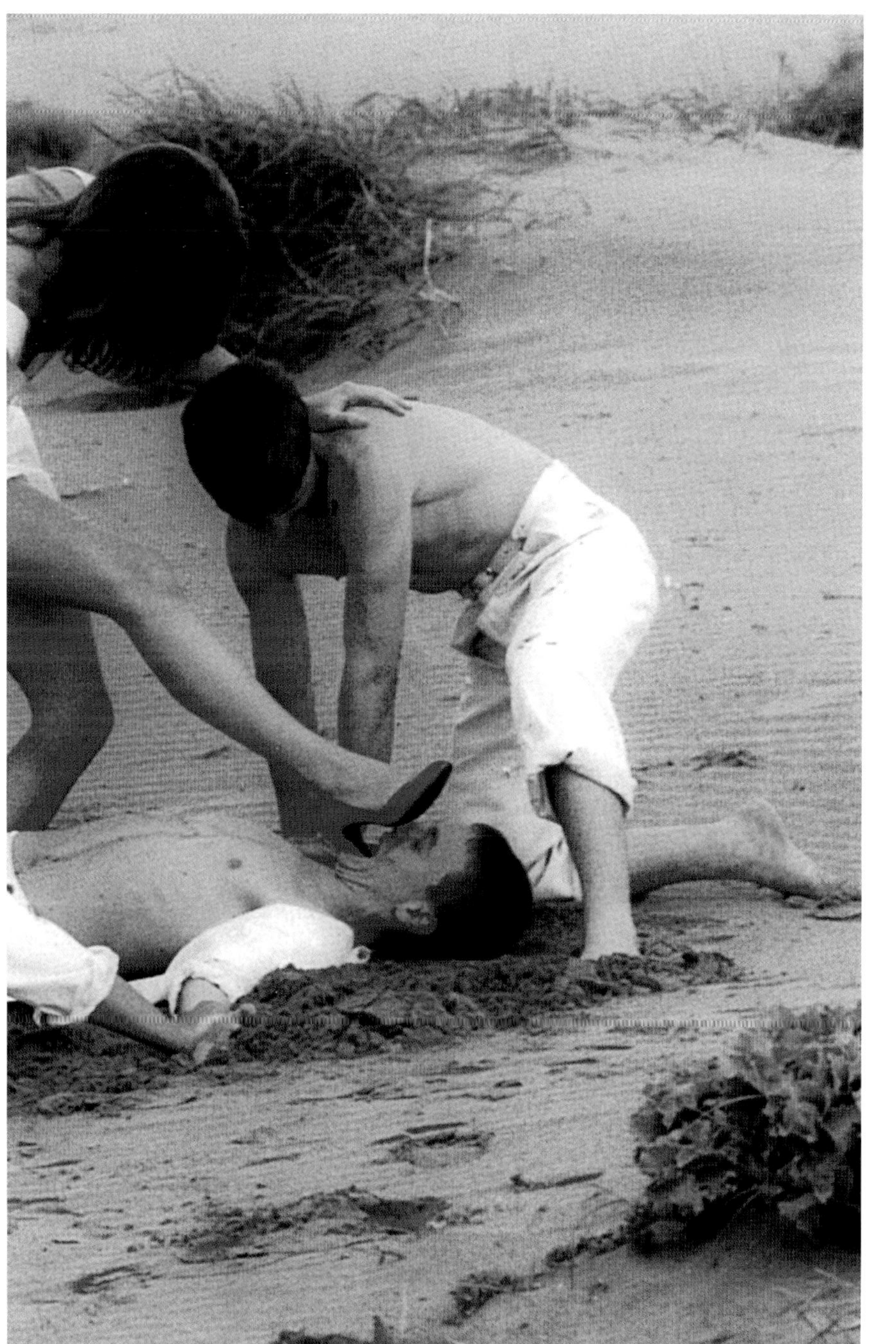

Tenebrae

PLAYFUL REVISIONISM

Pasquale Iannone on the Spaghetti Western

Artwork by Reinhard Kleist

The 1950s is usually considered to be the Hollywood Western's richest period. In 1956, the genre's undisputed master John Ford made the film that for many remains one of the greatest Westerns of them all – *The Searchers* – but it was perhaps less-heralded directors like Budd Boetticher, Anthony Mann and Delmer Daves that pushed the Western into exciting new territory. Murkier themes and tones were introduced to a genre whose central dynamics had traditionally been very clear-cut. In terms of aesthetics, the Western benefited greatly from the introduction of widescreen technology in the early-to-mid 1950s, with pictures like Mann's *The Man from Laramie* (1955) and Boetticher's *Ride Lonesome* (1959) making striking use of the new format. However, as the 1960s loomed on the horizon, all these formal and thematic innovations could not mask the fact that far fewer Hollywood Westerns were actually being made. This drop in output allowed directors from outside the US to craft their own takes on the most quintessentially American of genres and it was a wave of Italian 'horse operas' that charged onto the screen with greatest force and fervour.

The antecedents of the 'Spaghetti Western' can be traced back to the 1940s when directors such as Pietro Germi, Giuseppe De Santis and Alberto Lattuada drew heavily on Western iconography. In Germi's 1949 film *In the Name of the Law* (*In nome della legge*), for instance, a city lawman arrives at a Sicilian town to take on the mafia. By no means is revolutionary in terms of its style, *In the Name of the Law* nonetheless very effective in drawing on elements familiar from the Hollywood Western – characterisation, landscape – to tell of indigenously Italian phenomena. It would take another decade or so for a more dramatic Italian reinvention of the Western to take place and the man who masterminded it was Rome-born Sergio Leone. *Fistful of Dollars* (*Per un pugno di dollari*, 1964), *For a Few Dollars More* (*Per qualche dollaro in più*, 1965) and *The Good, the Bad and the Ugly* (*Il buono, il brutto, il cattivo*, 1966) – his *Dollars* trilogy - were the first European Westerns to establish a bold new formal and thematic approach and they served as templates for hundreds of Spaghettis.

It's interesting to note how Leone began his playful genre revisionism not with a Western, but with a historical epic. He had been in the film business since he was a teenager, serving as screenwriter, assistant and/or second unit director. He even had a small cameo in Vittorio De Sica's 1948 neo-realist classic *Bicycle Thieves* (*Ladri di biciclette*). His feature debut came in 1961 with *The Colossus of Rhodes* (*Il colosso di Rodi*) where he was given the opportunity to subvert what was usually a high-minded, straight-laced genre. Just a matter of months later, Leone was back manning the second unit, this time of *Sodom and Gomorrah* (1962), another sword-and-sandal extravaganza. The shoot was turbulent to say the least, with Leone and director Robert Aldrich at frequent loggerheads. Leone felt he had given a unique spin on the epic with *The Colossus of Rhodes* and was unimpressed with Aldrich's drier style. As costs continued to rise, Leone left the production (accounts vary as to whether he was sacked or left of his own accord). During this time, Leone became interested in the work of Japanese director Akira Kurosawa and was particularly struck by *Seven Samurai* (*Shichinin no samurai*, 1954) and *Yojimbo* (1961). Here, he felt, was a filmmaker with an intelligent, witty take on established cinematic tropes, here was a model to aspire to. Famously, *Yojimbo* became such a close model for *Fistful of Dollars* that Kurosawa's production company Toho would launch legal proceedings.

You need only watch the first five minutes of *Fistful of Dollars* to see just how different Leone's approach was to the Hollywood Western and to see that despite all the influences that fed into the film - 18th century playwright Carlo Goldoni was another of his declared reference points - it gave the genre as a whole a real shot in the arm. With great affection, François Truffaut once said of fellow French director Jacques Becker that he made two-hour films about subjects that only really needed fifteen minutes and this is something that also comes to the fore in Leone. In defiance of tight Hollywood narrative structure, Leone, like Becker, makes unconventional use of film rhythm, of cinematic time. A perfect example of this is the opening sequence of Leone's *Once Upon a Time in the West* (*C'era una volta il West*, 1968) where gunfighters lay in wait for the arrival of Harmonica (Charles Bronson) at a train station. It's a scene that could have easily been covered in a couple of minutes, but the director chooses to stretch it out; lingering, heightening details that are usually lost in more scrupulously plot-driven films. In his 2014 memoir *Fear* (*Paura*), *giallo* maestro Dario Argento (who collaborated on the screenplay for *Once Upon a Time in the West*) tells of how he and co-writer Bernardo Bertolucci sat down with Leone to watch *The Searchers*. When the screening was over, Leone asked them both what the most important element of the film was. "We both blurted out the most obvious answers such as John Wayne's acting," Argento recalls. "Sergio looked at us and shook his head: 'No, the most important elements of *The Searchers* are not the characters, but the

atmosphere, the landscape.'"

For his *Dollars* trilogy, Leone employed full widescreen but his framing and composition differed considerably from the CinemaScope Westerns of Boetticher and Mann. He retained wide shots of vast parched panoramas but he went to the other end of the spectrum too, filling the letterbox frame with extreme close-ups of faces (sometimes just eyes). Rather than opt for an established film star, Leone cast Clint Eastwood, the tall, lean protagonist of US Western series *Rawhide* (1959-65) to star in all three films. Swathed in a poncho and with a small cigar jutting out the corner of his mouth, Eastwood's characters were laconic, blue-eyed, bearded and anything but verbose. Across the trilogy, Eastwood would be joined by a host of memorably grizzled actors – Gian Maria Volontè, Eli Wallach, Lee Van Cleef – and Leone has them toil and struggle in the oppressive heat, his camera alive to catch every sweat-drenched moment. Volontè and Van Cleef's appearances led to several more Italo-Western roles, especially for the latter.

The now-iconic status of *Fistful of Dollars* and indeed all of Leone's Westerns is down as much to sound as image. Even those who have never seen the films will recognise many of their musical cues, especially the main theme for *The Good, the Bad and the Ugly*. The work of Leone's former schoolmate Ennio Morricone, the music for the *Dollars* trilogy set the standard for all Italo-Westerns and even when Morricone was not called upon himself, replacement composers were often told to evoke his style. Breaking away from the tradition of lush orchestral scores, Leone and Morricone agreed on a more experimental soundscape, using sounds from folk and pop music (electric guitar, Jew's harp, harmonica) as well as making full use of the expressive power of the human voice (the whistles of Alessandro Alessandroni, the wordless vocals of soprano Edda Dell'Orso). "Some of the music was written before the film, which is unusual," Morricone told the *Guardian*'s Will Hodgkinson in 2006. "Leone's films were made like that because he wanted the music to be an important part of it, and he often kept the scenes longer simply because he didn't want the music to end. That's why the films were so slow – because they were following the pattern of the music." Leone's practice of choreographing sequences to Morricone's music would continue right up until their final collaboration *Once Upon a Time in America* (1984), but the most famous scene of this kind came in *Once Upon a Time in the West*, where Claudia Cardinale's character Jill McBain arrives at Flagstone train station and the camera rises high to Morricone's swelling strings.

By the second half of the 1960s, thanks largely to Leone, the Italo-Western had become internationally famous. A slew of Spaghettis were made, both in Italy and across the globe. Some of these, like Damiano Damiani's *A Bullet for the General* (*Quién sabe?*, 1966) and Carlo Lizzani's *Requiescant* (1967), emphasised the political or allegorical element, while others, such as Giuseppe Colizzi's *Ace High* (*I quattro dell'Ave Maria*, 1968) and Enzo Barboni's *They Call Me Trinity* (*Lo chiamavano Trinità...*, 1970), stressed the humour. Among the hundreds of titles, only a few were able to match the films of Leone in terms of ambition and artistry. With echoes of *Fistful of Dollars*, Sergio Corbucci's *Django* (1966) starred 25-year-old Franco Nero. Together with Terence Hill, who would play Django in Ferdinando Baldi's 1968 prequel *Django, Prepare a Coffin* (*Preparati la bara!*), Nero was one of the few Italo-Western sex symbols. He plays a Civil War veteran who arrives at a Mexican border town with bloody revenge on his mind. Controversial at the time thanks to its heightened violence, *Django* spawned scores of unofficial sequels but Nero only returned to the role some 20 years later in Nello Rossati's *Django Strikes Again* (*Django 2 - Il grande ritorno*, 1987).

After Leone and Corbucci, the third Sergio to distinguish himself in the world of the Italo-Western was Sergio Sollima. He made two films back-to-back between 1966 and 1967 that are essential titles in the canon. Both feature evocative Morricone scores and both have Tomas Milian in tandem with actors familiar from Leone's Westerns. *The Big Gundown* (*La resa dei conti*, 1966) sees Van Cleef as an ageing bounty hunter on the hunt for a young Mexican (Milian) while *Face to Face* (*Faccia a faccia*, 1967) tells of the clash between two very different sensibilities - a middle-aged professor (Volontè) and a young outlaw (Milian).

Critic and filmmaker Alex Cox has rightly identified the lifespan of the Spaghetti Western as roughly a decade, its golden period bookended by Leone productions *Fistful of Dollars* and *My Name Is Nobody* (*Il mio nome è Nessuno*, 1973). However, the trend's afterlife has been a rich and diverse one, its influence seeping into many different art forms. In terms of cinematic disciples, we need look no further than the work of Quentin Tarantino, who has to date made two decidedly Corbuccian Westerns. *Django Unchained* (2010) references *Django* while 2015's *The Hateful Eight* (yet to be released at the time of writing) looks to have been influenced by *The Great Silence* (*Il grande silenzio*, 1968). With

The Hateful Eight, Tarantino also finally secured the services of Morricone to compose an original score after years of cherry picking through the composer's back catalogue. The composer's influence on music more generally has been profound. Indeed, it's hard to think of a film composer who's left more of a mark on pop music, whether it's Arizona band Calexico, Devon outfit Muse or Mancunian miserabilist Morrissey. In 2007, a tribute album called *We All Love Morricone* was released featuring Morricone covers by artists as varied as Roger Waters and Yo-Yo Ma. Highlights of the album include modern versions of Morricone's pieces for the Spaghetti Westerns of Leone. Jazz royalty Quincy Jones and Herbie Hancock contribute a brassy re-imagining of the main theme from *The Good, the Bad and the Ugly* while Metallica perform a characteristically storming version of 'The Ecstasy of Gold' from the same film. The fact that artists from such diverse backgrounds have a shared passion for the images and sounds of the Italo-Western – sometimes even more than for the classic Hollywood Western itself – is testament to the Spaghettis' inexhaustible appeal.

Day of Anger

SNOW JOB: A BRIEF HISTORY OF CANADIAN EXPLOITATION CINEMA

Paul Corupe on Canuxploitation

Artwork by Jim Rugg

Blowing in like a balmy chinook wind across the frost-bitten prairies, Canada's exploitation film industry has long aimed to inject a little sex, violence and sleaze into the sometimes stuffy arthouse scene. Over the last 65 years – but especially during the anything-goes 'tax shelter' era of the 1970s and '80s – the Great White North fostered a proud tradition of weird and uncompromising B-movies from across all genres. Sometimes grouped under 'Canuxploitation' – a term I came up with in 1998 – these films are finally winning the battle of respectability against disapproving Canadian critics and tastemakers who, not so very long ago, accused them of being little more than flawed facsimiles of the latest Hollywood trash.

The humble beginnings of Canadian genre cinema can be traced back to the late 1950s, but the real story starts in 1939 with the founding of the National Film Board. One of the only games in town, the NFB was originally established as a government agency to crank out wartime propaganda films, but moved into sober and self-serious social documentaries after World War II. But by the 1950s, NFB veteran filmmakers like Julian Roffman, William Davidson and Norman Klenman got the itch to break out on their own to make dramatic features. Since Hollywood maintained a tight grip on distribution and exhibition north of the border, they hoped that by producing low budget sensationalist films, they could attract the interest of a big American studio.

That's the reason why many of Canada's first 'modern' films were exploitation pictures rather than the self-serious dramatic works later Canada began making in earnest a few years later. Early juvenile delinquency films such as *The Bloody Brood*, *A Cool Sound from Hell* and *Ivy League Killers* (all released in 1959) were stark black and white features bursting with dope pushers, slang-spouting beatniks and switchblade battles. But despite the salacious approach, filmmakers struggled to get their work shown on local screens, and the experience left many feeling frustrated about their future prospects.

All that started to change with Roffman's 3D breakthrough *The Mask* (1961), which managed to secure distribution from Warner Brothers. This horror film – Canada's first – featured a memorable gimmick, asking viewers to don special mask-shaped 3D glasses whenever the character on the screen put his own mask on. Inspired by Roffman's success, a few other horror films followed, including mad scientist yarn *The Vulture* (1966) and the H.G. Lewis-inspired *Playgirl Killer* (1967). At the same time the NFB was gearing up its own introspective dramas,

Canada's fledgling film industry was more defined by a quick run of cheapie sexploitation flicks like nudie cutie *Have Figure, Will Travel* (1963), stripper revue *French Without Dressing* (1965) and thrillers *The Naked Flame* (1964) and *Adulterous Affair* (1966) – flesh-baring films that playfully challenged Canada's frigid reputation.

It wasn't until the early 1970s that things really took off. Following years of industry pressure, the government formed the Canadian Film Development Corporation in 1968 which it gave $10 million to loan to qualifying films (though the money wasn't always paid back). In addition, producers took advantage of increasingly popular rules that allowed investors to save tax on money used to produce Canadian movies. At first, backers could write off 60% of their investment, but the threshold increased to 100% in 1975, proving to be an irresistible tax break for well-heeled professionals. With these financial enticements in place, the floodgates opened. Hundreds of Canadian films were released during what is now known as the 'tax shelter' era, a boom period that stretched from about 1972 to 1982, peaking in 1979 with 66 films officially in the can. Though many of these productions imported aging Hollywood actors, the rest made up for a lack of star power and budget with distinctive exploitation thrills like deadly shootouts, kinky sex, and giant killer creatures.

Many of the filmmakers picking up cameras in the 1970s were considerably less experienced than the journeymen that helped establish the industry in the 1950s. Chief among them was University of Toronto student David Cronenberg, whose early films like *Stereo* (1969) and *Crimes of the Future* (1970) landed him at Cinépix, a Montreal based theatrical distributor that moved into production during the 'tax shelter' era with a series of locally shot French-language sex comedies. His first proper feature following the hour-and-a-bit *Stereo* and *Crimes of the Future*, *Shivers* (1975), was a sometimes transgressive story of sexually transmitted, aphrodisiac-emitting parasites that infest a modern apartment complex, creating a literal orgy of terror.

Cronenberg's early classic also spawned Canadian cinema's biggest controversy to date, with local critic and columnist Robert Fulford bluntly asking Canadians whether this publically funded film was the kind of cultural product we should be putting tax dollars into. His article, 'You Should Know How Bad This Film Is. After All, You Paid for It', is a watershed moment in the history of Canadian cinema, the precise point where industry grumblings and critical condescension about the tax shelter's focus on sex and violence turned to public accusations. But Cinépix and more open-minded film writers rallied behind the film, boosting Cronenberg's own notoriety and ensuring he remained in the director's chair for follow-ups including the Marilyn Chambers-starring revisionist vampire tale *Rabid* (1977) and the exploding-head entry *Scanners* (1981).

Other innovative filmmakers emerged alongside Cronenberg to break new genre ground. Ivan Reitman was also a university student when he began putting together risqué sexploitation pictures with his friends, but had his first hit with 1973's *Cannibal Girls*, a cheeky independent horror effort starring future *SCTV* players Andrea Martin and Eugene Levy. When that film was picked up by American International Pictures, Reitman also ended up at Cinépix, where he produced films for Cronenberg and directed his own classic, the 1979 summer camp comedy *Meatballs*, honing the skills he would use a few years later in Hollywood to make *Ghost Busters* (1984).

While not a born Canadian, Bob Clark was also a key director of the 'tax shelter' era. He began his filmmaking career in Florida, but ended up making his home north of the border after completing zombie flick *Dead of Night* (1974, aka *Deathdream*) for Toronto-based Cinépix rival Quadrant. While here, he crafted one of the decade's iconic slashers, *Black Christmas* (1974), in which obscene phone calls to a sorority house turn deadly – a stylish effort that's an acknowledged influence on John Carpenter's sub-genre defining *Halloween* (1978). Around the same time, Clark brought his former collaborator Alan Ormsby up to Canada where the two worked on *Deranged* (1974), a grotty, darkly humorous serial killer movie that features early work from effects artist Tom Savini.

Other notable tax shelter films include the *Ilsa* series, featuring Dyanne Thorne as the titular whip-wielding sadist. Co-produced by Cinépix and exploitation magnate Dave Friedman, and based on a script by a moonlighting University of Toronto professor, the naughty Nazi conquered 42nd Street in the gleefully tasteless *Ilsa: She Wolf of the SS* (1975), which shocked viewers with castrations, naked electrocutions and torture involving diseased maggots. Two official sequels followed, including *Ilsa the Tigress of Siberia* (1977), which placed the character back in Canada where she takes over the Montreal mob and recruits local girls for scuzzy brothels.

Less campy but equally effective, William Fruet's *Death Weekend* (1976) is a rape-revenge tale that takes place in the secluded natural beauty of rural Ontario. Likewise, Peter Carter's *Rituals* (1979) offered an intriguing deep woods horror story about doctors on an annual camping trip who are stalked by a mysterious figure. For fans of pure schlock, Ed Hunt's sci-fi *Starship Invasions* (1977) featured Christopher Lee and a clunky robot targeting earthlings with a suicide ray. And there was even an oversize Bigfoot stomping through Toronto in the Italy/Canada co-production *Yeti, the Giant of the 20th Century* (*Yeti - Il gigante del 20° secolo*, 1977) – something for virtually every taste.

Although some critics felt that the tax shelter experiment was already a miserable failure by the 1980s, there's no denying that the steady stream of exploitation films were getting slicker and more polished. The George C. Scott-led haunted house picture *The Changeling* (1980) and Bob Clark's raunchy peephole comedy *Porky's* (1981) were no longer relegated to just the drive-ins, but made big money at home and abroad. The slasher horror cycle was bolstered by leading Canadian entries like *Prom Night*, *Terror Train* (both 1980) and *My Bloody Valentine* (1981). But, perhaps rethinking whether these films offered a uniquely identifiable Canadian experience, the government slashed the tax shelter by half at the end of 1982 – just a few months before Cronenberg's mind-bending *Videodrome* (1983) hit cinemas and cemented the director's reputation as one of Canada's most original and visionary filmmakers.

The reduced 50% shelter didn't quite wipe out Canada's exploitation film industry, at least partially because of the bubbling demand for home video releases. Canadian producers continued to ransack every conceivable genre for straight-to-video releases, wallpapering rental outlet shelves with knock-offs, sequels and eccentric vanity projects. The record-breaking box office gains of *Porky's* birthed goofy T&A comedy imitators like *Screwballs* (1983), *Oddballs* (1984), *Goofballs* (1987) and *Fireballs* (1989) – films with more balls than brains. The McNamara brothers, Michael and Martin, Toronto-resident kickboxing twins, produced no-budget martial arts epics that included *Twin Dragon Encounter* (1986), while high concept horror like the ludicrous techno-thriller *Murder by Phone* (1982) and heavy metal demon battles of *Rock 'n' Roll Nightmare* (1987) flourished alongside surreal kids' movies like the nightmare-inducing *The Peanut Butter Solution* (1985).

By 1988, the Canadian government completely abandoned the tax shelter system in favour of provincial programs. While the shelter's last gasps did include standouts like satanic panic-inspired *The Gate* (1987) and creepy mannequin tale *Pin* (1988), emerging filmmakers including Atom Egoyan and Guy Maddin were more auteur-minded than their exploitation film counterparts, and began to take Canadian film in a new direction. Even Cronenberg started drifting away from his horror roots after 1986's *The Fly*.

The result was slim pickings for Canadian genre fanatics, who had to make due with direct-to-video action movies, such as local impresario Jalal Merhi's self-starring martial arts films *Tiger Claws* (1991) and *TC 2000* (1993) and, improbably, three separate films about using Alexander the Great's sword to fight in underground combat tournaments: *The Swordsman* (1992), *Gladiator Cop* (1995) and *G2* (1999, aka *Mortal Conquest*). But as flying fists and feet dominated, Canadian-lensed horror took a backseat with tepid, unwelcome sequels like *Scanners II: The New Order* (1991), *Witchboard III: The Possession* (1995) and *Prom Night IV: Deliver Us from Evil* (1992), among others.

All that changed with the release of the teen werewolf antics of John Fawcett's *Ginger Snaps* (2000), a smart genre effort that almost single-handedly brought horror back into the spotlight with its story of a werewolf curse that complicates two sisters' struggles with puberty. Despite receiving only a video release in the United States, the film became a huge cult hit and garnered critical acceptance in Canada, resulting in two sequels. More importantly, the *Ginger Snaps* franchise helped lay the foundation for a new generation of genre filmmakers from across the country, who were already busy rediscovering tax shelter hits like *Black Christmas*, *Deranged* and *Videodrome* on VHS and DVD. Since then Canada has seen another young crop of young talent take the reins, including Ottawa's Lee Demarbre of *Jesus Christ Vampire Hunter* (2001) fame, Nova Scotian Jason Eisener, the director of *Hobo with a Shotgun* (2011), the Winnipeg-based Astron-6 collective with *Father's Day* (2011) and *giallo* spoof *The Editor* (2014) and the Soska Sisters out of Vancouver, with *Dead Hooker in a Trunk* (2009) and *American Mary* (2012). Together, they've helped carry on the tradition of Canuxploitation, but with a new awareness of the country's exploitation film past.

And that's important, because Canada's relatively brief film history is complicated – a litany of false starts, funding woes and much handwringing over whether the end product really represents us. But while many once worried that spending all our resources making sick and sleazy genre films would hurt our national reputation, these are the Canadian films that have stood the test of time, continuing to draw in new fans from across the globe. And some of us wouldn't want to have it any other way.

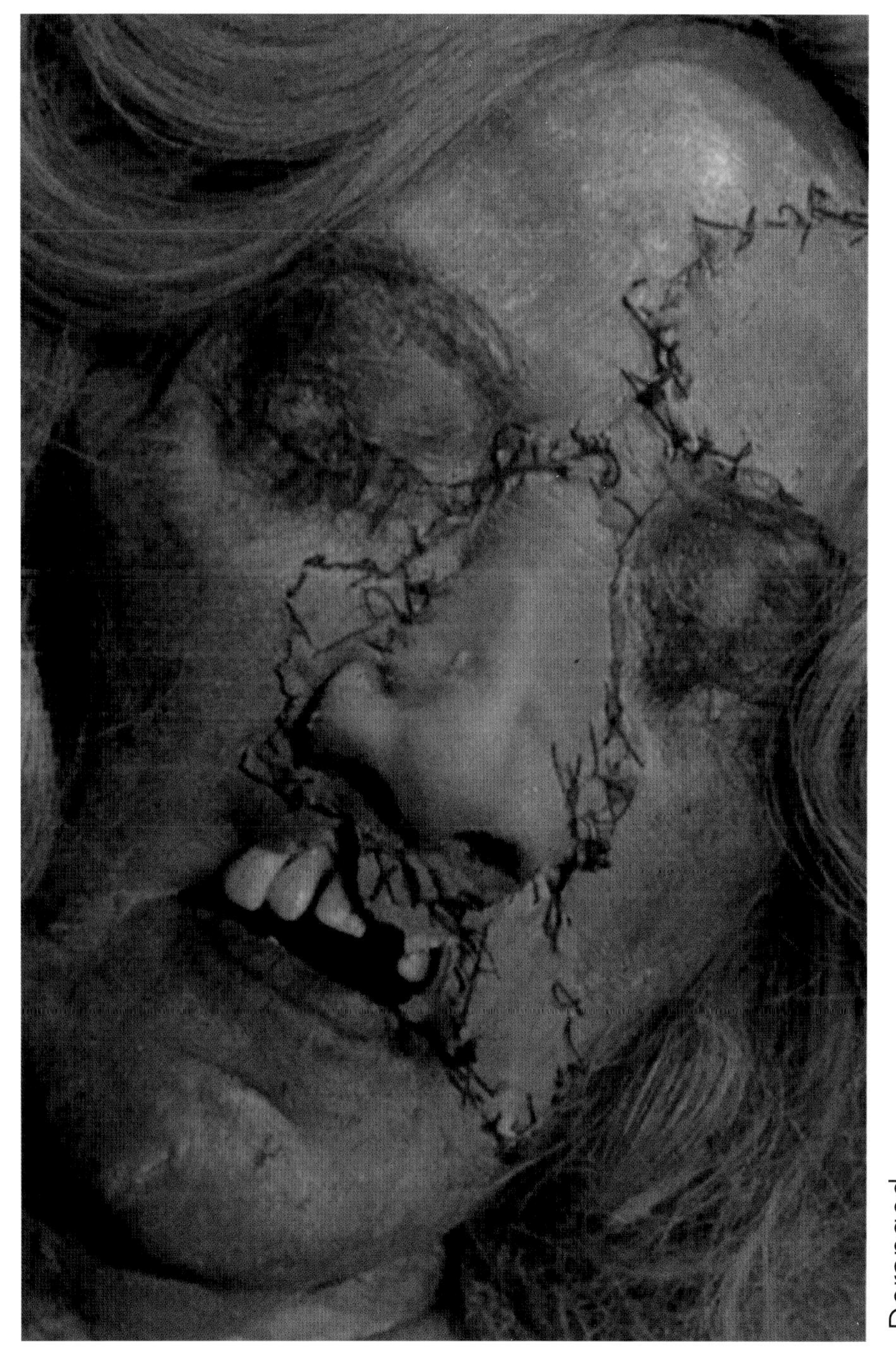

Deranged

BEHIND BARS
NO ONE CAN HEAR YOU SCREAM!

Robin Bougie on Pornochanchada

Artwork by Robin Bougie

The women-in-prison (WIP) genre may well be mostly forgotten by the mainstream now, but there was a time when the genre was so popular and ever-present that every single country with a film industry had at least one entry in it. Most of the them originated from the same places that cult cinema has always been fostered and expertly managed: America, Italy and Asian countries such as Japan and the Philippines – but South American countries such as Brazil also came correct with their fair share of chicks-in-chains.

Brazil's 'pornochanchada' exploitation genre saw its heyday between 1977 and 1985. Low budget 'chada' movies (a nickname administered by their adoring fans) are a sibling of the pink films of Japan, the Italian Sex-Comedy, and the 'roughies' of the 1960s American sexploitation film industry. It is a vulgar skin-tastic genre that solely existed to shock, titillate and bust the cherry of cultural taboos such as rape, misogyny, bestiality, necrophilia, and other forms of kinky sex. If you're new to 'Latsploitation' – and the majority of us are simply because so few of these movies have ever been translated into English – you're in for a treat.

Regardless of the strict censorship and ridged Catholic doctrine that Brazil faced in the era in question, state-run film companies were eager to support pornochanchada for two simple reasons:

1. They were proven money makers.
2. Despite their many exploitive tendencies, the movies were not all critical of the current regime that was in government.

In fact, more and more production companies became dependent on the lowly chada movies to help them compete with the juggernaut that was the American film industry; an outside force that was slowly taking over the Brazilian theatrical market.

With a sleazy filmography any exploitation filmmaker could be proud of, including *Bruce Lee versus Gay Power* (*Kung Fu Contra as Bonecas*, 1975), *The Insatiable Female Fugitives* (*Fugitivas Insaciáveis*, 1978), *Amazon Jail* (*Curral de Mulheres*) and *Bacchanals on the Isle of the Nymphets* (*Bacanais na Ilha das Ninfetas*, both 1982), writer/director Oswaldo de Oliveira could well have been considered the Joe D'Amato of Sao Paulo's Grindhouse district. But it was with his 1980 film *Bare Behind Bars* (*A Prisão*) that he created his masterpiece of sin.

Darker and more cynical than your average light-hearted pornochanchada, Oliveira's movie still invoked comedy and tongue-in-cheek madness, if only to help offset the carnal debauchery taking up the majority of its runtime. Indeed, *Bare Behind Bars* could well be the filthiest and most pornographic women's prison movie ever made outside of the XXX classification. Keep in mind the exploitation genre has a ripe and storied history of misrepresenting films with wildly inappropriate cover art and deceptive titles that are designed to draw you in and take your money. It's what the genre was built on, and this carnival barker history of hucksterism and sleight-of-hand is what makes an otherwise cheap and tawdry effort like *Bare Behind Bars* such a breath of fresh air. The movie doesn't dare take itself seriously for an instant, and you're getting exactly what you're being sold: naked women in prison. In fact, there aren't many scenes in this disreputable classic where fully clothed people even take up screen space. It's all furry beaver shots, natural jugs, 69-ing, masturbation and the cold grey steel of prison iron.

Its execution may be a lesson in transgressive Latsploitation, but the plot is pretty standard WIP fare. We have a psychopathic sadomasochist warden who takes perverse pleasure in the agony of her detainees (whom she looks to sell off on the white slave trade market), a guard who has concerns about the excessive abuse and nefarious treatment of the gals, oversexed inmates planning a prison break, and all kinds of quivering young Latin flesh, not the least of which belongs to what fans of the genre call the 'new fish' – the new girl on the cell block who always serves as a primary character.

Prison is never supposed to be a very nice place to stay, but this dirty, unregulated shit-pit houses multiple female criminals crammed into squalid conditions where only rats provide a sympathetic furry ear. Here, nubile young souls can't stay out of trouble (or in their clothes) no matter how hard they may try. These South American lovelies are resolved to the torturous confines of this wretched South American penal institution, where dire sadism, sexualised degradation, and forced sex are proudly presented in place of palliative justice. Indeed, if these sweaty, splayed lovelies are lucky enough to avoid the torture chamber, it will only be because they've bravely bartered their beautiful bods or submitted to the wanton Sapphic desires of the prison's dizzy Marilyn Monroe-esque nurse.

It's not always cruddy in the hoosegow, though. Don't forget that female prisoners get to shower together as a means of bonding. Here, a multitude of them regularly get lathered up against each other while squealing, giggling and wiggling a whole lot. Far from a sausage party, Oswaldo saw to it that few nude dudes appeared in front of his camera in this onerous ode to female slavery.

What world is this? This is a trashy, mean-spirited reality where straight razors are smuggled inside tight feminine buttholes, severed penis is fed to dogs, raspberry pudding can throw one into rapturous delight, ferocious cat fights happen for no discernible reason, outdoor gymnastics are done in the nude, dildos are passed around from cell to cell, prison riots are quelled by blowing the inmates clothes right off of them with pressurised water, pineapples are utilised inappropriately, and rich dykes are always tickled to purchase a foxy incarcerated bitch to use as a personal plaything.

The talent are uniformly stunning (with the exception of a vile lunch-lady), but bad dubbing transforms already ludicrous dialogue into nearly transcendental camp. Sure they're flippin' hot, but the performances range from the mediocre to the downright vaudevillian. And good taste and restraint? They're totally alien concepts – as witnessed in the final grotesque reel of the film when female escapees bust into a house and sexually abuse a young boy whom they force to witness the murder of his mother and the castration of his father. A WIP movie where the lusting, busting inmates are also kiddie-fiddlers? We are through the looking glass here, people. Pure trash.

The abuse of the innocent isn't the only cultural sacred cow gutted and bled out; also present are some frankly jaw-dropping racial stereotypes. We're talking Mammies and black guys eating watermelons. Is there any wonder this movie was banned for decades in the UK and given an X-rating in the US?

In order for depraved and cringe-inducing material of this variety to work as well as it does, a filmmaker must be shameless and unapologetic, and Oswaldo De Oliveira fits the bill.

With the end of the military regime and the introduction of hardcore porno, by the mid-1980s the pornochanchada market had been dealt a severe death blow. It was an all-too-familiar decline to fans of the American sexploitation genre, which suffered similarly in the early 70s when triple-X fare such as *Deep Throat* (1972) made its orifice-packed presence known.

Yes, the degenerate chada sex movie era had come to an unceremonial close, but to the majority of English-only speakers worldwide, Brazilian softcore sex cinema is only in recent years being presented, hungrily unwrapped, and gobbled up by a whole new generation of cult film fans.

***This essay originally appeared in the Arrow Video edition of* Bare Behind Bars.**

YOU BETTER WATCH OUT

Kim Newman on Christmas Horror

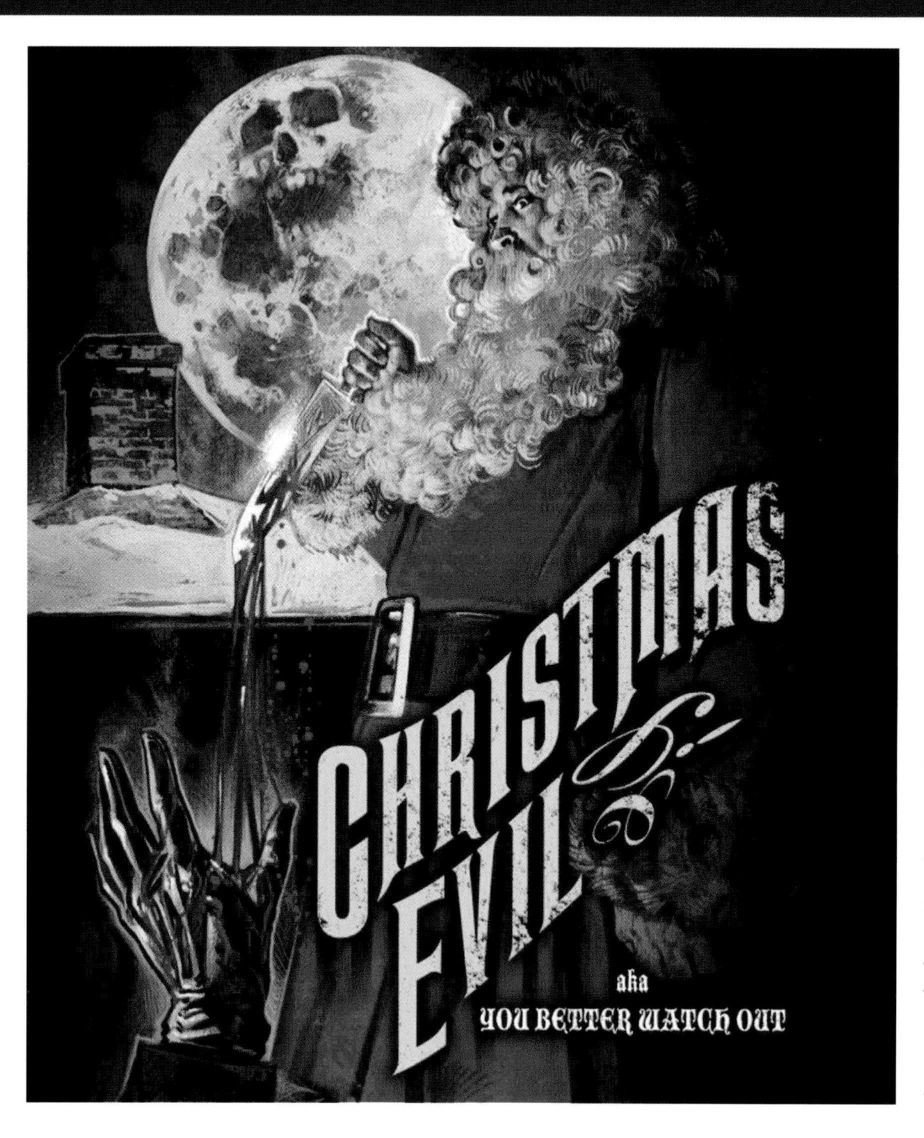

Artwork by Graham Humphreys

Charles Dickens' *A Christmas Carol* (1843), taking cues from German festival practices imported to Britain by Prince Albert, more or less established the institution of Christmas as celebrated in Britain and America. It's often forgotten that the novella is as much concerned with the excluded, the miserable, the emotionally poverty-stricken and the dead as it is with merry-makers, puddings and parties. "Every fool who prattles of Christmas should be buried with a sprig of holly through his own heart," sneers Ebenezer Scrooge. Regardless of the never-quite-convincing happy ending, the regularly filmed tale is responsible for the association of Yuletide with ghosts and the gruesome. Though the term 'Dickensian Christmas' came to be associated with holly and family gatherings and a happy exchange of presents, *A Christmas Carol* also sets its most depressing moments – Scrooge's vision of his unloved, lonely death, picked over by scavengers – at Christmas. Dickens' last (unfinished) novel, *The Mystery of Edwin Drood* (1870) contains a potent antidote to the nostalgic glow of *Carol* as a derelict woman passes around a succession of institutions on Christmas Day, forever shut out of any hope of cheer.

In the 1890s, M.R. James, provost of Eton, read his ghost stories aloud to the pupils as a Christmas treat; and, in the 1970s, the BBC picked up the tradition by presenting an annual adaptation of James in a slot known as *A Ghost Story for Christmas*, which slipped a few quiet chills and a strange sense of *fin-de-siècle* despair into a schedule otherwise concerned with Christmas episodes of soaps and sit-coms and the regular Morecambe and Wise special. The use of holiday trappings for a horror movie made John Carpenter's *Halloween* (1978) a hit, but the genre got round to its own scary holiday only after it had deployed tinsel and cheer for contrast in Theodore Gershuny's *Night of the Full Dark Moon* (1972, aka *Silent Night, Bloody Night*) and Bob Clark's *Black Christmas* (1974). The twentieth century, purely cinematic, equivalent of *A Christmas Carol* is Frank Capra's dark-hued masterwork *It's a Wonderful Life* (1946), another work whose hard-won happy ending does not really detract from the long, miserable path taken to get there. One of the most referenced and quoted movies of all time, *It's a Wonderful Life* has come to stand for Christmas and, as such, has featured in many works that set out to attack the institution with a savagery unmediated by Capra's bedrock sense of community and family. A more elaborate, horrific revision of Capra's tone is Joe Dante's *Gremlins* (1984), a gleeful trashing of everything America holds sacred about Christmas, which it conflates with the orgiastic abandon of a

Roman Saturnalia.

Because he is the figure who encapsulates all modern meanings of Christmas, even taking aboard the holiday's pre-Christian pagan aspects as a winter solstice festival, Santa Claus – aka Father Christmas, Saint Nick, Kris Kringle, etc. – has come in for a lot of grief in anti-Christmas movies. Santa has been forced to duel demons in the Mexican *Santa Claus* (1959), abducted by aliens in *Santa Claus Conquers the Martians* (1964), evicted by Rossano Brazzi in *The Christmas That Almost Wasn't* (*Il Natale che quasi non fu*, 1966), got mixed up in a drug bust in *The French Connection* (1971), zombified by a master villain from the future and gunned down by Tim Thomerson in *Trancers* (1984) and abducted by Jack Skellington in *The Nightmare Before Christmas* (1993). The most excessive anti-Santa movie is the cheapjack British slasher picture *Don't Open Till Christmas* (1984), in which a knife-wielding maniac (Alan Lake), traumatised because he literally saw Mama kissing Santa Claus, murders a succession of deadbeats and winos dressed up as Father Christmas. Even supposedly pro-Santa films – the ghastly *Santa Claus*, the surprisingly dour *One Magic Christmas* (both 1985), the negligible *Ernest Saves Christmas* (1988) and the smug *The Santa Clause* (1994) – make a fairly feeble case for this beloved old figure of universal benevolence and charity. It is no surprise, therefore, that Saint Nick should strike back, creating the busiest of all Christmas-themed horror sub-genre movies, the psycho Santa slasher film. Many children are disturbed by the whole idea of an all-powerful character who can get into their house at night and knows everything about them, and many versions of the tradition[1] have a nasty moral undertone, with Santa punishing bad children as determinedly as he rewards good ones. "He knows when you've been bad or good," runs the song 'Santa Claus is Coming to Town', "so be good for goodness sake."

Obviously, the idea of Father Christmas as a homicidal maniac strikes a deep chord, for it has been used over and over again. The perfect touchstone of the genre is the first episode of Freddie Francis's *Tales from the Crypt* (1972), adapted from a horror comic by Johnny Craig ('All Through the House', *The Vault of Horror*, 1954). Joan Collins has just bludgeoned her husband to death under the Christmas tree

1 - The folkloric version of the myths of Santa Claus and Father Christmas, who were once less interchangeable than they have become, was set in stone by the poem 'A Visit From St. Nicholas' (1823), more commonly known as 'Twas the Night Before Christmas'. Published anonymously, it is generally taken to be the work of Clement Clarke Moore, though a case has also been made for Henry Livingstone Jr.

when an escaped madman dressed as Santa begins to terrorise the neighbourhood. Robert Zemeckis remade 'All Through the House' in 1989, as the pilot for the *Tales from the Crypt* TV series, before defecting to the tinsel side of the holiday in *The Polar Express* (2004) and directing a CGI 3D stab at *A Christmas Carol* (2009). More psycho Santas turn up in *The Silent Partner* (1978), with Christopher Plummer as an especially fiendish bank robber in Father Christmas drag; the sorority-set slasher *To All a Goodnight* (1980), which features several red-suited madmen; the obscure anthology *Campfire Tales* (1991), in which an axe-wielding 'Satan' Claws punishes a wicked youth; the franchise-spawning *Silent Night, Deadly Night* (1984), which was oddly controversial; *3615 code Père Noël* (1989), a French template for the less horrific *Home Alone* (1990); and an increasingly demonic run of revisionist myths, *Santa's Slay* (2005), *Rare Exports* (2010) and *Saint* (*Sint*, 2010).

The greatest of the cycle is Lewis Jackson's *You Better Watch Out* (1980, aka *Christmas Evil*), with Brandon Maggart as the most sympathetic of the psycho Santas. A put-upon employee of a rapacious toy company, Harry Stadling (Maggart) lives for Christmas and seems to be the only person in snowbound New York actually to believe in goodwill rather than greed. All year Harry keeps tabs on the local children to see if they've been naughty or nice and, on Christmas Eve, driven mad by the cynical exploitation he sees all around, he gets into his padded red suit and takes to the streets as a pro-Noël vigilante. Besides giving away toys embezzled from his employers to a group of handicapped kids, Maggart uses a lead soldier to gouge out the eye of a Christmas-hating lout and manages to charm children even while he is killing their rotten father with a sharp ornament. This odd mix of psycho wish-fulfilment, urban sleaze and strange innocence climaxes with a touch of *Miracle on 34th Street* (1947) as Maggart's van crashes off an embankment during a police chase and takes to the skies, flying Northwards while sleigh bells jingle on the soundtrack. Jackson's movie, produced by toy tycoon Ed Pressman, is still underrated, though its admirers include John Waters, who said "I wish I had kids. I'd make them watch it every year, and if they didn't like it, they'd be punished."[2]

---

2 - John Waters, 'Why I Love Christmas', National Lampoon, December 1985; reprinted in *Crackpot: The Obsessions of John Waters* (Fourth Estate, 1988).

The celebration of Christmas as decreed by 'Twas the Night Before Christmas', Charles Dickens, Norman Rockwell (and the Coca-Cola company) and Walt Disney Enterprises is for many a tyrannical regime, emphasising the shortfall of their own family lives (or lack thereof). Despite the good-cheer around the Cratchit table, this fantasy Christmas is available only to those who have the money (and room) for a full-sized tree and a turkey dinner for the whole family. Much of the appeal of Christmas-themed horror is that this illusion is shredded, and those smug, mostly well-off celebrants are assaulted by primal forces, be they gremlins or Santa psychos, which embody the resentment that must be felt towards them by audiences who, even subliminally, cannot look at an idealised representation of Christmas without sparking associative thoughts of malice, horror and shivers. The strength of Jackson's film is that it takes this Scrooge-like mean-spiritedness and despair as a given, and then struggles hard to come round to the notion of Christmas as a time of giving and forgiving and the truly miraculous.

***This essay originally appeared in the Arrow Video edition of* Christmas Evil.**

ENOUGH IS NEVER ENOUGH

Joel Harley on Food Horror

Artwork by Gary Pullin

"Smooth. It tastes real good. Tasty. Sweet. Whatever that could be, it's mighty good."

When a mysterious white, unctuous goo begins to ooze from the very Earth in Larry Cohen's *The Stuff* (1985), man's first instinct is to eat the stuff and market it as a fabulous new dessert sensation. The flaw in this thinking is revealed when those who consume it are turned into rabid stuff-hungry zombies. Well, if you will insist on eating any old crap you might find growing out of the Earth's various orifices, this sort of thing is going to keep happening. It's like the British horsemeat scandal all over again.

But then, folk in horror and cult cinema have a curious knack for eating the inedible. From dangerous dessert sensations through to awful overeating and earlobes in the custard, the misuse and abuse of food is a powerful tool in horror filmmaking. At its most base level, the manipulation of food for nefarious purposes is an easy way to revolt and disgust one's audience; a nifty short cut to the gag reflex. It's no coincidence that the master of horror himself, Alfred Hitchcock, had a complicated relationship with food, using it to great effect in his movies, from *Rope* (1948) - where a meal was famously served on the same trunk which held a dead body - to *Psycho* (1960). A famous yo-yo dieter, the director suffered bouts of self-loathing followed by periods of overeating. He also suffered from a curious food-related phobia himself. "I'm frightened of eggs," Hitch once told an interviewer, "have you ever seen anything more revolting than an egg yolk breaking and spilling its yellow liquid?" Well, sure, when you put it like that...

In 1922, cinema's love-hate relationship with food began, with F.W Murnau's *Nosferatu, eine Symphonie des Grauens*. Vampires had been around long before then, but Murnau's unofficial adaptation of Bram Stoker's *Dracula* (1897) was the first to bring the bloodsuckers to the big screen. As Count Orlok's rat-toothed, bat-eared agent of the undead suckled his way to horror infamy, so the first course was served. While the consumption of blood is more intimate than the horrors offered by Cohen and his Stuff, its effects are no less catastrophic. Both are an extremely addictive substance, for one thing, turning those who might partake into a sort of vampire. There's a sexual element to bloodsucking that, while very much downplayed in *The Stuff*, isn't entirely removed from Cohen's use of imagery and biology. The B-movie master and his special effects men couldn't have failed to notice the Stuff's resemblance to a certain white, micro-orga(ni)sm-packed goo very much instrumental to human (and otherwise) reproduction. Ahem. But enough is enough of that!

As the Stuff breeds quasi-zombies, so we must note that the living dead are at least as important to horror cinema as the vampire. George A. Romero was the first to depict ravenous stomach- and brain-eating with his zombies in his seminal *Night of the Living Dead* (1968); whilst the flesh-munching continued unabated in follow-ups *Dawn of the Dead* (1978) and *Day of the Dead* (1985). "Choke on 'em!" shouts *Day of the Dead*'s Captain Rhodes in the sub-genre's greatest kill sequence of all time. Should have stuck with the Stuff. It's much harder to choke on goo. Not that the fellow on the film's poster seems to be having much trouble with that, the Stuff clogging his eyeballs and throat as he clutches his face in terror. There's a homage to *The Blob* (1958) there too, that sentient creeping, leaping, gliding, sliding hunk of goo surely being among Cohen's many B-movie influences.

Granted, the 'zombies' of *The Stuff* are considerably less dead than most, but the mob mentality remains the same. Even man's best friend falls before the sinister cravings that the Stuff brings with it. "I'll get you some more!" one poor fellow cries, savaged by his own dog when he runs out of dessert. Scenes in which a family pursue their non-Stuff eating son are reminiscent of the *Star Trek: The Next Generation* episode 'The Game' (1991), in which the controversial Wesley Crusher attempts to fend off his videogame-addicted friends and crewmates. There's more than a nod to the Pod People of *Invasion of the Body Snatchers* (1956 and 1978) too, with the family all being very insistent that their reluctant relative 'join' them forthwith.

It's all the fault of the Stuff of course, the vile-but-delicious goo being responsible for turning the people into zombies. In a similar way, bad food turns people into zombies in *Degrassi of the Dead* (2007) – thanks, genetically-modified vegetables – and the short films *It Came from the Fridge* (2004) and *Sick Day* (2006). As with *Dawn of the Dead*, *The Stuff* is a satirical critique upon America's consumerist culture, particularly inspired by the dangers of smoking, drinking and overeating. With a series of slick spoof television adverts, iconic packaging for the Stuff itself, and a catchy tagline ("Enough is never enough!"), Cohen uses his B-movie platform to discuss such pertinent issues as addiction, consumerist greed and corporate hunger. These, he suggests, are the side effects of putting such crap inside one's body, and this is the government's indifference when it is revealed to be less than healthy. Certain foods might indeed be bad for our health, but would the powers that be care, so long as it sells? As *Super Size Me* (2004) proved, the big corporations are happy to take our money, side effects – obesity and zombification included – be damned! Are you eating it? Or is it eating you? Who cares: just re-market, dilute it and call it 'The Taste' instead. It worked just fine for Menthols, lite beer and Diet Coke.

As important a cinematic movement as vampires and zombies is the lowly cannibal. Tobe Hooper's *The Texas Chain Saw Massacre* (1974) is king of the backwoods cannibal movie – its 'head cheese' the sub-genre's signature dish. As Leatherface butchers a poor innocent hippy with a massive sledgehammer and impales another on a meat hook, there's even a little guilt, as we recognise in that the way we farm and treat our animal neighbours; ethics be damned, the suspicion is that mankind would probably eat just about anything, if it tasted good enough. We are a species that invented foie gras, after all. Is there nothing mankind won't harvest and eat? Dress it up all you like, with your fava beans and your nice Chianti, but something still died to get on that plate of yours. This thought is taken to its mass-produced, marketed and inevitable conclusion with the accidental cannibalism of *Soylent Green* (1973). It's people, people!

There are plenty of movie monsters and villains that would use food as their *modus operandi*, then, but there are also the many occasions in which it is used as a tool to revolt and terrify, tickling our gag reflex and making us feel more than a little ill. Most notably, there's the 'gluttony' segment of David Fincher's *Se7en* (1995), which should put all but the most hardened horror fan off of spaghetti for a very long time. A cult gem, *Feed* (2005) depicts the crimes of a man who feeds his victims to death, while Peter Jackson's *Braindead* (1992, aka *Dead Alive*) gives us a revolting dinner sequence in which our hero's zombified mother, struggling with a bowl of custard, winds up eating her own decayed ear. There's maggoty steak in *Poltergeist* (1982), Linda Blair spewing pea soup everywhere in *The Exorcist* (1973), and perhaps the most unthinkable meal of all in Pier Paolo Pasolini's infamous De Sade adaptation *Salò, or the 120 Days of Sodom* (*Salò o le 120 giornate di Sodoma*, 1975). At the same end of the spectrum, witness the delightful dinner chomped by Divine at the climax of John Waters' *Pink Flamingos* (1972). Or don't, if you value not being sick.

Elsewhere, Japanese and South Korean cinema continues to upset stomachs everywhere with some of the most horrifying (mis)uses of food in history. In the modern classic *Oldboy* (*Oldeuboi*, 2003), there's anti-hero Dae-su Oh, eating a live octopus. Meanwhile, in the disturbing and terrifying *Dumplings* (*Jiao zi*, 2004), it's revealed that the secret to staying young is the liberal consumption of human foetuses. It may well give you cause to think twice about that side order of dumplings with your takeaway dinner. The food bites back rather more literally in Noboru Iguchi's altogether less serious *Dead Sushi* (*Deddo sushi*, 2012), in which the sushi in a small Japanese hotel comes to life and begins attacking the guests. The zombie apocalypse has rarely looked so tasty.

Back to the US, and there's a similar effect at play in *Poultrygeist: Night of the Chicken Dead* (2006) when an army-themed fast food joint unwittingly builds an outlet on an Indian burial ground. Like *The Stuff*, *Poultrygeist* is a gruesome skewering of the fast food industry, with greedy restaurateurs and soulless corporate types coming in for the sort of battering that only Troma can deliver.

Next on the menu is *Attack of the Killer Tomatoes!* (1978) and its sequels, *Return of the Killer Tomatoes!*

The Stuff

(1988), starring a young George Clooney, *Killer Tomatoes Strike Back!* (1991) and *Killer Tomatoes Eat France!* (1992). Here, sentient man-eating tomatoes threaten the very fate of the world. Meanwhile, the *Child's Play* franchise (1988-2013) gets a food-based rip-off in Charles Band's *The Gingerdead Man* (2005) and its multiple sequels. The first film stars Gary Busey as killer Millard Findlemeyer, re-incarnated as a gingerbread man in order to wreak vicious vengeance upon those he holds responsible for his own death.

Less sentient, but often mentioned in the same breath as *The Stuff*, is James M. Muro's *Street Trash*, the 1987 shocker in which a liquor store owner finds a case of a drink called Tenafly Viper in his cellar. Selling it to winos at one dollar a bottle, he unwittingly causes a literal hobo meltdown, with those who drink it turning into puddles of human goo. Like *The Stuff*, it's unabashedly cult, mixing its practical effects with a cheap punk vibe and crude satire. Where Cohen aims his satirical scope at the Fat Cats at the top end of the corporate ladder, Muro's film is much more street level, the 'trash' of the title referring to the disenfranchised working class who might fall victim to this poison drink.

Cohen himself would go on to use dodgy dinners to repel his audiences after *The Stuff*, most notably in his script for *Captivity* (2007), in which Elisha Cuthbert's kidnapped model is force-fed a number of repellent courses (including maggots, a hand and – so she thinks – her own dog) through a funnel. Unlike the kitsch and fun *The Stuff*, *Captivity* leaves a bad taste in the mouth, thanks to its mean spirit and predictable twist, and has very little of use to say. The influence of Cohen and his Stuff, nevertheless, remains notable. It can be seen in at least two episodes of *Futurama* (1999-2013). The first of these, 'Fry and the Slurm Factory' (1999), sees young man-out-of-time Fry discovers that his favourite drink – the titular Slurm – is in fact the product of a gigantic slug-like creature. *The Stuff* is directly referenced in Fry's exclamation of "soon enough is not soon enough!" echoing the famous "enough is never enough" line of the Stuff's commercials. It's worth noting that the colourful writing on the Slurm cans bears more than a passing resemblance to the pots of Stuff available from all good supermarkets. In a later episode, entitled 'The Problem with the Popplers' (2000), the crew of Planet Express find a delicious new food called popplers growing on a faraway planet. As the popplers become an insanely popular, marketable and profitable taste sensation (sound familiar?) it is revealed that they are not only alive, but the product of a furious alien dictator. Whoops.

Thankfully, just as the blood and gore of Romero's *Night of the Living Dead* and Hitchcock's *Psycho* was mere chocolate syrup and Linda Blair's vomit was but pea soup, so the real-life stuff of *The Stuff* wasn't quite as nasty as the film would have one believe. Buckets of Häagen-Dazs ice cream was used for filming purposes, in addition to various yogurts, and – in one scene – the foam from a fire extinguisher. Only really a nightmare if you happen to be lactose intolerant, then, or have a fear of brain freeze.

From head cheese through to plates of spaghetti, a live octopus and cans of Slurm, we've seen all manner of monstrous meal consumed onscreen over the years. This has served many a purpose, whether it be to terrify, disgust or satirise, but... but it could never happen, right? Entertaining as *The Stuff* might be, it's always been particularly peculiar that its characters should start tucking into creamy muck straight from the ground. That is, after all, how we ended up with giant rats, wasps and worms in the utterly ridiculous *The Food of the Gods* (1976). Well, maybe it wouldn't happen quite like that, but Dad's description of the Stuff sounds awfully familiar. "There's something alive in yogurt. It's called benign bacteria. We eat plenty of things that are still alive that are good for us. All micro-organisms move." Remember that, next time you're glugging from a friendly pot of Bifidus Digestivum-infested yogurt.

Enough may never be enough, but I think I'm full for now, thanks.

***This essay originally appeared in the Arrow Video edition of* The Stuff.**

The Stuff

TEENAGE MUTANT COMET ZOMBIES

James Oliver on Empty City Sci-Fi

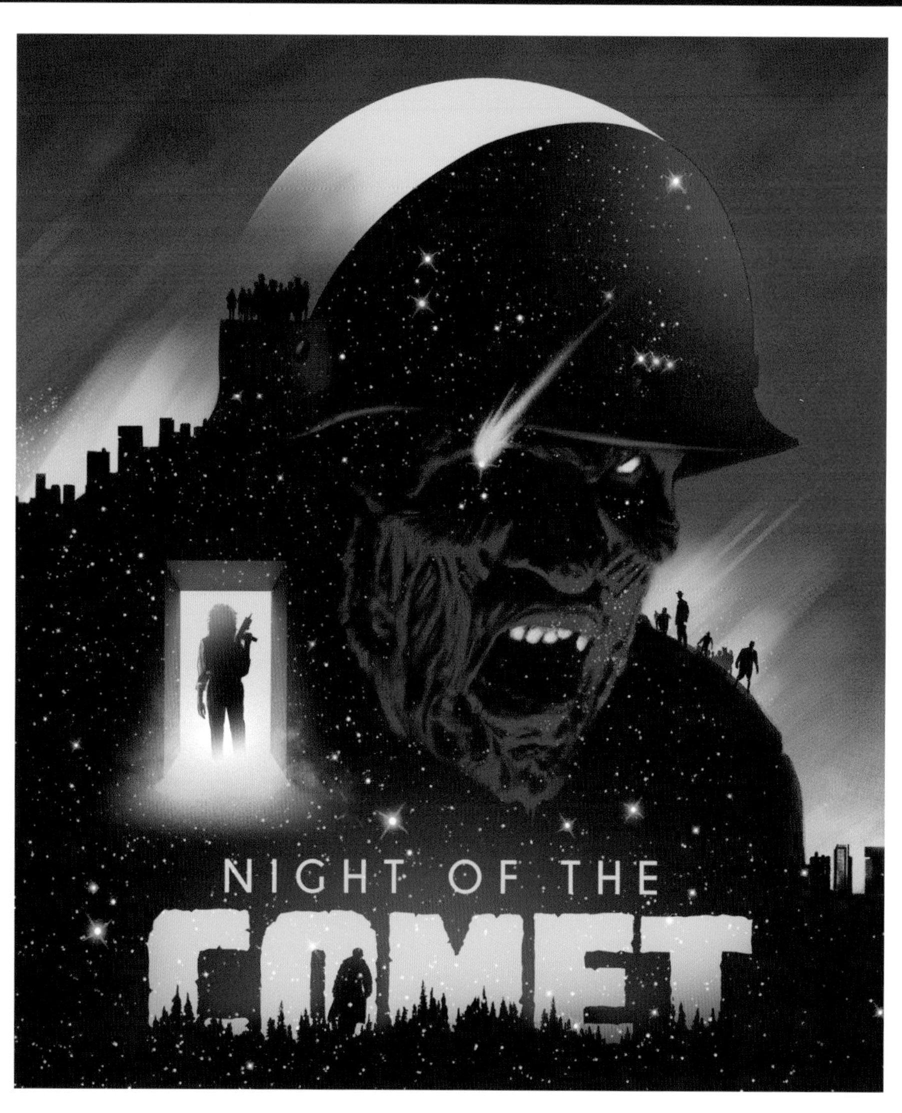

Artwork by Gary Pullin

The end of the world has been nigh for centuries now, if not millennia. It would take a veritable library to record how this perennial anxiety has been reflected in art works across the centuries, in paintings, plays, poems, novels, symphonies and songs. Inevitably, it features in films as well.

But in all those iterations, whether musical, literary or visual, has the twilight of humanity been faced with the perkiness of *Night of the Comet* (1984)? This might be the most purely entertaining depiction of the aftermath of a catastrophic event, not just in movie history but possibly... well, ever; those medieval Doom paintings are hardly known for their levity.

Then again, Thom Eberhardt, writer and director of *Night of the Comet*, had an advantage over the pessimists of the Middle Ages. He was inspired more by affection than by fear, informed by his liking for the type of film that begins with 'The End'. World civilisation had already ended many times in movies when he came to write *Night of the Comet*; Eberhardt decided his film would pay tribute to one of his favourite subsets of the apocalypse genre, the 'Empty City' film.

The conventions of the 'Empty City' film are simple: there's been some kind of catastrophic event and places that previously teemed with life (mainly, as you will have guessed, cities) are now inhabited only by the few souls who survived, for whatever reason. Those survivors have to wrestle with the consequences of what happened. And, usually, with each other.

The very first film to be set in the aftermath of some kind of nuclear bomb, *Five* (1951) – "Four Men and One Woman are the Last Five People on Earth!" shrieked the poster – shows the survivors trying to create a new Eden, with one character predictably playing the serpent. *The World, the Flesh and the Devil* (1959) – "The Most Unusual Story Ever Told!", to continue with poster tag lines – is set in an empty New York, and touches on racial prejudice as Mel Ferrer objects to Harry Belafonte propagating the human race with white woman Inger Stevens.

Given that films of this type could be made on the cheap, with few cast members and some easlly-snatched location work, it's hardly surprising that it was a sub-genre beloved of that notorious cheapskate Roger Corman: from *Day the World Ended* in 1955 – tagline: "HUMAN EMOTIONS STRIPPED RAW! The terrifying story that COULD COME TRUE!" – to *Gas! Or It Became Necessary to Destroy the World in*

Order to Save It in 1970 – "Invite a few friends over to watch the end of the world!"– he could proudly boast that no other director had ended life as we know it more often.

More specific influences on *Night of the Comet* were *The Day of the Triffids* (1963) and *The Omega Man* (1971). *The Day of the Triffids* – "BEWARE THE TRIFFIDS... they grow... know... walk... talk... stalk... and KILL!" – much altered from John Wyndham's original 1951 novel, features a peculiar meteor shower that renders most of the world blind thus sending society into a tailspin. (It also features – per the poster – homicidal plants that can move about, but that's not germane right now). *The Omega Man* – "The last man alive... is not alone!" – was taken from Richard Matheson's 1954 novel *I Am Legend* (previously filmed as *The Last Man on Earth* in 1964, and later as *I Am Legend* in 2007) and features Charlton Heston as one of the few survivors of a devastating plague, who battles nocturnal vampire mutants created by the infection.

Night of the Comet – whose tagline, just to be fair, was "It was the last thing on earth they ever expected" – hardly conceals its roots. Indeed, it actively celebrates its awareness of film history, opening with the sort of portentous narration that graced many a low budget B-movie of the 1950s and nodding to film culture by making a plot point of the pristine print of *It Came from Outer Space* (1953) that Larry the projectionist sends to a collector for copying.

But there's so much more to the film than a game of spot-the-influence: "Oh look – there's a nod to *Dawn of the Dead*". For a start, it's a film with ideas, and concerns, of its own to explore. Just as the classic science fiction films of the 1950s reflected (some of) the disquiet of the era in which they were made – when, amongst other things, scientists had invented weapons that might destroy the world and when ideological conflicts threatened a flashpoint which might cause such things to be used – so *Night of the Comet* touches on some of the anxieties of the 1980s.

This was, let's not forget, a time when the Cold War was at the frostiest it had been for decades. Ronald Reagan's first term had seen a more confrontational approach to the Communist bloc – 'the Evil Empire' – than the détente of the 1960s and '70s, and a ready deployment of nuclear weapons. It's an element that invariably gets airbrushed out of nostalgic surveys of the decade but anyone who was young at the time – even kids as self-absorbed as Reggie and Sam in the movie – grew up with the distinct possibility of Mutually Assured Destruction lurking at the back of their mind.

So *Night of the Comet* is much more than the airheads-survive-the-apocalypse movie that it might have been. Eberhardt has stated that one of his starting points was listening to two ordinary teenage girls as they struggled to confront the sheer, terrifying enormity of what nuclear holocaust actually meant. Although Eberhardt treats the subject in a more-or-less light-hearted way and filters it by way of homages to previous genre films, *Night of the Comet* is alert to those same, fundamental fears, most obviously in Samantha's tear-filled recognition that everyone, including the boy she had her eye on, is dead.

Cold War sensibilities are displayed in other areas too. Consider the principal human villains, the bloodsucking scientists who lurk in the underground bunker. Dressed in drab, conformist grey jumpsuits (such a contrast to the vibrant colours favoured by the Belmont sisters) and guided by a bland utilitarian philosophy that makes no regard for freedom or individuality ("Whatever the majority wants," as Audrey White sardonically notes), they represent the sort of hive mind mentality that was so often associated with communism during those years.

There's a brief, and rather more direct, acknowledgement of a real-world Cold War issue. Daddy Belmont is said to be "in Honduras", fighting the Sandinistas; these were the leaders of El Salvador at the time. Believing them to be communist stooges, the United States, working from bases in Honduras, actively sought to destabilise the Sandinistas, a campaign widely criticised for its questionable legality and brutality.

Given her father's involvement in Latin America, it places an interesting slant on her relationship with Hector, a Latino. As they bicker in the radio station, she brings an unmistakable racial edge to the argument: his gun, apparently, is only good for "date night in the barrio". Was it only gunplay she learnt from her father? That she is able to overcome any prejudices is to her great credit, and to the film's – Hollywood traditionally fights shy of inter-ethnic couples.

But ultimately, no matter the political/thematic backdrop, this is a film driven by its characters. It is those characters who anchor the film, who give the film the heart which makes it so much more than a string of homages: the fun is balanced by the genuine emotional connection the audience develops with our heroines.

True, Reggie and Sam do not, at first, seem to be obvious candidates to weather the post-apocalyptic storm: their horizons initially stretch no further than the mall. When faced with the once-in-a-lifetime, whole world-uniting experience of watching the comet, Reggie stays inside: as Larry, her boyfriend says, "It's not like you can't see it on television". (But then, most of the people who survive the comet are, almost by definition, slackers, the sort of folks who don't regard the whole once-in-a-lifetime, whole world-uniting experience thing as a big deal.)

The older generation are certainly not impressed by the kids: "Don't be an over-achiever," Reggie's boss tells her. "You'll fit in better with your age group." Except that the film takes great delight in proving these people wrong. It builds towards the new family unit, with Reggie playing the concerned mother, keen to instil the importance of obeying the traffic signals into her brood, but she and her sister have both proved their mettle before then. Not only are both proficient in using automatic weaponry (thanks Daddy!) but both are better suited to surviving the brave new world than most of the men – Reggie is too fly to be killed by the zombie in the alley, unlike poor old Larry.

Valley girls they might be, but the film paints both Reggie and her sister as brave and resourceful – it's Sam who rescues her sister from the bunker, while Hector does the dull, mechanical work of wiring up the explosives. And unlike so many male filmmakers, Eberhardt understand 'strong female characters' don't have to become warrior women – ass-kicking is only one of the many things they can do, and they'd rather go shopping anyway.

Even if they have the occasional ditzy moment, this is a very genuine portrayal of two teenage girls and the film likes both of them far too much to mock. Although much of the surface details date it to a very specific era – the tinny synth 'n' saxophone music and its tonsorial equivalents (that big hair!) make this primo '80s filmmaking – the heart of the film still feels fresh because its two lead characters are so well drawn, so well played and so damn likeable. It is to be regretted that neither Catherine Mary Stewart (Reggie) nor Kelli Maroney (Sam) ever had a script that allowed them to shine this brightly again (although no doubt genre fans will remember Stewart's turn in *The Last Starfighter*, another great sci-fi film from 1984, with great affection).

Intriguingly, for a film with such obvious antecedents, *Night of the Comet* has proved to be extremely influential, inspiring a number of other films which attempt the same trick of placing unlikely characters inside a foursquare genre format and sweetening the mix with humour. Most obviously, there's *Tremors* (1990), in which a couple of good ol' boys do their best to deal with an underground monster straight out of a '50s creature feature. Writer-director Joss Whedon has professed admiration for *Night of the Comet* too, citing it as partial inspiration for *Buffy the Vampire Slayer* (1992 on film, 1997-2003 on television).

More recently, there's *Shaun of the Dead* (2004). It doesn't take much to see *Night of the Comet* as one of that film's (numerous) influences, most obviously in the graceful juggling of comedy, character moments, and genuine genre thrills. It's also possible to find trace elements of *Night of the Comet* in *28 Days Later* (2002); although a much more serious film – and one that shares some common influences (like *The Omega Man*) – it repeats moments from Eberhardt's film (an abandoned car in the middle of the road, for instance) and builds to a confrontation with malevolent authorities at a heavily militarised base. Hmm.

Such things are only to be expected of a film with such a pronounced cult following. If its smart, witty handling of the genre was a little too sophisticated to meet with general approval upon original release in 1984, then it has ensured a strong afterlife, and its reputation continues to grow. Far more than 'just' a pastiche, *Night of the Comet* both celebrates the genre and contributes to it, updating the concerns of the golden age science fiction films for a new era and a new generation. Far more importantly, it remains thoroughly entertaining; and in an age like ours, when the world again feels increasingly apocalyptic (war, terrorism, environmental collapse... take your pick), such things are welcome indeed.

***This essay originally appeared in the Arrow Video edition of* Night of the Comet.**

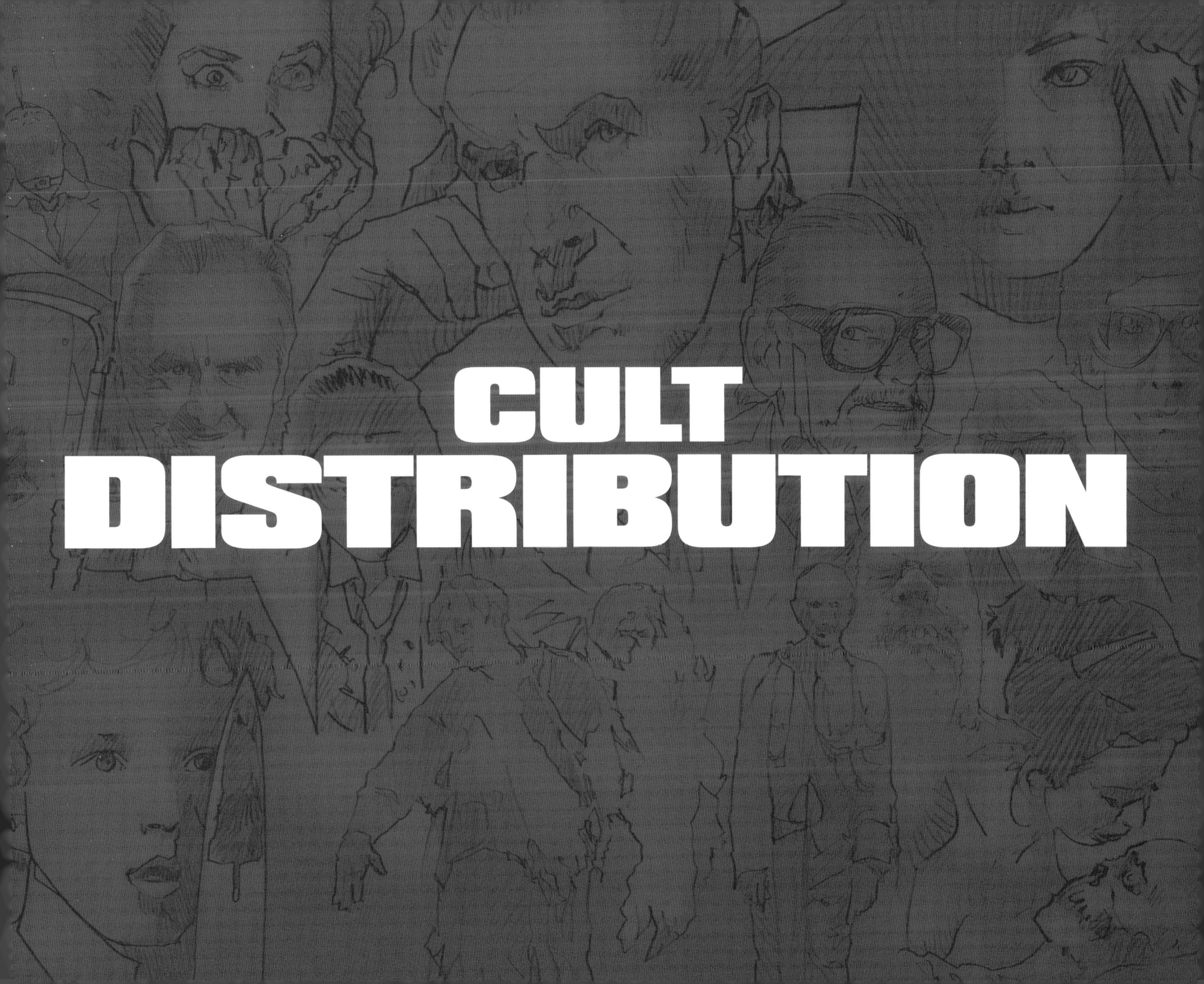
CULT
DISTRIBUTION

THE GOLDEN AGE OF EXPLOITATION

Robin Bougie on the Early Days of Cult Cinema

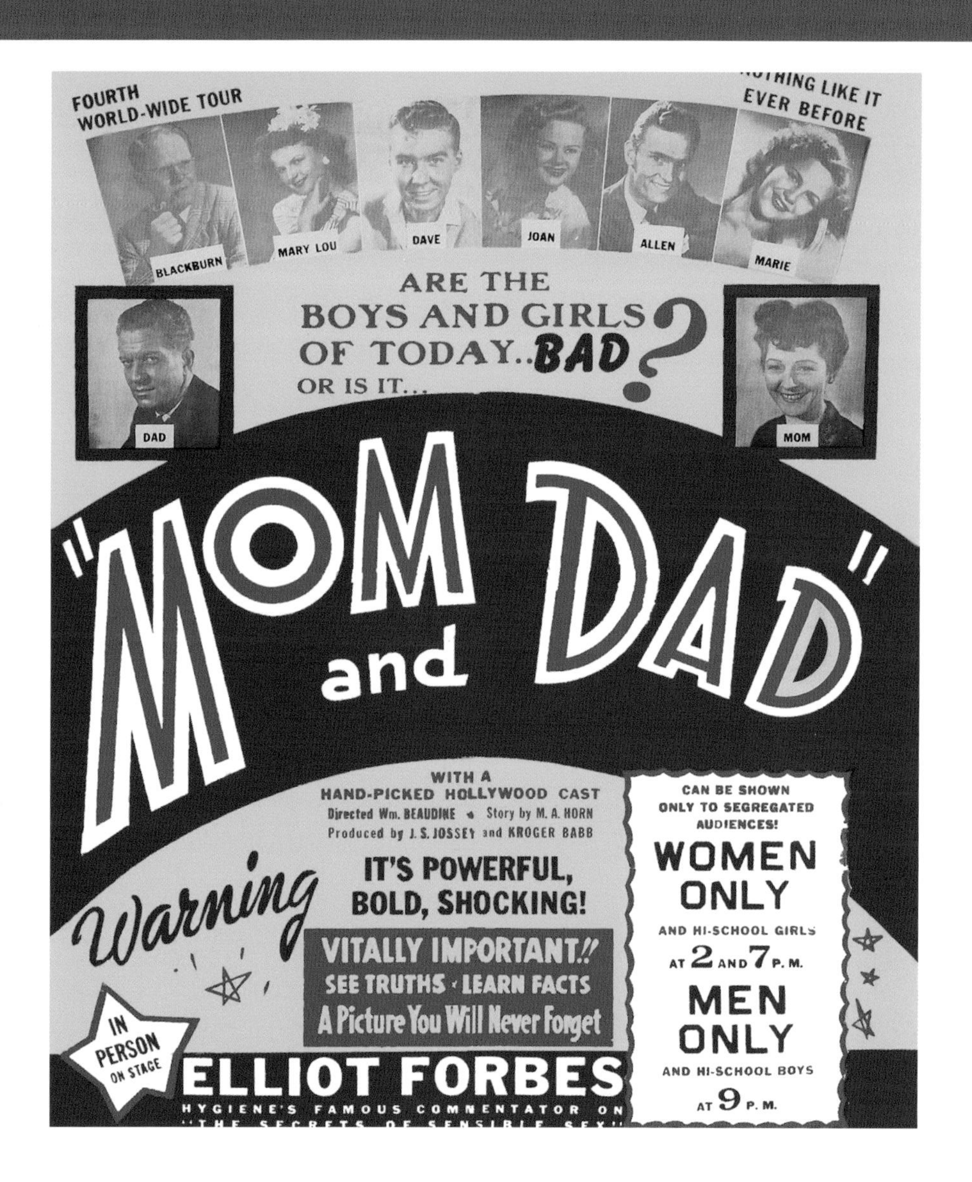

In the 2010 documentary *American Grindhouse*, film journalist Eric Schaefer aptly notes that "exploitation is as old as the movie itself", but the genre of 'exploitation', as film fans know it, really began on February 17th, 1930. Sure, there were roughly 10 years' worth of cinematic sleaze droplets that had fallen on an unsuspecting public up to that day – vintage movies like *Wild Oats*, *The Solitary Sin* (both 1919), *Pitfalls of Passion* and *Is Your Daughter Safe?* (both 1927). But it was 1930 when the floodgates opened and a wave of sin washed across the American plains, cascading out of every major city and town. Amazingly, that tidal wave of exploitation entertainment was birthed from the most unlikely of sources: censorship.

Or, more specifically, self-censorship. On February 17th 1930, Hollywood had created its own production code, the Motion Picture Production Code aka the Hays Code, and in doing so had effectively wrenched the reigns of censorial control away from church groups and various other institutions – both federal and private – that were looking to put an end to the filth that was "polluting the hearts and minds of all good Americans". In this act of distraction, a fertile ground was sown not for mainstream Hollywood (who had to formally submit every film they made to ensure they adhered to a list of strict DO NOTs and BE CAREFULs) but instead for a group of low budget exploitation roadshow producers. Unlike the rest of the industry, most of them did not operate out of California, but rather places like Texas, Florida, New Jersey and New York.

These filmmakers saw the Production Code list of verboten topics (white slavery, drunkenness, drug addiction, sympathetic depictions of the underworld, gambling, rape, nakedness, ridicule of the clergy, profane and vulgar language, miscegenation, wilful offence, and sex perversion) as their personal golden checklist in a bid to make money, and provide America what it was told it wasn't allowed to see. From 1931 to 1934 the increasingly frail economy during America's Great Depression meant that Hollywood studios were rarely seeing profits and cinemas were closing. The majors responded by offering double-bills, slashing prices and getting audiences to play games such as 'Screeno', a form of bingo that gave audiences the chance to win cash prizes. But the independents didn't need any of that. They had something the mainstream could no longer provide.

The working class men that openly defied the Production Code status quo were dubbed the "Forty Thieves", and they operated outside of the system while creating their own distribution network. They would take their movies around a depressed and impoverished country - in person - and set up at carnivals, cheap grindhouses, taverns, and anywhere else they could quickly get a crowd together using handbills and posters featuring promises of shocking, daring, and altogether true tales of vice and perversion!

There were the sex hygiene/childbirth/promiscuity/abortion movies such as *Damaged Lives* (1933), *The Road to Ruin*, *High School Girl*, *Modern Motherhood* (all 1934), *Damaged Goods* (1937), *Sex Madness* (1938), *Unborn Souls* (1939), *Birth of a Baby* (1940), *No Greater Sin* (1941), *Because of Eve* and *Street Corner* (both 1948).

There were the "shocking" drug movies like *Sinister Harvest* (1930), *Narcotic* (1933), *The Pace That Kills* (1935), *Reefer Madness*, *Marihuana* (both 1936), *Assassin of Youth* (1937), *Devil's Harvest* (1942), *Wild Weed* (aka *She Shoulda Said No!*) and *The Devil's Sleep* (both 1949).

The vice, prostitution and white slavery films such as *Reckless Decision* (1933), *Guilty Parents* (1934), *Gambling with Souls* (1936), *Slaves in Bondage*, *Smashing the Vice Trust* (both 1937), *The Wages of Sin* (1938), *Mad Youth* (1940), *Escort Girl* (1941), *Confessions of a Vice Baron* (1943) and *The Flesh Merchant* (1956).

The nudist movies like *Elysia (Valley of the Nude)*, *This Naked Age* (both 1933), *Unashamed: A Romance* (1938), *Garden of Eden* (1954), *The Naked Venus* (1959) and *Hideout in the Sun* (1960).

The burlesque pictures such as *Hollywood Revels* (1946), *Vegas Nights* (1948), *Midnight Frolics* (1949), *Everybody's Girl*, *Too Hot To Handle* (both 1950), *Love Moods*, *Lili's Wedding Night*, *Striptease Girl* (all 1952), *A Virgin in Hollywood* (1953), *Tijuana After Midnite*, *Varietease* (both 1954), *Teaserama* (1955) and *Buxom Beautease* (1956).

The 'exotics', which featured naked - or nearly-naked - native girls, such as *Virgins of Bali* (1932), *Inyaah (Jungle Goddess)* (1934, aka *Jungle Virgin*), *Angkor* (1935, aka *Forbidden Adventure*), *Jaws of the Jungle* (1936), *Devil Monster* (1946), *Curse of the Ubangi* (1946), *Outrages of the Orient* (1948 aka *Atrocities of the Orient*), *Karamoja* and *Mau-Mau* (both 1955).

Less common were underage marriage movies like *Child Bride* (1938), forced-sterilisation features like *Tomorrow's Children* (1934), artificial inseminationsploitation in *Test Tube Babies* (1948), lesbian cinema like *The Third Sex* (1934, aka *Children of Loneliness*), and unclassifiable weirdness such as *Maniac* (1934) – which featured a man eating a cat's eyeball – and the Lenny Bruce-scripted *Dance Hall Racket* (1953).

While the major film production houses in the 1930s had anywhere from 20 to 50 permanent executive and department heads, not to mention sometimes over a thousand employees per studio, the exploitation mavens often had anywhere from one to five people running the whole shebang, with anyone else who took part in the making of the movie totally free from an employee contract and hired purely for a basic wage on a per-picture basis. Their performers were generally less skilled than those found in Hollywood's output – usually up-and-comers looking to get work, or sometimes you would spot character actors and elderly stars that had fallen out of favour with the studios and had to slum it up to pay the bills. It didn't matter. In exploitation, it's the concept that sells the product, not the star power.

Budgets could be as low as $8,000 and as high as $25,000, but a large percentage of whatever money could be utilised went to the cost of film processing. Because money was often raised privately, budgets were threadbare and technological gimmicks like colour and widescreen were avoided. The large majority of vintage exploitation movies were black and white, shot with often stationary cameras using one or two – maybe three at the maximum – takes per scene. They employed minimal set design, and were filmed in five days or usually less, with burlesque films almost always shot in a single day.

A favourite and oft-used scam was to use the feature to panic and titillate the crowds about an issue of the day (venereal disease, sex addiction, pot, or what have you) and then sell them cheaply-produced pamphlets and tracts (known as pitchbooks) to put their mind at ease as they left the venue. The master of that ploy was the legendary Kroger Babb, who was responsible for the most successful exploitation film of the golden era, a 1945 childbirth movie known as *Mom and Dad*.

Billed as "America's fearless young showman", Babb sold *Mom and Dad* with some of the most professional hucksterism ever witnessed in the history of film promotion, impressing even his jaded contemporaries. Millions of men, women and teenagers saw this massively popular roadshow in screenings separated by gender, and it's been said that, during the time just after World War II, ol' Kroger had over 25 units on the road simultaneously, each presenting the evening's entertainment with its own 'Elliott Forbes', the "eminent hygiene commentator". He was a gentleman (usually an old out-of-work vaudeville comedian) with glasses and a lab coat who would instruct the audience to buy a booklet that cost "a mere dollar". The total cost of printing and binding the pitchbook was eight cents.

Incredibly, *Mom and Dad* was still playing drive-in dates well into the 1970s and was ultimately added to the National Film Registry in 2005. Some estimates place the film's total haul at $100 million smackeroonies. Sued over 400 times for the movie and unable to duplicate such vaunted success, a disappointed and cranky Babb later dropped out of exploitation filmmaking, and tried to get rich with a failed pyramid scheme called the Idea Factory and a wonky weight loss plan called the Astounding Swedish Ice Cream Diet. Neither caught on.

Producers regularly recycled characters, storylines, props, costumes, footage, and anything else they could from earlier efforts – including entire movies! "That was part of roadshow-ing," producer David F. Friedman noted in the 1989 documentary *Sex and Buttered Popcorn*. "You changed the title. You couldn't afford to make a new picture every three months, but you could afford a new main title. Nobody knew the difference. I never had anybody ask for their money back." Indeed, some movies were known over time by as many as five or six titles, allowing them to stay in circulation for decades.

Friedman came into his own more towards the end of roadshow distribution history, in the late 1950s and early 60s, but a fascinating lineage of B-movie grindhouse kings preceded him in the time of the Great Depression and beyond. Producers like J.D. Kendis (responsible for *Jaws of the Jungle* and *Slaves in Bondage*), Willis Kent (*Confessions of a Vice Baron*, *Lili's Wedding Night*), Dwaine Esper (*Maniac*, *Reefer Madness*, *Sex Madness*), S.S. Millard (*Is Your Daughter Safe?*), the Sonney family (*A Virgin in Hollywood*), and George Weiss (*Too Hot to Handle*, *Dance Hall Racket*).

One of the Forty Thieves had a very unique beginning. Gidney Talley was a Texas cinema chain owner who was approached by Universal Pictures one day in 1948. The Hollywood studio giant, greedily licking its chops while witnessing the amount of money that Babb was making with *Mom and Dad*, had produced a copycat picture called *Bob and Sally* (1948, aka *The Story of Bob and Sally*), which starred Gloria Marlen and Ralph Hodges. Universal executive Cliff

Work had really stuck his foot in it, producing an exploitation movie based around venereal disease, whoring, alcoholism and abortion, with the hopes that the Hays Code might look the other way. With the conservative Joseph I. Breen now the head of the Production Code office, however, they most certainly did not, leaving the discredited suit holding an expensive and unmarketable boondoggle.

Desperate to make anything back on *Bob And Sally* and save his job, Work dropped it in the lap of Talley for pennies on the dollar, and Talley marketed his new acquisition roadshow-style just as Babb had, except this time he could have a tagline boasting of "an all Hollywood cast!". He made massive profits, and would eventually join forces and create an exploitation huckster all-star team with Babb, Irwin Joseph, David Friedman and Floyd Lewis, forming the company known as Modern Film Distributors. One of their most successful releases, *Because of Eve*, would be the very first one to show full frontal nudity in domestic cinema. A year later Friedman would take the movie through New England, the most staunchly Catholic section of America. "I cleared over $150,000", Friedman boasted to film historian Eddie Muller in his 1996 book *Grindhouse*. "It was my biggest run ever."

The golden age exploitation movies shrouded their suggestive concepts and provocative imagery under the mantle of education and edification, a cautious ploy that was also later utilised in the early years of American hardcore pornography in the 1970s. This was pushed forward with a brief statement for the audience explaining the necessity of displaying a particular evil for the sake of helping the community know exactly what it is they *shouldn't* be doing. A little speech that was there to throw the law off and to allow the hang-wringers in the audience to feel better about witnessing moral transgressions. Having both a 'hot' and 'cold' edit of the movie in the truck of the car was found to be a smart move by directors through trial and error, who made use of this editing ploy to accommodate local censorship rules or taste and thereby play municipalities that might have been harder to penetrate in the quest of making a buck.

Even with those safeguards in place to keep Johnny Law at bay, it was common for local police to show up with a newspaper-worthy obscenity bust in mind. Spotters were employed, and the second word spread about a raid, the projectionist flew into action – making a few quick cuts on special flagged spots on the reel -- turning what would certainly be considered a 'dirty movie' (never blatant pornography, of course, but lurid for the time) into something that would end up putting the frustrated coppers to sleep. As soon as the flatfoots were gone, the 'square-up reel' came out (a safely guarded collection of racy, skin-filled footage), which never failed to satiate what would otherwise usually become a rowdy and unhappy crowd.

In 1954, the conservative head of the Production Code, Joseph Breen, retired. *Variety* noted "a decided tendency towards a broader, more casual approach" in the enforcement of the Code (case in point: the somewhat salacious Tennessee Williams adaptation *Baby Doll* getting passed and allowed to play cinemas in 1956) and, as the 1950s came to a close, the US Supreme court finally ruled that nudity was not obscene. They instead decided that material that catered to "prurient interest" was – which is, of course, much harder to prove – leaving plenty of room for filmmakers to skirt the issue. This legal development and hit films like *Some Like it Hot* (1959) and *Psycho* (1960) being released without code approval totally defanged the Production Code and saw Hollywood's self-censorship ease right off until the code was abandoned entirely in 1966.

Quite frankly, the Forty Thieves were forced off the dirt road and into the highway gridlock that was the system simply because the public was now having a harder time telling the roadshows and exploitation pictures from mainstream movie-house fare. American International Pictures had brought the sinful juvenile delinquent film to the forefront in mainstream cinemas and drive-ins, and young audiences were flocking to see them. Hundreds of what became known as 'nudie cuties' were released in the USA between 1959 and 1963, which soon transformed into the era of rough and twisted sexploitation spearheaded by Russ Meyer, Joe Sarno, Lee Frost and Harry Novak, which then morphed again into the many colourful and celebrated exploitation sub-genres of the 1970s.

No Greater Sin

IT CAME FROM SUPER 8!

Douglas Weir on Super 8

Artwork by Gary Pullin

When Super 8mm film was developed by Eastman Kodak in 1965 as an upgrade to the ageing Standard 8mm format its uses were not bound to only that of the home movie market, though that was the original objective. The idea behind Super 8 was to alter the size and shape of the perforations that ran down the edge allowing for a larger exposure area than Standard 8 resulting in sharper images. Kodak also made room for another new addition that followed in 1973, a combined magnetic audio track that ran down the opposite edge. Though available before, this was the first time it had been standardised. With these improvements to a still very popular medium, film distributors began to think seriously about a new distribution format aimed specifically at the living room.

Up until 1965 films distributed on Standard 8 were confined to the restrictions of image quality and were mostly old black and white silent films and short cartoons. It was still regarded as specialist. When Super 8 arrived whole films could be potentially distributed directly into the home with superior image quality in colour, with sound and even – with a special lens for your projector – in CinemaScope!

The market was flooded with cartoons, sporting events such as boxing and football, 'specialist' films available from behind the counter, documentaries and Hollywood shorts and feature films presented in a format that became known as the digest. Digests were, very simply, edited down versions of feature films that maintained the absolute basics of the films plot (if they were well edited) within the confines of the reels length. The most popular lengths of digest were seven minutes (200ft) and twenty minutes (400ft). Depending on the size of your wallet, other more expensive options were available such as several reels of 400ft film. If you were lucky enough to have a capable projector (again, not cheap) then you could be watching *The Towering Inferno* (1974), *Jaws* (1975), *King Kong* (1976) or *Superman* (1978) projected on a big screen in the comfort of your own home. In some cases, due to US/UK theatrical distribution holdback, films such as Star Wars could be bought as Super 8 digests several months before being released in UK cinemas. Sub distributors such as Castle Films, Ken Films, Derann Films Services and Arrow Films made a killing licensing titles from Hollywood until the big studios started to get in on the act and distribute Super 8 films themselves.

With Super 8 distribution being big business through the 1970s, things began to quieten down in the '80s due to the popularity of VHS and eventually LaserDisc. However, the nail wasn't finally in the coffin until Kodak discontinued Super 8 Sound film in 1998 and Derann Film Services, at one time the world's largest sub-distributor of Super 8 films, closed its doors in 2011. Right up until the end, films such as *Toy Story* (1995) and *Independence Day* (1996) were available to own as brand new Super 8 prints.

This essay originally appeared in the Arrow Video edition of* The Incredible Melting Man*.

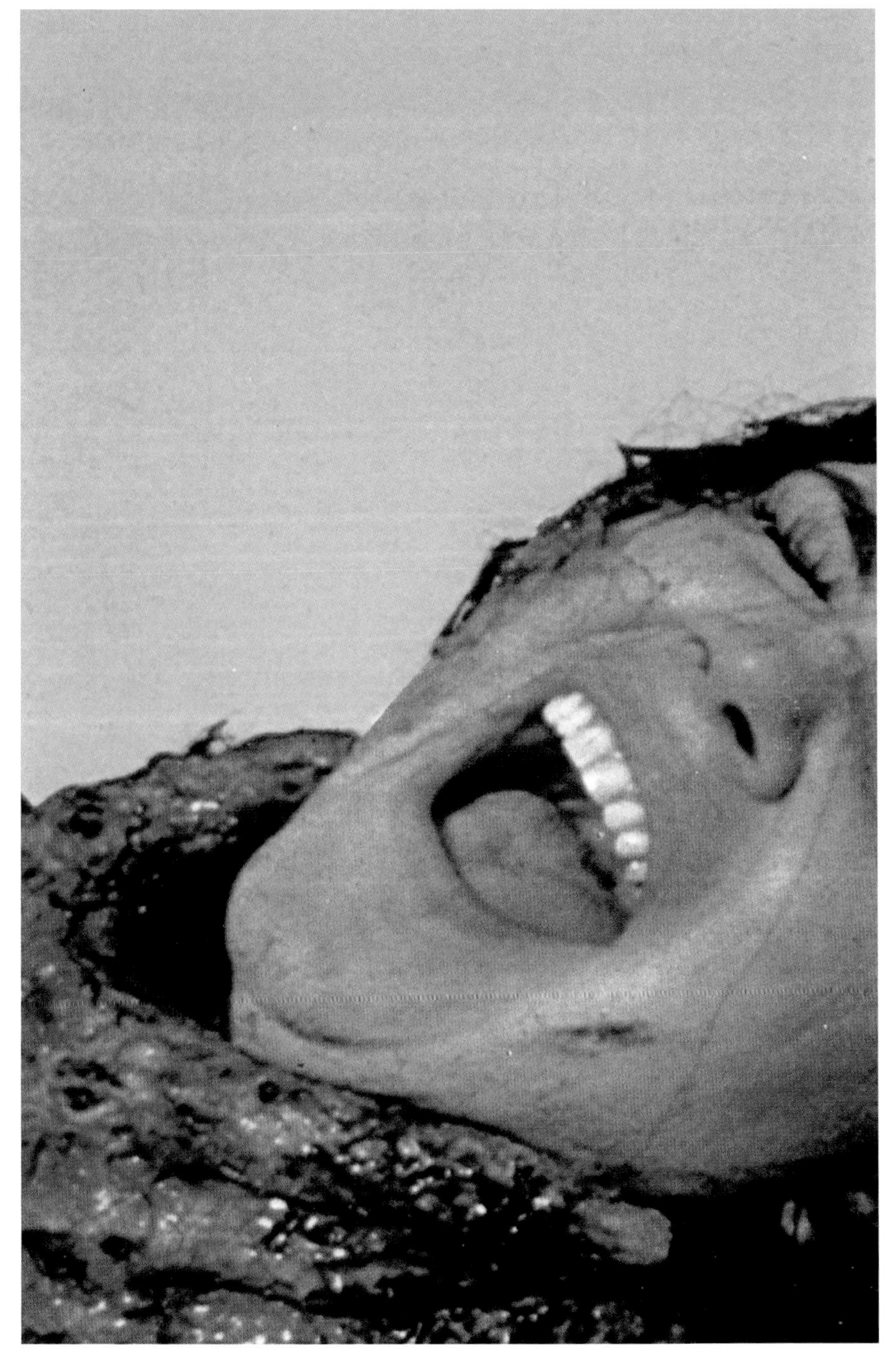

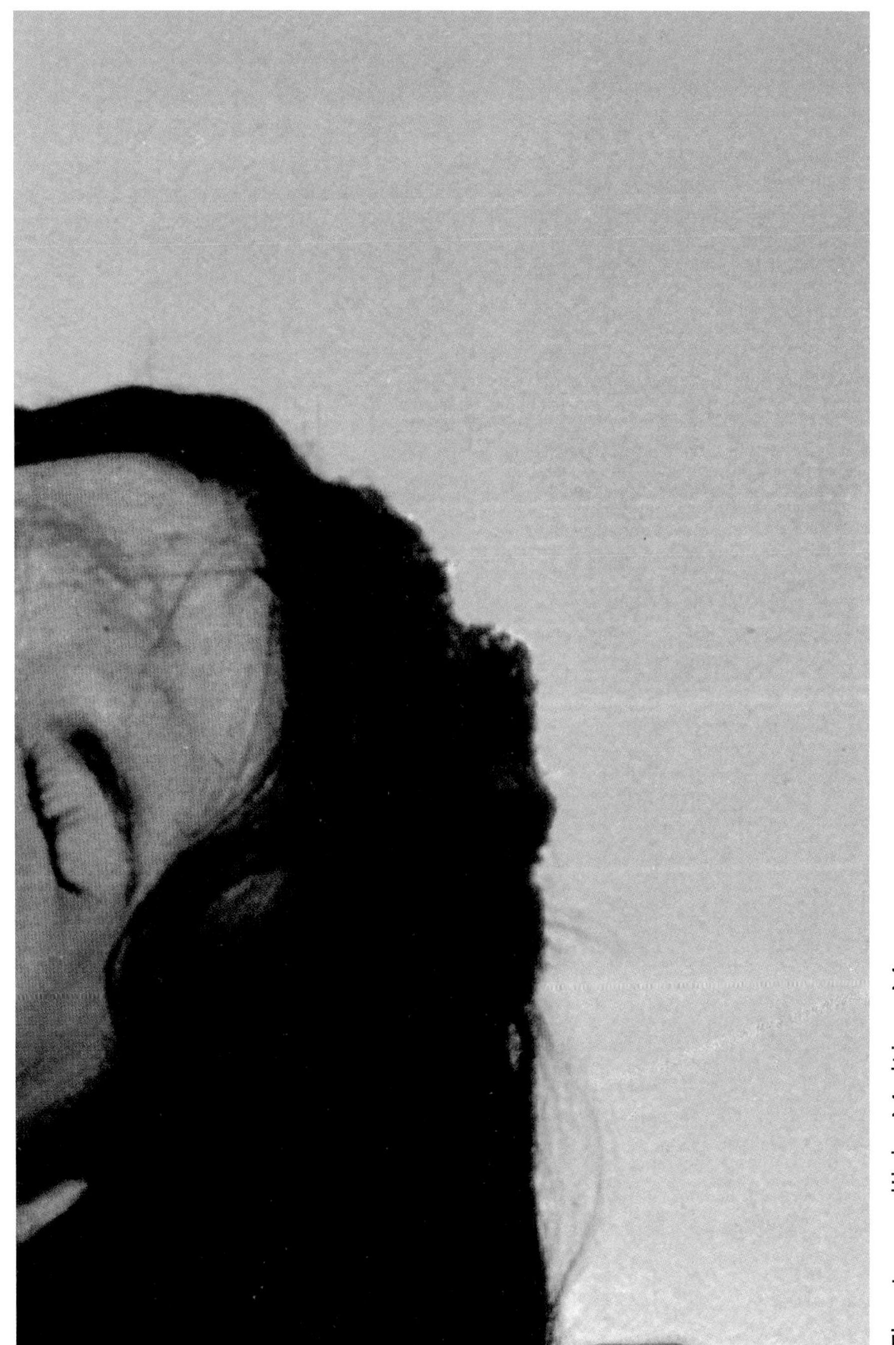

HIGH STREET HORROR

Michael Brooke on the Video Nasty

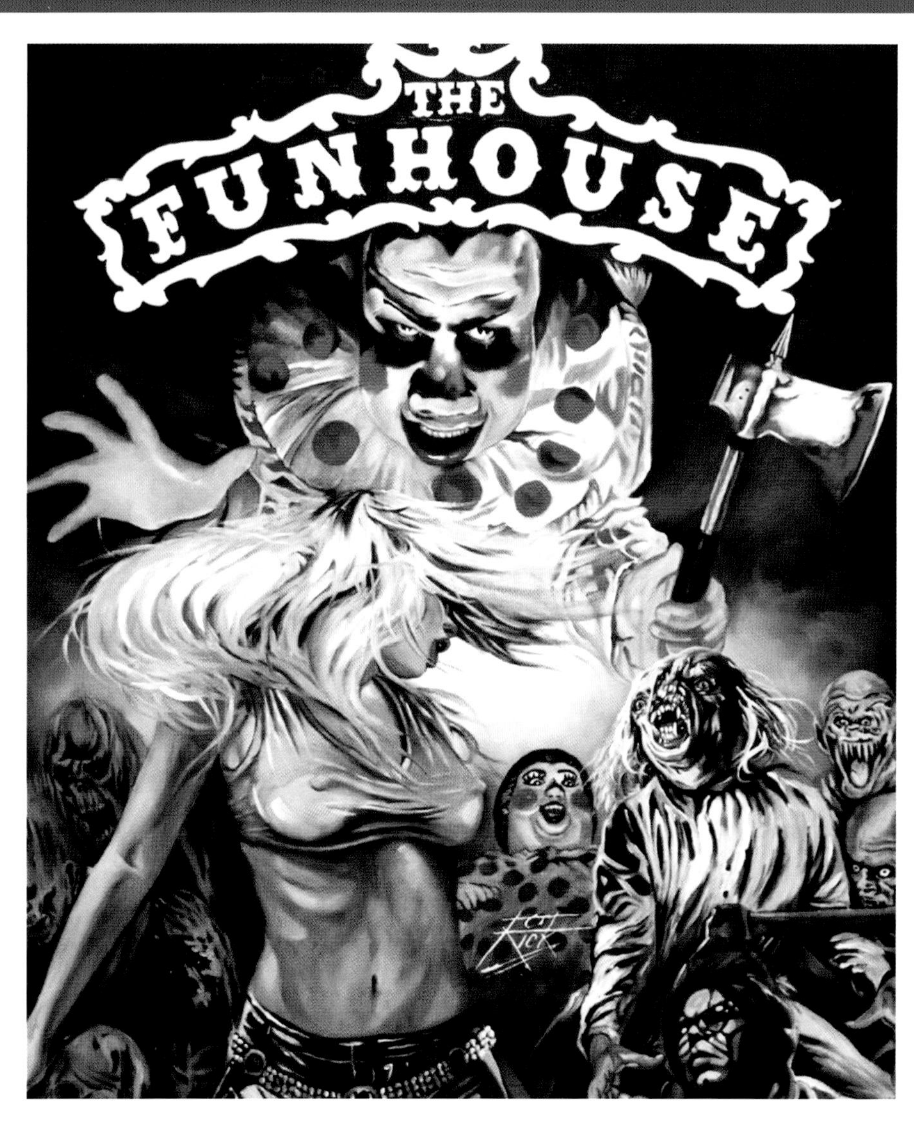

Artwork by Rick Melton

Seldom has a single simple phrase gained such malevolent and continuing currency as 'video nasty'. Surprisingly so, in fact, because it's so essentially twee: not as much as 'video horrid' or 'video beastly' might have been, but in the same general etymological area – and it's this implied naïveté and suggestion of pearl-clutching fits of the vapours that makes it such a peculiarly British phenomenon. But it led to one of the UK's great moral panics of the late twentieth century, with consequences that remain firmly in place to this day, notably the fact that Britain is one of the few countries that legally requires not only that all commercial video releases that aren't documentaries or music videos to be pre-vetted by a state-sanctioned censor but that the distributors in question should pay for the privilege (and on a per-minute basis).

The first use of the term 'nasty' or 'nasties' to describe the kind of films allegedly being watched by a substantial number of the nation's children (a common if frequently unsupported theme), seems to have been in a *Sunday Times* article dated 23 May 1982, headlined 'How High Street Horror is Invading the Home'. This appeared just under a fortnight after the *Daily Mail* started the ball rolling with 'The Secret Video Show' (12 May), and by the 28th the *Daily Express* clambered aboard an accelerating bandwagon with 'This Poison Being Peddled as Home "Entertainment"'. Well before the first actual prosecutions took place that summer, the term 'video nasty' had become firmly embedded in the public consciousness.

It's worth noting at this point that the video cassette recorder had been unusually successful in Britain compared with many other countries. Cinema audiences had been declining precipitously throughout the 1970s, and the fact that television was largely to blame was acknowledged by two of that decade's most successful homegrown genres being TV sitcom spin-offs or softcore sex comedies. Going to 'the pictures' became a desultory prospect, with former picture palaces carved up into boxy two- and three-screen affairs with screens the size of beach towels. This gave cinemas a short-term financial boost, but they offered a vastly diminished big screen experience. Accordingly, cinema audiences plunged from 193 million in 1970 (itself a pale shadow of 1946's record of 1.6 billion) to an all-time low of 54 million in 1984.

And no wonder: by then, the small screen's bow had developed a substantial new string. No longer forced to make do with just three television channels (a fourth launched in November 1982), VCR owners (or renters, another common phenomenon) had access to a huge range of DIY programming via one of the era's few genuine British growth industries: the high street video rental shop. Sometimes these weren't even standalone businesses but adjuncts to others: it was very common to see newsagents offering videocassettes for rent. The major cinema distributors should by rights have seen this as a heaven-sent opportunity, but fears about piracy (a worrying new issue for them) made them very hesitant to get involved – so in their place a load of independent labels sprang up. And since most were run on a shoestring, they naturally gravitated towards the kind of titles that were cheap to license and easy to sell, ideally with the most sensationalised advertising possible. Even better, because this was a wholly new medium, there was no regulation at all, besides that laid down by existing criminal laws governing things like animal cruelty or pornography. There was also nothing legally preventing children gaining access to video recordings. For a naturally conservative and censorious country like Britain, this was asking for trouble. Several months before the video nasty panic began in earnest, complaints were registered with the Advertising Standards Authority about the content of certain video sleeves and posters.

So what is a video nasty? The popular cliché says that it's something considered too horrific for British cinemas, which was cut or banned by the British Board of Film Censors (which is what the initials BBFC represented for much of the Board's existence), which is crammed to overflowing with gratuitous sex and violence (ideally in combination), and which will instantly deprave and corrupt anyone who comes into contact with so much as a frame – or even, in many cases, just the advertising artwork. Look at the titles: *SS Experiment Camp* (*Lager SSadis Kastrat Kommandantur*, 1976) *Gestapo's Last Orgy* (*L'ultima orgia del III Reich*, 1977), *The New York Ripper* (*Lo squartatore di New York*, 1982) – who could possibly defend this filth? As George Bernard Shaw once said to an aspiring playwright who tried to pull the age-old trick of sticking two pages of his new opus together to prove that Shaw hadn't read it all before dismissing it, "you don't have to eat a whole egg to know it's rotten".

Certainly, some of the video nasties were rotten: indeed, their presence on the various lists of suspect titles issued by the Director of Public Prosecutions for potential seizure was arguably the best thing that could possibly have happened to them, adding genuine political cachet to what was only ever intended by their makers as cheap and crude exploitation – to this day, aficionados seek them out purely because they were part of the 'DPP 39' (or 72, if you include listed but acquitted or never-prosecuted titles). But the lists also included work by such celebrated genre directors as Dario Argento (*Inferno*, 1980), Mario Bava (*Bay of Blood/Reazione a catena*, 1971), Luigi Cozzi (*Contamination*, 1980), Lucio Fulci (multiple titles), Tobe Hooper (*Eaten Alive,* 1976 aka *Death Trap*; *The Funhouse*, 1981) and the early work of then-unknown major talents such as Abel Ferrara (*The Driller Killer*, 1979) and Sam Raimi (*The Evil Dead*, 1981). There was even a fully-fledged Cannes-winning arthouse movie (Andrzej Đuławski's *Possession*, 1981) which, like several of the films on the DPP lists, had been passed uncut by the BBFC with an X-certificate for normal cinema viewing by the over-18s. Indeed, some nasties have subsequently been classified uncut with 15 certificates – including *Contamination*, *The Funhouse*, *Don't Go in the Woods* (1981) and *The Forgotten* (1973 aka *Don't Go in the Basement*) – suggesting that they never really lived up to the tagline "the ultimate experience in gruelling terror" so memorably bestowed on *The Evil Dead*.

Much to the surprise and alarm of Raimi and his colleagues, *The Evil Dead* became viewed in some quarters as the ultimate video nasty, and constantly mentioned as such in outraged dispatches from the tabloid front line. And yet the film was clearly made with its tongue planted firmly in a rotting cheek – the present author saw the film uncut on its original release at London's Prince Charles Cinema in March 1983 (the full version 'accidentally' ended up on its projectors) and can attest first-hand to the fact that there were as many belly laughs as involuntary screams. Indeed, if it hadn't been for one clearly fantastical element of sexual violence (the scene in which Ellen Sandweiss wanders out into the possessed forest and is raped by a tree), it's likely that the film would have been far less controversial. BBFC records recall that examiners were divided over the film, with some (including BBFC Secretary James Ferman) considering it so absurdly excessive as to be hard to take seriously and others professing to be genuinely disturbed by it, so a few cuts were made to lessen some of the more extreme moments and the film was duly passed for cinema release, opening to largely excellent reviews. It was this same censored version that was released by Palace Video, one of the UK's more enterprising independent labels, although that didn't stop it from being regularly seized and cited as amongst the worst of the worst, the 'number one nasty'. It was eventually formally acquitted on obscenity charges, but not until 1985, by which time the commercial damage had already been done.

By summer 1982, the issue of video nasties was being regularly raised in both Houses of Parliament. The first serious attempt at regulating the video industry was put forward in December by Labour MP Gareth Wardell (this was never a party political issue), which would make it an offence to provide unsuitable videos to children and young people. Wardell's failure to win government support led to newspapers like the *Daily Mail* ramping up its anti-nasty campaign, just before the simultaneous theatrical and video release of *The Evil Dead*. Shortly afterwards, in April 1983, veteran anti-obscenity campaigner Mary Whitehouse wrote to every Member of Parliament urging them to consider stricter video legislation. This was in the immediate run-up to a General Election, and once Margaret Thatcher's government had been re-elected by a landslide, Conservative MP Graham Bright put forward a Private Member's Bill proposing far more comprehensive regulation of the video industry than Wardell had done, this time with Thatcher's strong personal support.

That summer, the Director of Public Prosecutions issued the first list of titles that would face seizure and prosecution (in the process providing horror fans with useful tips), and on November 1st Bright arranged a now-notorious screening of the most lurid extracts from some of the better-known video nasties for his Parliamentary colleagues. Unsurprisingly, given both the lack of dramatic context (as was pointed out at the time, the careers of Alfred Hitchcock and Luis Buñuel could have been rubbished via identical methods) and the fact that MPs weren't the original target audiences, the compilation achieved its aims, and the Bill sailed through Parliament with remarkably little opposition, despite the heroic efforts of individual MPs like the future newspaper columnist Matthew Parris (then a Conservative MP) and of sceptical academics like Guy Cumberbatch, who neatly debunked the shock-horror statistics about children's exposure to the nasties (a *Daily Mail* headline that appeared during one of the Parliamentary debates bluntly stated that "HALF OF CHILDREN SEE FILM NASTIES") by asking groups of schoolkids about deliberately made-up titles. Naturally, the vast majority claimed to have seen them, and some even proffered lurid descriptions of their non-existent content.

However, this fell on deaf ears, not least because the mainstream film industry thoroughly approved of what eventually became the 1984 Video Recordings Act, as it created conditions that were far more favourable to them. Economies of scale meant that a large-scale release cost much less to be BBFC-vetted on a per-unit basis than one aimed at a cult audience, and the majors were much less likely to be handling anything potentially contentious – although in the early days of video regulation, the BBFC was substantially more draconian when it came to cutting video releases, on the grounds that cinemas were better at preventing impressionable children from seeing them.

With only a few tweaks since 1984, the Video Recordings Act remains on the statute books to this day. Thankfully, the BBFC significantly liberalised its internal guidelines in 2000, to the effect that they no longer cut films intended for adults unless they breach the criminal law (genuine animal cruelty, unsimulated underage sexual activity and extreme sexual violence being the most frequently proscribed subjects). As a result, most of the original video nasties are now legally available in the UK, in most cases in vastly superior presentations than were ever released in the 1980s (where films were invariably reframed to the 4:3 aspect ratio and often cut – sometimes because either an uncut video master wasn't available or the distributor wasn't clued-up enough about the film to notice).

DEVIANT WISCONSIN ROMANCE

Graham Rae on Horror Festivals, Fanzines and *Nekromantik*

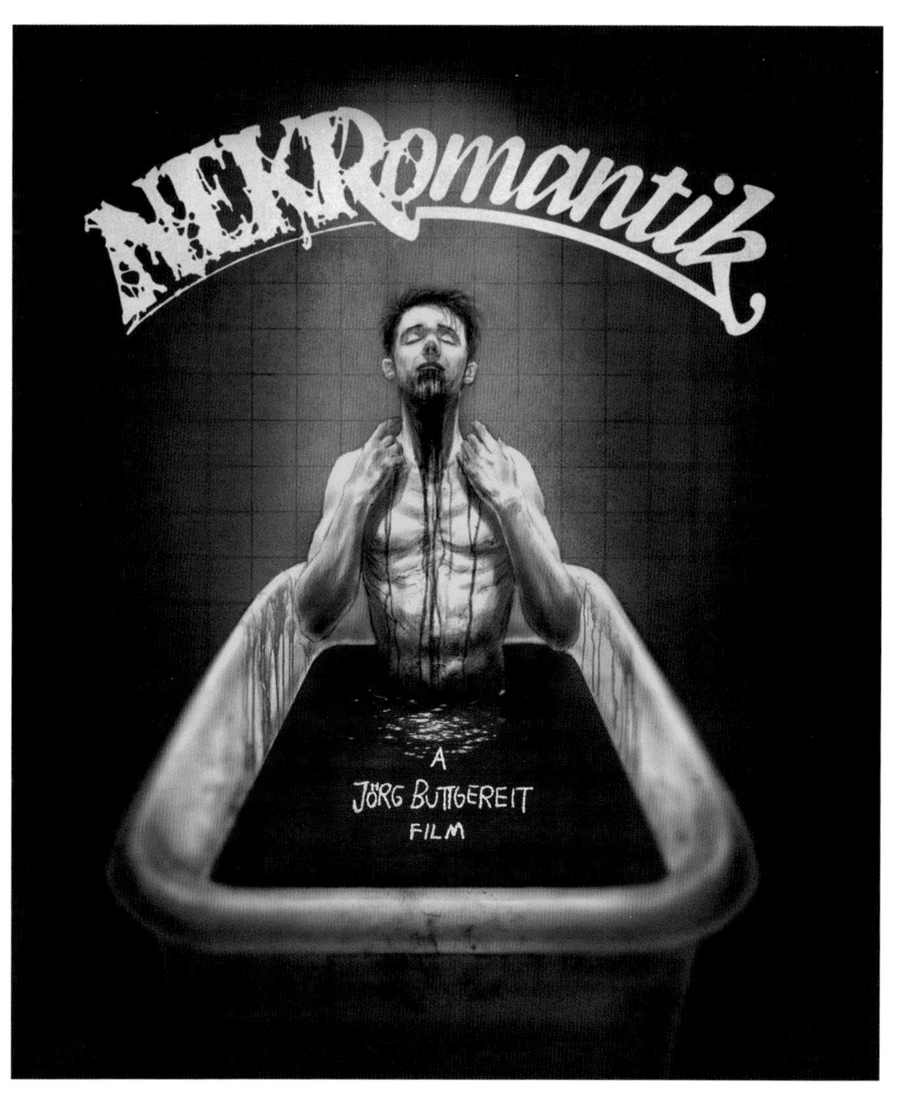

Artwork by Gilles Vranckx

I was all of 18 when I first saw *Nekromantik* (1987) at the infamous, seminal 24-hour Shock Around the Clock horror film festival screening at the Scala in London in 1988. I had gone down there with my uncle Gary on an overnight bus from Scotland, and we had great fun wiring into a case of Budweiser, cheering along with the crowd at the gory deaths in each new atrocity exhibition. The fare ranged from fun American nonsense like *Maniac Cop* (1988) to excellent Spanish excrement like *Slugs* (*Slugs, muerte viscosa*, 1988). We drank and roared as the underground rumbled ceaselessly along below us, the vibrating adding to the charged 'atmosfear' of the event.

Then came *Nekromantik*, and everything changed. It was the last film shown to a tired, jaded audience, drunk on booze and blood. The German work, which was the controversial talk of the festival, started. A couple argued in a parked car. The woman got out and pissed in close-up, then got back in. Instantly this was different from the more escapist fare we had been shown up until this point. They drove off. They crashed. Dark black threatening storm clouds of superb music boiled on the soundtrack, bursting open to drench the unwary, unprepared viewer with a grim landslide of transgressive images: a woman cut in half. Body parts harvesting. More pissing. A collection of body parts. A corpse tenderly fucked by an insane-but-happy necrophile couple. A cat killed and cut open, its intestines used for soap. Slasher film satire. Bloody murder, more necrophilia. Then an auto-erotic suicide to top them all, sending us stunned out into the early King's Cross morning beaten and bloody and bruised. This was what we had come all this way down for.

I instantly became obsessed with this beautiful, black death diamond of a film, getting a German-language bootleg (I still know the whole film in German, and can tell exactly what people are saying anywhere during the runtime) on the UK tape-trading circuit, and watching it constantly. It came out at a bleak, conservative time in the UK, a few years after the risible and fascistic 'video nasties' movement had taken gory uncut films off the video shop shelves and blighted the lives of some fans who were fined for having uncut prints in their homes. Jörg Buttgereit's film was an oft-seized 'indecent or obscene' videocassette, and getting a Notice of Seizure Under the Customs and Excise Acts 1979 letter through the door from H.M. Customs and Excise put a tense legal shiver down the spine of many a horror fan in the late 1980s, myself included.

Nekromantik was utterly groundbreaking and epochal, something which belonged to my generation and mine only, a true original. It was a sleazy, flyblown, subterranean classic that I had discovered on my own without anybody handing me it, travelling hundreds of miles to see it, something nobody else in Scotland knew about. It was far beyond anything I had ever seen during the early '80s on video from the local video shops, the more playful, sometimes cut cult exploitation fare so breathlessly hyped and demonised by the papers and the Tories in one of the most ludicrous political ploys from a repressive administration notorious for them.

The film felt like the work of somebody suffering from deep depression, with each frame tainted with an atmosphere of bleak, black despair, which fit my own deep teenage depression like a glove. It was obvious that the director was an uncompromising artist, and we were seeing his own obsessions up there on the screen, unflinchingly and graphically rendered, without apology, without censorship, without warning. I was reading a lot of true crime material at the time, and this strange German's rendition of his insane characters ran true on some deep and pure level, getting the pathologies right, not condescending to the audience. But it was a mournful, melancholic romance film too, a meditation on lost love, on the finality of death. I confess I had a teenage crush on Beatrice M at the time. It also had a sense of humour, albeit humour as black as any you were likely to come across. *Nekromantik* had it all and more.

I had written to Chas Balun of the now-legendary *Deep Red* fanzine asking him if I could be a foreign correspondent. I was a teenager writing to him on a manual portable typewriter from my bedroom in my parents' house, with no contacts in the film world whatsoever. But that's part of what *Nekromantik* was about – punky, spiky DIY, not letting the authorities (just as repressive in Germany as in the UK) in any arena dictate what you could or couldn't do, just throwing enough mud at a wall and seeing what stuck. Chas said go for it. Among the first stuff I sent him I wrote the film's first ever US review, for which I still get American people telling me to this day turned them onto *Nekromantik*. It's bizarre, quite frankly. It made the film a huge underground curiosity in the States, and apparently meant it was being taken more seriously outside of Germany than it was inside the country. Guess they were just too close to it. Or couldn't get far enough away from it. Whatever. It was their loss.

Jörg became my favourite filmmaker for the next few years, with my understanding of his themes widening as his other feature film works came out. His poetic low-budget, oddly feminist, audience-baiting films are about the loneliness of perversity,

Nekromantik

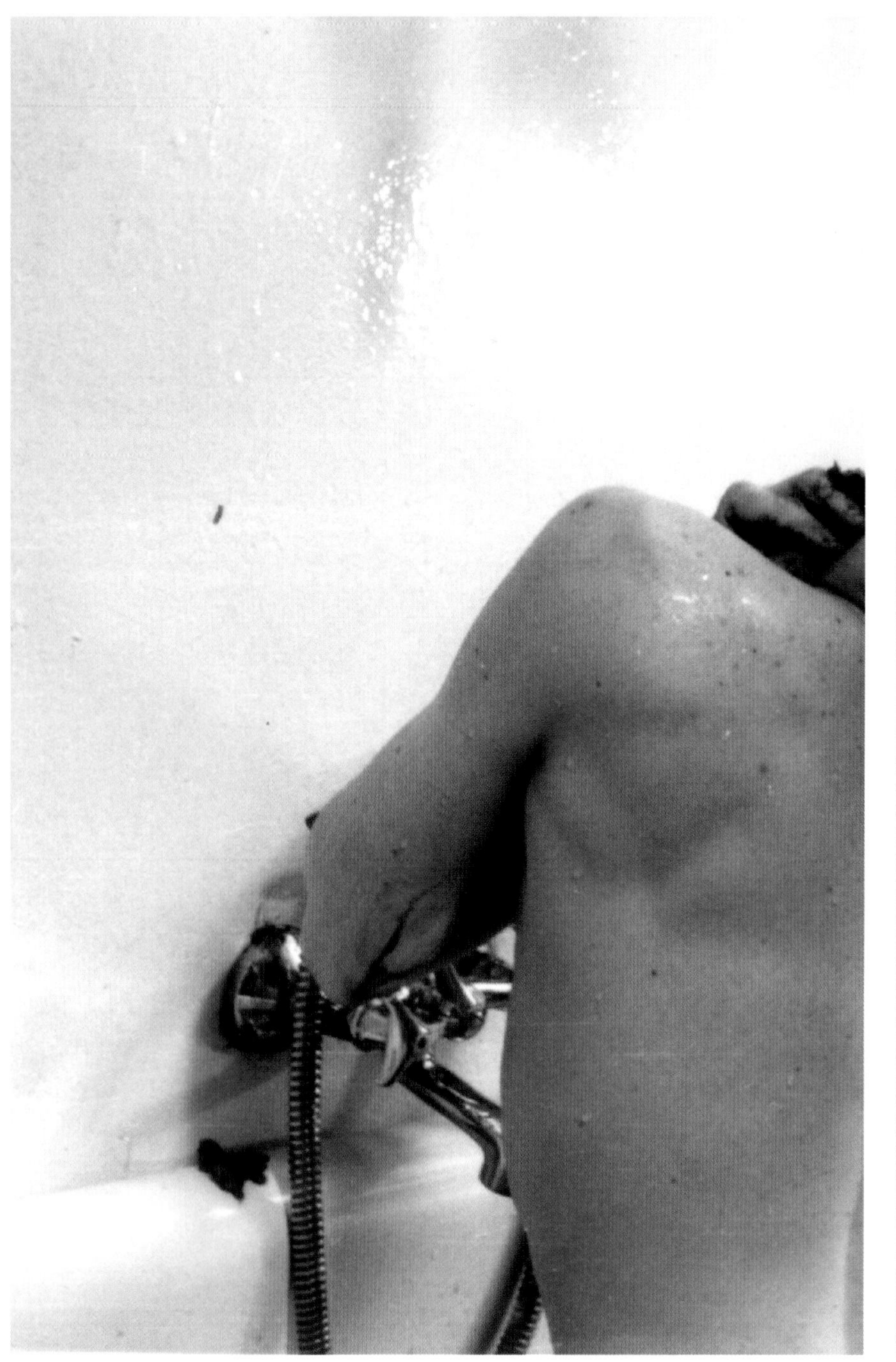

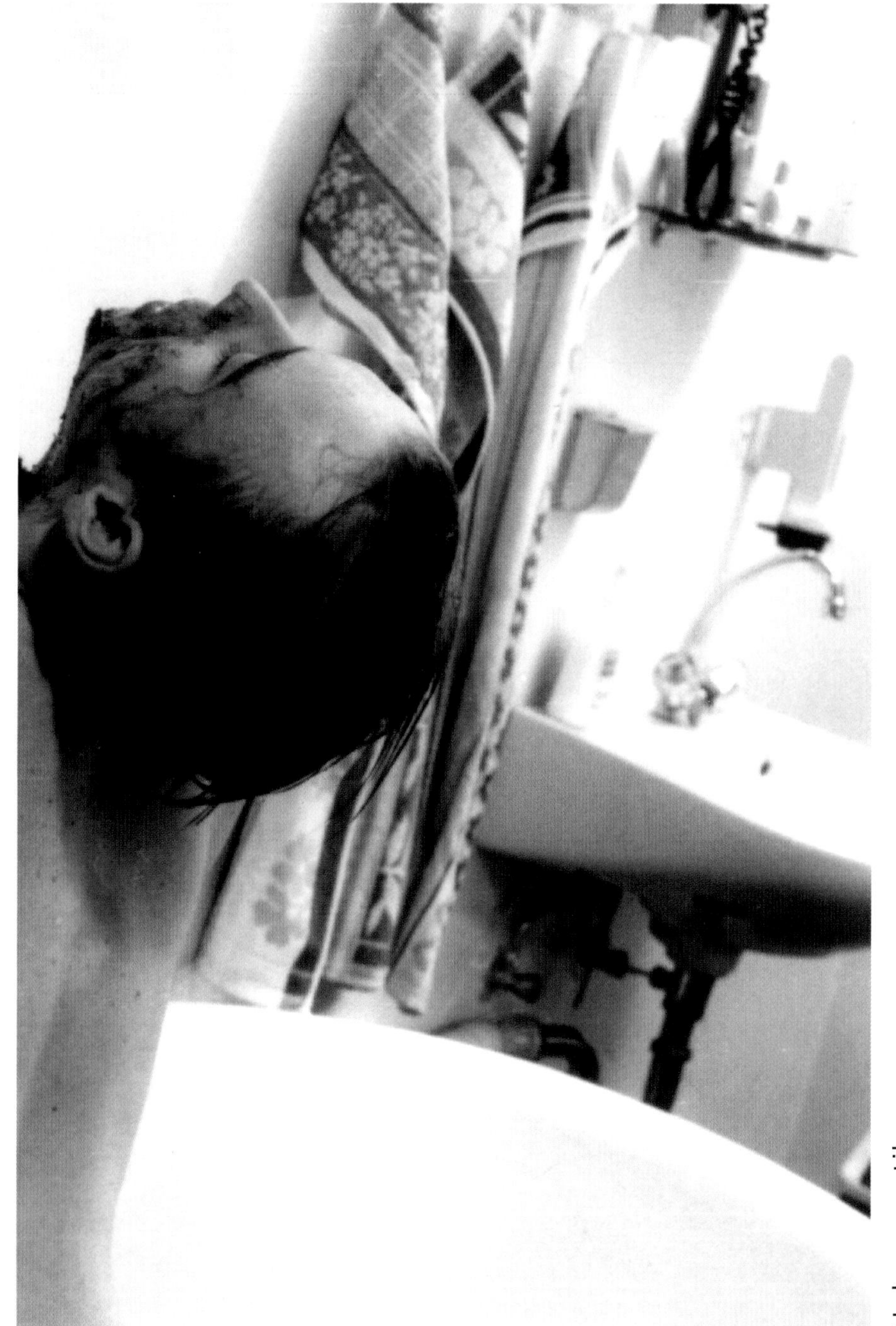

the frailty of the human condition, and the bitter tears of the flesh-loathing damned. His characters exist like fat black widow spiders pulsating in the enmeshing webs of their own pathologies, way beyond normal human relationships, unable or even unwilling to escape their madness, dealing death to anybody who cares or dares to wander into their obsessive psychopathic radius. There is no God here, no law, no final authority but death and its attendant sadness, the inescapable cessation and putrefaction of the body, from which a few final moments of taboo sexual joy can still be wrung.

Jörg always played it straight, albeit with an occasional pomposity-deflating, serious-art-mocking hilarious nod here and there to lighten the mood. Scared of rejection by the living, these poor lost diseased souls were people from the undiscovered squalid margins of society. Their real-life counterparts filled the true crime shelves with disgusting and horrifying and depressing and occasionally poignant stories of their lives gone terribly irreparably wrong, psychiatrist-teased jail-confession intimations at their reactions to lack of intimacy, frantically masturbating themselves or others to death looking for a final *lustmort* orgasm and release from their earthly tormented flesh prisons.

Jörg told me that people always asked him where his inspiration came from, and they were always referencing movies when they did. He said it was weird that nobody ever figured out that a lot of his inspirations came from real life. This is genuinely the case, with *Nekromantik* being no exception. In July 2012, I jokingly invited Jörg to come down to Chicago, where I now live, from a horror fest he was attending in Indiana, and we could do some touristy things. So it figures that, along with John Szpunar, whose excellent Barrel Entertainment label put out several of Jörg's works on DVD years ago, we ended up travelling several hundred miles north into Plainfield, Wisconsin on July 11th to visit the grave of Ed Gein, the 1950s madman whose infamous and horrifying murders and unusual tailoring methods have, of course, entered morbid American pathology mythology, spawning endless films based on his sickness: *Psycho* (1960), *Three on a Meathook* (1973), *Deranged*, *The Texas Chain Saw Massacre* (both 1974), *The Silence of the Lambs* (1991). And *Nekromantik*.

Now, I don't mean that the film is a literal rendition of the mentally subnormal farm-dweller's visceral crimes against humanity. But Gein's influence on the mood and atmosphere and somewhat... *unusual* décor choices of Rob and Betty is clearly visible. At the time the film came out, nobody grasped the fact that all those severed body parts lying around, and the necrophilia, came in part from the Gein case. The scene with the rabbit being skinned was inspired by the farmer being traumatised as a child by his parents slaughtering a pig in front of him. In the movie, this horrible scene starts love and death intertwining in the young Rob Schmadtke's mind, which will, in time, become a full-blown pathological obsession with death and dying in this troubled young man.

Jörg first encountered Gein's pernicious, pervasive presence on the page in his teens, when a friend of his had a true crime paperback about the murderer. Later on, he saw an issue of *Weird Tales* magazine with a picture of Gein on the cover. Because the cover looked like the work of Jack Davis, who drew *Mad Magazine* covers, and with the director being a *Mad* fan, he picked it up and became fascinated – obsessed – with Edward Theodore Gein's extreme and insane case of mother fixation. As is evidenced by our trip, it is an obsession that stays with him to this day. In 2012 he brought out a play called *Kannibale und Liebe* about Gein in Germany.

On the necrophilia front, I mentioned the book *Killing for Company: The Case of Dennis Nilsen* (1985) to Jörg on his Chicago trip, a true crime tome about the homosexual necrophile serial killer who plied his deadly trade on the streets of London. Though he had forgotten all about it, Jörg instantly recalled how it had been an influence on the film, with the scenes of Betty lying around reading to the corpse. Not to mention the necrophilia, of course. There is a scene in *Nekromantik 2* (1991) which recreates a photo from *Killing For Company*, where the plastic bagged remains of a dismembered body have an air freshener sitting on top of them to kill the rotten smell. So this real-life stuff was going in deep with Jörg, and he was partly consciously recreating it in his films for an added authority won from reality.

Whilst his other loves may have been superheroes and Godzilla, there was and is a definite fascination with real-life horror in the man and his work. It can be difficult, though, to apportion appropriate praise/blame for the different strands of the filmed horror, because if you don't include Franz Rodenkirchen (who co-wrote Jörg's four feature films, and came up with demented scenes like, say, the climax to *Nekromantik 2*) and producer Manfred Jelinski into the equation you don't get a true picture of three men working as a seamless horror-film-making machine.

Other influences on *Nekromantik* included *The Texas Chainsaw Massacre* (most noticeable in the violent violin screeching on the soundtracks of Jörg's films, and the barbed wire round the necrophile couple's bed), and the little-seen November 1971 story 'Cleanup Crew', by artists Greg Irons and Tom Veitch, from *Skull Comics* #3. As noted by horror authority Stephen R. Bissette, that nasty wee tale of a worker who cleans up after car crashes, and cavorts with his wife in human guts, quite clearly sketched out parts of *Nekromantik*. But Jörg was not above auto-cannibalism as well, and his short film of two years earlier, *Hot Love* (1985), prefigures a lot of the *Nekromantik* action, including suicide, necrophilia, a cat given as a present (though here it's a small stuffed toy), and romantic rejection. *Hot Love* had been bitterly made by the director after a break-up with his girlfriend of the time, and the wounded anger and agony of romantic rejection resonates through both films. A risk, of course, which necrophiles no longer have to worry about – unless their partner runs off with the body, that is.

***This essay originally appeared in the Arrow Video edition of* Nekromantik.**

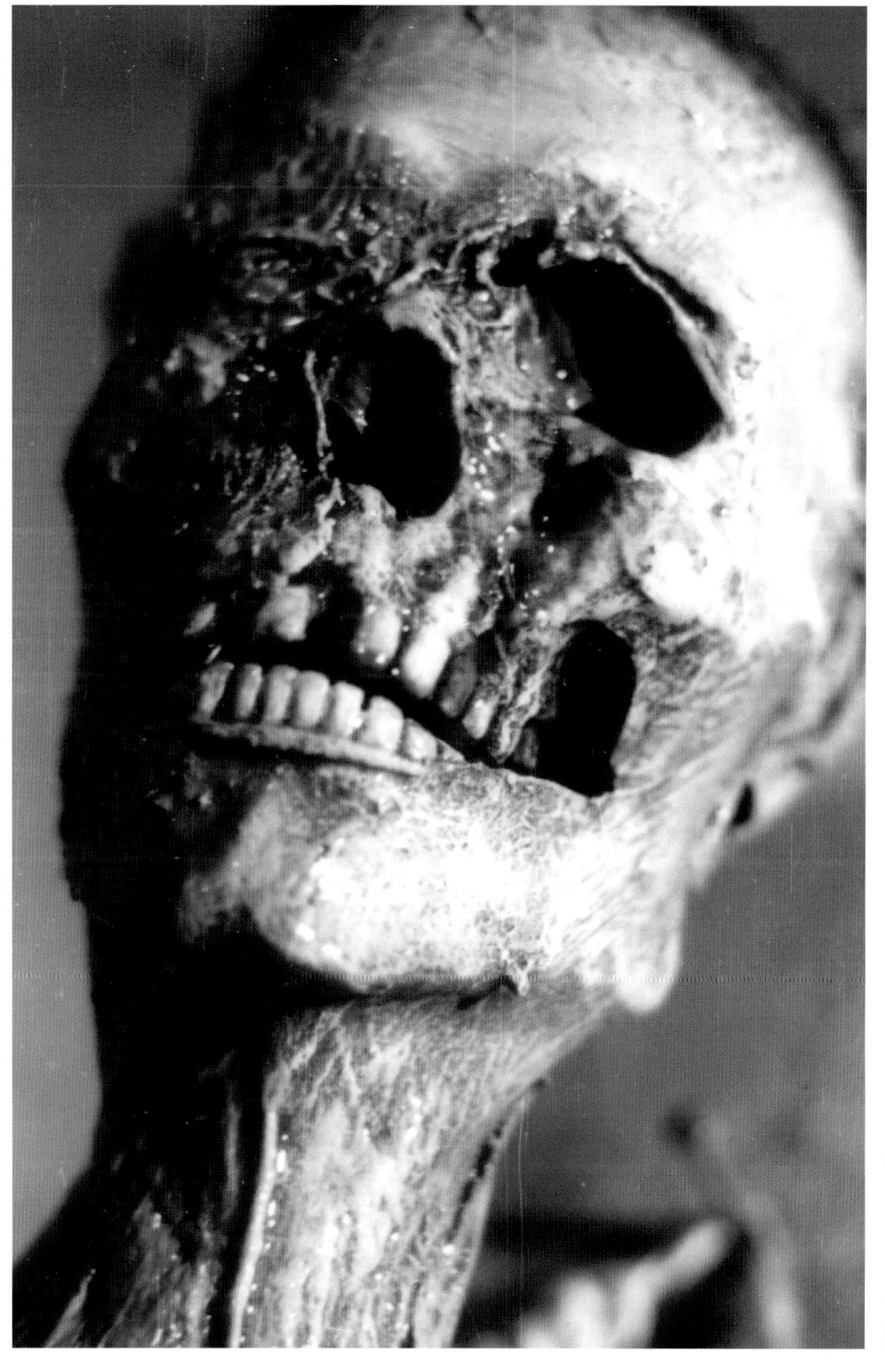

Nekromantik

OPENING THE FLOODGATES

Kevin Gilvear on the Asian DVD Explosion

Artwork by the Twins of Evil

If you were already hopelessly in love with Asian cinema by the turn of the millennium and happened to join the right forums and review sites in the wake of the internet revolution, then gaining intel on the latest happenings in the east was a walk in the park. And if you were new to it all? Well, it only ever takes one film for someone to decide that they want to discover more. It was an exciting time to be a part of. Specifically, by 1999 we were dealing with three major Asian powerhouses, and with the latest in digital media distribution we were starting to become spoiled for choice. It's worth breaking down some of the contributions from these countries – Hong Kong, Japan and South Korea – along with select distributors who were instrumental in capturing the attention of loyal and, dare I say, obsessive fans, as well as helping to introduce new ones to a golden era in home entertainment.

With regards to Hong Kong cinema in the late 90s, companies such as Tartan were occasionally supporting the scene, but a noticeable shift came at the tail-end of the decade with the arrival of Hong Kong Legends (HKL), which quickly rose to become a major leader in its field. Founded in 1999 under the watch of label manager Brian White and cinema expert Bey Logan, its mission was to serve up the best in in HK action cinema, dedicating its resources to remastering and restoring classic films primarily from the 80s and 90s, which had turned the likes of Jackie Chan, Chow Yun Fat, Jet Li and Sammo Hung into household names. Such dedication to their releases – not only from a visual and audio standpoint but also in terms of providing brand new interviews and informative commentary tracks – yielded huge respect from genre fans; they didn't quite nail every release but they did help to create topics of debate in an area which provided the perfect springboard toward discovering other bright gems within the Asian film industry.

HKL came along at just the right time; no other distributor in the UK was giving Hong Kong action cinema this kind of attention. It helped that new, creative talent was seeping through to Hollywood, which directed more attention toward Asian filmmakers. Word of mouth spread across the web and a new generation of action film fans soon discovered that *The Matrix* (1999) owed its debt to a far greater power than its revolutionary visual effects – folk were subsequently discovering genres and sub-genres they never knew even existed. As business decisions go, however, not even HKL was averse to using the Wachowskis' turn-of-the-century sci-fi spectacle to boost sales. Arguably, you had two groups: the seasoned fans who wanted to see their beloved films presented to their absolute best; and those who were simply curious as to how modern mainstream blockbusters were being influenced once word got out. By 2000, the obsession with Hong Kong action cinema had really come into full force with the release of Ang Lee's Oscar-winning *Crouching Tiger, Hidden Dragon* (*Wo hu cang long*), with producers clamouring to replicate its success. Meanwhile, the likes of Jackie Chan – who had made a successful attempt at conquering the American market by 1998 – was helping to broaden audiences' taste with his inimitable brand of death-defying martial arts and slapstick humour. There was really no escaping how entwined Hollywood and Asian action sensibilities would become as the 'noughties' shaped a new era in action cinema.

A taste for Asian filmmaking naturally led toward people making further discoveries, and imports were the way to go. Hong Kong, of course, naturally made for easy access. They were readily providing mandatory English subtitles on their DVDs, and with online retailers such as YesAsia offering fantastic shipping deals, free from import duties, the time couldn't have been any better for the most cash-strapped amongst us. Cue the unearthing of Category III exploitation greats and blisteringly funny turns from iconic performers like the Hui Brothers and Stephen Chow – essentially a chain reaction of just wanting more than certain companies were able (or willing) to provide given current market trends.

In 1999 the west also witnessed Japan's horror renaissance, when Hideo Nakata led the charge with his seminal *Ring* (*Ringu*, 1998). This period helped usher in a host of imitators wanting to get in on the long-haired, pale-skinned creepy lady, climbing all over the walls to much success, certainly enough for Hollywood to take notice. Distributors were quick to capitalise on this seemingly unstoppable 'J-horror' wave. In the UK, Tartan, for example, created an entire sub-label designed solely for 'Extreme' releases, which featured auteurs like Nakata, Kiyoshi Kurosawa (*Bright Future/Akarui mirau*, 2003), Shinya Tsukamoto (*A Snake in June/Rokugatsu no hebi*, 2002) and Takashi Miike (*Audition/Ôdishon*, 1999), until it inevitably wore itself out. Nonetheless, they served as a critical outlet for Japanese cinema fans living in the UK for a little while, with the earlier established Manga Entertainment having provided further 'extreme' output via its anime products in the wake of the cyberpunk boom ten years prior. Given that Japanese distributors are notoriously picky when it comes to providing English translations on their releases, we were lucky to get what we could, with the grey area of fan-subbing being the only real alternative if you were hungry to discover further genres. Even back then we just didn't have many companies taking on the more alternative Japanese features. That would change just a few years later, however.

Just as *The Matrix* managed to aid western distribution companies in selling their niche products for the sake of reaching a far wider audience, so too the arrival of Quentin Tarantino's *Kill Bill* in 2003 sparked a massive resurgence in grindhouse cinema: everything from Toei's 'pinky violence' franchises to Nikkatsu's *roman porno* oddities had DVD producers in a frenzy. Highly respected US independent labels like Synapse, ArtsMagic and Discotek Media were already savvy to the scene, becoming partly responsible for the rise in imports. They were companies dealing with the epitome of cult cinema; an area that many of us had otherwise little access to outside of terrible VHS bootlegs (and even then you'd have to be extremely lucky). The astounding amount of attention geared toward films that weren't really designed to be remembered decades on was cause for major celebration and fans were quick to import from whichever countries were serving up uncut Japanese cinema. This became a key area of importance when researching availability on home video formats, leading to online discussion and paving the way for numerous film comparison sites such as DVD Basen and DVD Beaver, which would serve as one-stop solutions for all your uncut celluloid needs. Films like Miike's *Ichi the Killer* (*Koroshiya 1*, 2001), for example, which hadn't pleased the British Board of Film Classification, could be purchased in its complete form from the Netherlands (circa 2003). Such was the power of online warriors that extreme efforts were made to ensure that if you were going to purchase a Japanese film title, you'd bloody well do it properly.

Arguably the most impressive movement from 1999 was the quite out-of-nowhere South Korean new wave invasion, born from the country's economic restructuring of the 90s, which quickly won over admirers of Asian cinema with the release of Kang Je-gyu's *Swiri* (1999), or *Shiri* as it later became known in the west). Popularised as an homage to Hollywood 80s blockbusters, and featuring fight choreography reminiscent of HK cinema, *Shiri* became a smash hit in its homeland, eclipsing previous cinema attendance records held by the Hollywood juggernaut, *Titanic* (1998). It was massive in other Asian territories to boot, being heralded as a modern action classic. Naturally this led to widespread discussion online and with the quick DVD turnaround fans were importing, eager to find out what was up with a scene which hadn't been discussed on such a level prior. *Shiri* didn't see US or UK distribution until 2002, much as Stephen Chow's beloved *Shaolin Soccer* (*Siu lam juk kau*, 2001) wouldn't receive a western release until around three years after Hong Kong had put out a well-respected disc. It gave us bragging rights, you see!

Shiri ultimately kickstarted an intense amount of interest and, with South Korean distributors fortunately providing well-translated English subtitles, it was back to ordering more DVDs than we really knew what to do with and providing online opinions for those sitting on the fence. For a good few years, South Korea was a dominant force, putting out fresh movies that undoubtedly drew people away from the somewhat stagnant scene that was developing in Hong Kong and Japan by the mid-2000s; the former appearing more obsessed with shoving Canto-pop stars in its films and the latter lacking exposure outside of the horror genre until some years later. South Korean film was the conversation point. The arthouse scene was thriving thanks to workhorses like Kim Ki-duk, whose controversial output, such as *The Isle* (*Seom*, 2000), was enough to ensure that we had to witness much of his visions on unmolested import. Kim Jee-woon (*A Tale of Two Sisters/Janghwa, Hongryeon*, 2003; *A Bittersweet Life/Dalkomhan insaeng*, 2005) was turning heads as he proved time and again that there was no genre he couldn't do. Park Chan-wook was reinventing the revenge thriller with *Sympathy for Mr. Vengeance* (*Boksuneun naui geot*, 2002) and *OldBoy* (*Oldeuboi*, 2003). And a little comedy based on an internet tale, *My Sassy Girl* (*Yeopgijeogin geunyeo*, 2001) became the highest grossing South Korean comedy of all time, winning overseas admiration and earning a quickly forgotten Hollywood remake in 2008. This was a time of raw ingenuity, from hungry new talents; some who would defy conventions and others who were eager to compete head-to-head with the big-hitters. The attention this movement ultimately received firmly placed it into the history books. South Korea had opened its doors to the rest of the world and we embraced it with open arms.

Moreover, its DVD distributors would realise the power of the format as a collector's tool, affording releases with limited edition packaging, which sometimes had more effort put into it than the film it actually represented. This unusual method of distribution solidified the South Korean home entertainment industry as one of the best in the world, driving collectors wild, who were snapping up every deluxe edition they could: from swimming caps and fancy tin lunch-boxes, to KFC style takeaway packages and bizarre recycled cardboard boxes with cleaning products included! It was suddenly a wonder as to what we were really picking these things up for, but it was another feather in the cap, which united a growing community of Asian film lovers who also wanted their shelves to look real pretty.

As cult scenes go, none is greater than the power of the audience itself. Things may have changed a bit over the years but the power of fandom is very much alive. Niche distributors are still around, moving with the times as the digital format evolves and more importantly the best in the business are those who respect the fans; those who understand that word of mouth is paramount to success – nowhere is this more evident than in our ever increasing social media circles. Today is the best time to be an Asian film fan insofar as we've really never had it better in terms of what's available. Whether or not we see another online movement as it was fifteen years ago remains to be seen. Regardless, we'll always be out there discovering something 'new' to us.

Audition

CONTRIBUTORS

ROBIN BOUGIE is a porn comic artist and the creator of *Cinema Sewer* magazine, a periodical guide to the sickest and sexiest movies ever made.

MICHAEL BROOKE is a freelance film critic, historian and DVD/Blu-ray producer.

PAUL CORUPE is the creator of Canuxploitation.com and a regular columnist for *Rue Morgue* magazine.

DAVID DEL VALLE is a film historian, broadcaster and the author of *Lost Horizons: Beneath the Hollywood Sign* (2010).

DAVID FLINT is a freelance writer and the author of *Babylon Blue: An Illustrated History of Adult Cinema* (1999), *Ten Years of Terror: British Horror Films of the 1970s* (2001), *Zombie Holocaust: How the Living Dead Devoured Pop Culture* (2008) and *Sheer Filth!* (2014).

CULLEN GALLAGHER is a writer and curator whose criticism has appeared in the *Los Angeles Review of Books*, *Bright Lights Film Journal*, *Film Comment* and *Moving Image Source*.

KEVIN GILVEAR is a freelance writer and film critic specialising in Asian and cult cinema.

JOEL HARLEY is a film critic and regular contributor to *Starburst* magazine.

DAVID HAYLES is a freelance film critic.

PASQUALE IANNONE is a film critic and academic.

ALAN JONES is a film critic, broadcaster and the author of *Profondo Argento* (2004).

TIM LUCAS is a film critic, novelist and the author of *Mario Bava: All the Colors of the Dark* (2007).

MICHAEL MACKENZIE is an author and DVD/Blu-ray producer whose PhD thesis examined the *giallo*'s relationship with sociocultural upheavals in post-war Europe.

MAITLAND McDONAGH is a film critic and the author of *Broken Mirrors/Broken Minds: The Dark Dreams of Dario Argento* (1991) and *Filmmaking on the Fringe: The Good, the Bad, and the Deviant Directors* (1995).

TOM MES is the founder of MidnightEye.com and the author of *Agitator: The Cinema of Takashi Miike* (2004), *Iron Man: The Cinema of Shinya Tsukamoto* (2005) and *Re-Agitator: A Decade of Writing on Takashi Miike* (2013).

JOHN KENNETH MUIR is the author of *Horror Films of the 1970s* (2002), *Eaten Alive at a Chainsaw Massacre: The Films of Tobe Hooper* (2003), *Horror Films of the 1980s* (2007) and *Horror Films of the 1990s* (2011).

KIM NEWMAN is a novelist, critic and broadcaster whose non-fiction work includes *Nightmare Movies* (1984/2011) and the BFI Classics studies of *Cat People* (1999), *Doctor Who* (2005) and *Quatermass and the Pit* (2014).

ANTHONY NIELD is a freelance film critic, historian and DVD/Blu-ray producer.

JAMES OLIVER is a critic and film historian who regularly contributes to MovieMail.com.

VIC PRATT is a writer, historian and curator of fiction film at the BFI National Archive.

GRAHAM RAE is a writer on film and literature, and the author of *Soundproof Future London* (2011).

JASPER SHARP is a writer, curator and the author of *Behind the Pink Curtain: The Complete History of Japanese Sex Cinema* (2008) and *The Historical Dictionary of Japanese Cinema* (2011).

KENNETH J. SOUZA is a former film professor and the author of the forthcoming *Scared Silly: The Films of Joe Dante*.

MIKE SUTTON was a freelance film critic whose writing has appeared in *Cinema Retro*, the *Huffington Post*, *BFI Screenonline* and the *Digital Fix*.

STEPHEN THROWER is a musician, film historian and the author of *Beyond Terror: The Films of Lucio Fulci* (1999), *Nightmare USA: The Untold Story of Exploitation Independents* (2007) and *Murderous Passions: The Delirious Cinema of Jesús Franco* (2015).

CAELUM VATNSDAL is a writer, filmmaker and the author of *They Came from Within: A History of Canadian Horror Cinema* (2004).

DOUGLAS WEIR is a technical producer at the British Film Institute.

BEN WHEATLEY is the director of *Down Terrace* (2009), *Kill List* (2011), *Sightseers* (2012), *A Field in England* (2013), *High Rise* (2015) and *Free Fire* (2016).